Au

Number
Nine

"Percy Purdy" by Hannah Barrett

POETRY EDITORS | E. Tracy Grinnell, Paul Foster Johnson, Julian T. Brolaski
CONTRIBUTING POETRY EDITORS | Jen Hofer, Nathalie Stephens
ESSAYS, REVIEWS, NOTES & PROSE EDITORS | Julian T. Brolaski, E. Tracy Grinnell, Paul Foster Johnson
ART EDITOR | Rachel Bers
EDITORIAL ASSISTANTS | Christine Kanownik, Alice Whitwham

TYPESETTING & COVER DESIGN | HR Hegnauer
DESIGN | HvA Design & E. Tracy Grinnell
COVER ART | Hannah Barrett, "The Brother Vermouth," 2007, oil on linen, www.hannahbarrett.net

Aufgabe is published annually by Litmus Press. Single issues are $15; a subscription for two issues is $25. For institutional subscription rates and for information about individual subscriptions, contact the publisher directly.

Litmus Press is the publishing program of Ether Sea Projects, Inc., a 501(c)(3) nonprofit literature and arts organization dedicated to supporting innovative, cross-genre writing with an emphasis on poetry and international works in translation.

Litmus Press / *Aufgabe*
P.O. Box 25526
Brooklyn, NY 11202-5526
www.litmuspress.org

All Litmus Press publications are distributed by
Small Press Distribution
1341 Seventh St.
Berkeley, CA 94710
www.spdbooks.org

ISSN: 1532-5539
ISBN: 978-1-933959-15-3

Aufgabe is made possible, in part, by public funds from the New York State Council on the Arts, a state agency. Litmus Press is also supported by grants from the Council of Literary Magazines and Presses, our members, subscribers, and individual donors. All contributions are tax-deductible to the extent allowed by law.

Contents

Poetry | edited by E. Tracy Grinnell, Paul Foster Johnson
& Julian T. Brolaski with contributing editors
Jen Hofer & Nathalie Stephens 139

Essays, reviews, notes, prose | edited by Julian T. Brolaski, E. Tracy Grinnell & Paul Foster Johnson 325

Contributors' Notes 391

"The Dogeressa of Twynnsdon" by Hannah Barrett

The Salt of Structure: Miron Białoszewski & the Future of Innovative Polish Poetry

Mark Tardi

Nearly a decade ago I sat on my family's porch reading an issue of the *Chicago Review* devoted to new Polish poetry. As somebody who grew up in Chicago with Polish grandparents, Poland was simply part of my consciousness. Figures like Wisława Szymborska and Czesław Miłosz were well known and well respected; and as my grandfather often reminded me, it was a Pole, Copernicus, who "set the world right." But as I read through the issue, I remember having two distinct thoughts: first, that American poets like Frank O'Hara, Gertrude Stein and John Ashbery were having some impact on developments in Polish poetry; and my second thought—who is Miron Białoszewski? Since virtually all the poets in the *Chicago Review* issue cited him as a profound influence, I was resolved to familiarize myself with his work.

From that point on I started delving into whatever I could find of his in English—which wasn't much—and talking about him to whomever would listen. There were a few scattered poems in a few anthologies (often the same poems, actually), and the incredible *Memoir of the Warsaw Uprising*. But when I looked for Polish publications, I found numerous volumes including poetry, prose, even theatre pieces. A few years later, working as an editor at Dalkey Archive Press, I chanced to meet Ewa Chruściel and Katarzyna Jakubiak, then both working on their doctoral dissertations. It was with Ewa and Kasia over tea that I first asked, "So why hasn't Białoszewski been translated more?" At the time I found the awkward pause and look of exasperation they both wore puzzling; since then I've considered it quintessential, something of a given when discussing Białoszewski's work.

But I kept talking, wondering, peskily asking questions—unaware that Białoszewski himself had a parallel appreciation for the necessity of conversation. As he reflects in his *Memoir of the Warsaw Uprising*:

> For twenty years I could not write about this. Although I wanted to very much. I would talk. About the uprising. To so many people. All sorts of people. So many times. And all along I was thinking that I must describe the uprising, somehow or other describe it. And I didn't even know that those twenty years of talking (I have been talking

about it for twenty years, because it is the greatest experience of my life—a closed experience), precisely that talking, is the only proper way to describe the uprising.

Jennifer Moxley suggested in her preface to *Imagination Verses* that "poetry is the frustration of limits." I can think of few places where that frustration is more evident or productive than in Białoszewski's poetry—and in attempts to translate it.

His work is at once playful, meditative, provocative, perplexing, and elusive—and has a well-deserved reputation for simply evading. In no small part, for this reason, his poetry is largely unknown to readers of literature in English. In 1974, Andrzej Busza and Bogdan Czaykowski's translation of *The Revolution of Things* was published, which turned out to be the first—and only—book of Białoszewski's poetry to appear in English to date. As they write in their introduction:

> Bialoszewski's 'return to things,' although it is not without parallels in modern poetry, has interesting features of its own. Białoszewski responds to the pressure of ideological abstractions by fabricating a mythology of things and, in his later poetry, by abandoning himself willfully to the contingency of speech and situation. In a deeper sense, Białoszewski's 'return to things' had also ethical and even 'religious' dimensions. Like St. Francis, who talked to animals, Białoszewski talks to things, and since they let him be himself, he celebrates them.

Thirty-five years later, I am honored and thrilled to be celebrating Białoszewski's poetry in the pages of *Aufgabe*, including reprinting excerpts from the long out-of-print *The Revolution of Things*.

It turns out that Busza and Czaykowski's working method—collaborative translation—has been an invaluable approach to translating Białosewski and breaking out of the limits of our own subjectivity. As Kacper Bartczak suggests in his accompanying essay discussing Białoszewski's poetics in the context of public versus private functions of language, his poetry is "born on the boundary between usage and its deformations."

My aim with this project was to offer some points of convergence and proliferation, both on Białoszewski and contemporary Polish poetry today. It in no way purports to be exhaustive, but it is my deepest hope that the selections here offer what Michael Palmer might call "the hum of the possible-to-say."

In addition to three galleries of poems that span a wide range of Białoszewski's life, and an essay by Kacper Bartczak framing the difficulties inherent in Białoszewski's work, this section includes the work from a number of poets working in or from Poland. Some poets may be known to English readers; others are appearing for the first time—though certainly not the last.

Andrzej Sosnowski has been writing exceptional, elliptical poems for a couple of decades now, and also serves as an editor of the influential *Literatura naŚwiecie*. Others like Monika Mosiewicz and Przemysław Owczarek are connected with a loose association of poets called mŁódź Literackie (a pun on the Polish word "młody," which means "young" and Łódź, the place I've called home for two years) and the literary journal *Arterie*. Mosiewicz's work echoes aspects of Wallace Stevens, though her poems are ripe with neologisms, vibrant tonal shifts, and an appreciation for the absurd.

Owczarek's is a poetry that interrogates and unravels vestiges of romanticism in smart and unsettling ways. Kacper Bartczak is both a fine poet and an astute critic. His poems too are unsettling in how they are built from fractures, the moving parts exposed, but his dislocations speak from a convergence of Ashberian aesthetics and pragmatic contingency.

Poets like Ewa Chruściel and Białoszewski speak to the complexity of our contemporary condition: both are identified as Polish writers, though find themselves living elsewhere. In the case of Chruściel, she writes poems in both Polish and English that can be at once spiritually contemplative and unabashedly bawdy, and are always teeming with astonishment. In Białoszewski I see a poet who extends some of Białoszewski's ontological concerns with things and place, while having the rigor and daring to rebuild the sonnet form.

Poets like Justyna Bargielska, Aneta Kamińska and Katarzyna Szuster reflect energetic and divergent poetic possibilities. Bargielska's poems provide exciting disruptions of surface, twists and turns of voice from line to line, and in her most recent book *China Shipping*, she engages in collaborations with the visual arts. Kamińska's poems explore the space between the page and the possible: she works both within the frame of the book, as well as constructs hypertextual webs. Hers is a poetry that expands Białoszewski and Stein for the 21st century. Szuster, like Bargielska and Kamińska, shares a playfulness of tone, though her poems turn inward and evidence a sensitive yet biting emotional register with a flair for the occasional Jarnotesque odd animal.

This project was not without its challenges, and I am indebted to many. To E. Tracy Grinnell, for the editorial support, vision, and friendship; and without whom this project never would have seen the light of day. To Henk Proeme, for his blessing and support. To Ewa Chruściel, Gabriel Gudding, Kasia Jakubiak, and A.D. Jameson for those early conversations and coffees in Normal. To Justyna Jabłonska and Ilona Zineczko, for taking over with Widzewian gusto. To the Polish-American Fulbright Commission, for providing me the funding and time to make this project a reality. To my colleagues at the University of Łódź for welcoming me. To my family, for understanding. To Bill Martin, for his example and for reaching out. To Ray Bianchi, Waltraud Haas, Dominick Mastrangelo, Sawako Nakayasu, Agata Pietrasik, and Steve Thanos, for giving me perspective. To the Chicago Achievers, for abiding. To Kacper and Aśka Bartczak, for their kindness, friendship, and tennis court oath. And to all the poets and translators, whose work and generous spirit humbles me. Thank you all.

Lastly, my deepest gratitude to you, *mój żółwiczku*—for the support, patience, dedication, and sharp humor that made this all possible. Rock paper platypus.

This issue is dedicated to the memory of Bogdan Czaykowski, for starting the conversation.

Łódź, Poland
October 2009

Gallery I:

The Salt of Structure

Five Poems

Miron Białoszewski

Of the Revolution of Things

Translated by Andrzej Busza and Bogdan Czaykowski

And they go round
and round.

Piercing us in nebulae.

Try and catch
    a heavenly body
    one of those
    called "close at hand . . ."

And whose tongue
    has savored to the full
    the Milky Drop of an object?

And whose idea was it
    that dimmer stars
    go round the bright ones?

And who thought up
    the dimmer stars?

Study of a Key

Translated by Andrzej Busza and Bogdan Czaykowski

The key
has
the smell of nail water
the taste of electricity
    and as a fruit
    is tart
    unripe
    being
    all stone.

Translation From a Parasol

Translated by Katarzyna Jakubiak and Rick Hilles

I
a crow
a soft bell
a galleria's claw
a rondeau's beat
a galleria's claw
a rondeau's beat
that's the rain—the one
th'one
tone

—

Unfurl me ceilingly
over a bulb
and I will shine
Indian-like
inspired
    sun of
      the dilettante

Translation From a Mattress

Patterns – Matisses – Bonnard

Choir with trumpets—under me
sunken coils
sleep slugs sleep

Patterns – Matisses – Bonnard

Peelings

Translated by Gabriel Gudding and Katarzyna Jakubiak

(1)

and subtract words from things

a word does not shrivel

suffers no loss

but stripped of skins, the words
numb from old pronunciation

o fruits!
o-ranges!
o them!

blushed by beginning

o vegetables!
that put on weight

o words!
you

       put on

           a thing

(2)

pot
a
to
earth
dirt a
pple

chill
– slips out –
we
ird to peel
odd
to circle
– such a
moon

stronger th
an:

        a desert
        a gong
        a going
        a sunrise of men as seen from the till
        since childhood
        out of scale
        into scale
        an unknown top
        ography teet
        ers closer
        before this broad
        moon o
        f an
        xiety

(3)

who peers from behind
the potato's horizon?

on this end
    me

so which end
    is mine?

peering thing!
my quadrant!

the thing is:
it is
at once
in
side
and a
round it
self

and for each who circumpeels it
it is equally
his thing
and the earth

a peeled equator
circuminjured
a
round it
self

My Jacobs of Exhaustion

Translated by Andrzej Busza and Bogdan Czaykowski

Up above:
          clarion calls of shape
                    abodes of touch
          all seasons of senses . . .
Down below—I.
          It is from my breast
          that stairs of reality grow.

Yet I feel nothing.
No sweetness.
No color.
I am not even
          one of the Old Testament heroes
but worse than a flatfish
          stuck to the bottom to die
          bubbling up
          clusters of breath-balloons
worse than a potato-mother
          sprouting
          huge antlers of rootstock
          herself shrunk
          almost out of existence.

Strike me
O structure of my world!

Five Poems

Andrzej Sosnowski

Speedometry

Translated by Rod Mengham

One day a wind shall rise all through this house
rainbows eclipse windows like cataracts
a cold awakening we shall have of it
photos drop from the walls and all manner
of things deny one another their voices discuss being lost with each
spin of the dial
what can you say about wind
you can make a wish and keep it forever

Down on the deck we'll grub for old
letters the time between in cobwebs
on the face like charred canvas
bits of paint under the nails Mind that
blade too late Mould is a remedy
stale bread cobwebs and lots of sunshine
The sun will rise up through the house
and out through collapsed windows
what can you say about its dazzle
you can make a wish and keep it forever

By night life is horizontal
in the glow of ringroad neon the
orbital highways of Saturn And a breath-stopped child
cannons towards the road Flashing in his eyes
the aureole of headlamps bringing him back
to us singing the news
but we will be gleaning the rubbish from the fields
spinning a small black flame from plastic waste
what can you say about the cold ground
you can make a wish and keep it forever

Can you feel that surge through the voltage of your throat?
That's feeling like a blackout deleting all memory
The sun zips from west to east
it prickles the scalp turning the heat up
you can even warm your hands on it
They'll put charges under all these buildings one day
the dust cloud will square up to the occasion
and then bow itself out
but what can you say about this jolt of fear
you can make a wish and keep it forever

A Little Tasting

Translated by Rod Mengham

Let's have a kick about, quipped the boys
and dream of the perfect pitch, of playing like angels
Salicional, Flauto, Gamba, and in the middle range
clear and fine-grained and bending it beautifully
Vox Coelestis. It's Barcelona! or the same lineup.
But you exit midair through stained glass with Miss X

while the fog grows as hard as the ceiling
confounding the forecasts of early morning haze
polar intervals and a slight buildup of
crochet-like weeping and dissonance. Never mind:
we got to sledge the cathedral roof,
a prime bit of Gothic, with exceptional crispness
and the sheen of bells like a distant parachute.

Inside was an amiable priest, consecrating
a cheap reprint of our deathless authors.
One more drop? Not even hemlock bubbly?
And all the time, cigarettes were losing their flavor
bit by bit, alongside a general loss of breath.
These were only samplings, and nothing to slake the appetite,
only dismal premonitions for the end of the sales drive;
just as well our protagonists were safely at home.

So what is to be done? What indeed.
When our old mate the signalman comes
and instructs us to dance the Sardana
like authentic Catatonians
then I permit myself a little wine in my orangina
and a little orangina in my wine
and feel a bit queasy
from this 'Stained Glass' concoction.
I give up the ghost for good.
It's either that, or give up the gusto.

Autumn

Translated by Rod Mengham

They don't know when to stop, the mayor and his henchmen
with their hail of special offers to make life so racy
its mere shadow on the platforms
works like a music box
that moves us to laughter
while the wind bucks the leaves
and recovers the lifeblood inside
autumn gold. It must be time to weep
after all that holding back
from so much victimhood. And this one interjects
he is always out of breath
from jumping tracks by night
to catch the express of morning
while that one strangles a cry
as the smiles are unfolded
ironic as an old tux. It's autumn
when dreams take a crisp shape
as they slide this way from the ideosphere:
in girum imus nocte et consumimur igni

Resumé

Translated by Rod Mengham

Getting ahead of yourself by .25 of a second
lagging behind the self in the Polaroid
in a haze of identity, skipping a beat
but dragging my feet in the light
and dark that the shutter blends
in a grey synchrony.

No matter whether I lose or find myself
No matter whether I sleep or slump before the TV
in showers of mud and water and cascades of leaves
it's hell either way.
Autumn is out to captivate
and you try to redeem the captive hand
that was lost to the land of the living.

But there's no rhyming between two worlds.
Two flames converge on one cigarette
but the hand with the match is unmatched,
it lights, and having lit, moves on;
even in grey autumnal dawns
when we vanish in overexposure.

Summer 1987

Translated by Rod Mengham

So your dying lodged where I gave it shade,
a cradle to pause in and thoughts to inhale.
But then I woke up. The sun at its height
made me squint. I was armed to the teeth with a good mood
and the pills to prove it.

Then I pulled up my sleeves and dislodged my heart,
removed that black arm-band, the corona of memory.
You respired me. I took up fruit
with a vengeance (multivitamins to the rescue!)
which cheered up my working parts.

Without stopping, I trotted from here to there,
even galloped into marriage, while thinking "wedding march."
Finally, the workouts: gymnastics, athletics,
prosthetics; just stopping short of
an early grave.

But the daily round was on its last legs
and the nightly, the senses giddying up to
a premonition of this major episode
flailing on the earth's crust, a body
hammering at the point of rest.

I was absolutely barking and nose down
I missed my footing, went beyond the pale
forgot to breathe, a poriomaniac, legging it
endlessly—not all the way from Bordeaux to Nurtingen
but I could have.

Except the ground turned into a quaking morass
that my feet vanished into, then my ankles,
then—at night the bed was an oubliette
that gaped suddenly without so much
as a warning squeak.

Then a blank, a dim impression of
the small girl glimpsed through the rear window
of our apartment clenching a razor between
her teeth. I am thinking of that now
and of the deadly kiss.

Four Poems

Przemysław Owczarek

Santero

Translated by Katarzyna Szuster and Mark Tardi

I

birch boulevard. tiny chicken bones with copper oxide.
the trees have goose bumps.

why are you driving us, santero?
we didn't deserve autumn and midnight
although we're talking about teas, women and decks of cards.

clubs and spades. blueberries and bitter chokeberry. ridicule
and small fraud. every day the evening has fuller lips.
old Abram noticed it first and muttered:
so much land in the wrinkles. death is too greedy
for vitamins.

II

on the edge, september's shedding. at night wild boars crunch
water manna. kittens squeal

in the pond. were dumped there a year ago by Mrs. Prus
and we've been left looking for answers since. words hang like traction.

and nobody knows where they lead?

Coil

Translated by Katarzyna Szuster and Mark Tardi

You didn't come up with it, Mr. Almodovar

I've long wanted to be a chimney sweep. Though I don't wear stripes on my back and the curbs don't walk me home.

I know . . . you want? You want sleepy sectarian lyrics, the emphasis of a poet who licks the mirror. A hand brushing the buttocks like impeccable cream for shapely dandies. Recipes hidden in the cylinder or the handle of an umbrella. No way. The chimney sweep befits a bowler hat and a woman who at dawn can be pulled into the gate. Even if she's sixteen and wears braces. Don't look rabbits in the incisors. Be a cowboy, though the bulls don't want the cows anymore and the sun sets in the south. Says the mirror. Infiltrations of eyebrows and stalactites. Have a good look and tell me already. Yes, I can do it. I can walk on stilts on the ceiling. Slobber at the sight of manholes. Note down from the roof the betrayals of women who think they can cook well. Throw a rope. Come

down. You need to drink up. Absurd? It's a kingdom in which the sage H. with a child's face (you know that the kingdom belongs to the child) pulls the sword from the dungheap and the crazy mill creates a galaxy. Grab your sword. Go on. The corridor narrows. Just a centimeter. And there it is. Light. Turn around. What do you see? Yeah.

Hi, Dad.

Depths

Translated by Katarzyna Szuster and Mark Tardi

this Delaware autumn. frost
scalps the trees. ice fleece and lash.
scar. the sun is

        like a broken potato.
        and fog
        like melted butter.

believe me, the black woodpecker is a master of games
and style. it could look like Raymond Queneau.
meanwhile, cranes flew off and the meadow is no longer
a tapestry of Edo. noon brings a little impression
that in water becomes sepia (get it
in another line). i look for a woman.

she emerged from the depths. was carrying in her hands
a dead kingfisher. said:
touch it.

(is desire geometry?)

beware of the foxfires
trajectories under the skin

and snow.

Mnemosyne

Translated by Katarzyna Szuster and Mark Tardi

there was rain before the birth of kabbalah.

falls, as if to consume the scattered sparks.
find one, and you'll blow away

the sky. when I think about it, tadpoles fade away on my
hand.
a muskrat skeleton glides to the bottom. the skin took

hunters when trailing ghosts in the swamps.
for you ochre. stupor.
you chew corn, and your lips are like ergot.

i'd like to suck the fire out of them. it wasn't you
that braided in my hair dark

allegories, but the soil and its whisper in my feet. jump
on the waterfall like that child. when i tear off

clams from stones, i can feel their look.
gray eyes. in the sweet flesh

a little disease and song.

Five Poems

Ewa Chruściel

Snow

                        a   **martyr**

           of   **desire**

To be in love is like going out to check your mailbox. Do not get me wrong. If you love him how prove he loves you too. We began by evanescence. A remote chance that you meet in the mailbox. Do you see a mulberry tree in a mustard seed? The mailbox does not keep the record. I was afraid of my grandfather. He exuded coldness. And yet you were a spitting image of him. And I loved you more than any dictionaries. I studied hoopoes to contain you. You said not even grass has such thin hair. In time of suffering, I insulate myself with snow. For a moment white albatrosses fall from the sky and become their own species of nouns; pray why chase each stalk of wounded light? The beauty possessed wounds and dwindles. White anarchy of their feathers. In a moment, the Snow Destruction Company will come to level this paralyzing powder and carry it away to the gas chambers, slaughterhouses, camps. It is a sin against Holy Albatrosses— this Ingratitude. We suffer from excess. There is a nobility in asking the same thing over and over again. Each broken snowflake becomes a broken coastline. The line of infinite affection—squeezed into limited space. Engraved on the palm of your hand. Whose nerves exploded and scattered into the map of our suffering. The hour we knew nothing of each other.

What a beautiful Yinguo owl which nests on Ginkgo biloba trees perched briskly
in my mailbox! Who could lacerate it? Not even a fierce editor like me! After all,
the editors are human species who show themselves to be human, as Higginson
once wrote in *Atlantic Monthly*. It is well enough to remember this fact, when
you approach Me. I am *not a gloomy despot, no Nemesis or Rhadamanthus*
(. . .) *draw near me, therefore, with soft approaches & mild persuasions.*
Meanwhile, on a more personal note, I'm terribly jealous because I know
that the fact that I haven't heard from you in months means that you have no need
of my odd impossible companionship because you have two or three new boys.
Either that or you fought a duel with Agnieszka and you lost. Sorry if that's the case.
Please let me know where to send flowers.
P.S. 1. I had a sexy dream about you today. In this dream you were not even afraid
of me. The details are my own.
P.S. 2. I don't know what else to say! Perhaps I would gain the respect I've long
deserved and your timely response, if I were to have a short essay come out in
Playboy. Yes, *Playboy*. Snort at my dreams if you like, but I if I did get published
there, I may receive an invitation to the Playboy Mansion. I would be sitting
with the bunnies while you shiver in the New England snow.

pentecost 2

I go to Lunkers for Ana's birthday. He is a bird. I knew this story would be continued.
An electron sets out on a journey and another electron comes in. You said
you were afraid I would never call back. When they get closer, the attraction is
magnetic, so that one electron shakes off the photon and the other absorbs the
photon—gets a kick
and moves in another direction. Now we have our wasabi ginger staircase. What
an eruption of brown. Why are we so omnivorous? Sex is what we say and not
what we do. The paint will splash, dissipate. We could grow beautiful little almonds.
The snaky-twigged branches coil up. In dire worship, the air horny, clumped up.
I wade through tiny spinning atoms. Love is thick and yellow. The entire world is
an egg. The universe has every possible history (which history will choose us to live
on?) and yet one method. It—a crying infant—needs someone to produce the loud
shushing noise which imitates what the fetus hears inside the womb as blood
pulses through the placenta. I will never possess you. I just imagine holding you
for a moment, but really can you hold the water?

To   a   universe   of   sea-
horse

Unkempt philosopher of silence with a dermal cirri. *Baron rampante.*
Drumming vespers to an audience of bleached coral. Your zebra stripes
transplanted into medicinal plates. I bought myself a sextant to measure the
angle of your elevation, so I can always see where the current takes you. One
should not catch a joy as it floats. A snout hopper
of the ineffable. Little prince, how I would like to fetch you a juicy shrimp.
For heart is a secret seahorse. Choreographer of chromatophores. I see
underwater hourglasses waving through a spiral of rings. Coralline algae.
Orange sponge. Aria of anemones
and gorgonians. Abducted from your bed of emerald eelgrass and anapest
of hued pigment. What illness springs from a lost place? I am just on the
other side of the mirror. Lexicons trespass; there are cross-code breakdowns.
I am seized by your vertigo flapping of knobs and spines. A hermit with no
stomach. Epicure of jaffa cake. A beige enclosure. Built of Atoms & Light. We
began with evanescence.

They thistle in us. They speck in the morning. They tingle. Sorrelic
apparitions. There is a tigress mother wanting to trim your hair. They come
to us. Do you hear them? Some as heavy footsteps. Others—miniscule
kisses. Thin as grass. Rising and swaying parasols. They come with
swinging hips. They come as minnows. They try to get where they belong.
They come in wrinkles. They come as a host of molecules. They come as
hard-faced dybbuks. They swarm into this lighthouse. They have fancy
hats. With forget-me-nots. They pebble across the floor. They fall from
marigold trees and lie crucified on the road. Get up and sing. They come
and pinch like too much love. They trespass. They come to a wailing wall.
They dot. We are burying them every day. We are burying them in staccato
rhythm. They rise and accrete. They beat electric letters in the air. They
hop always to a higher branch. They come invincible. They come to torture.
They come to soothe. They come for romance. They flip and tremble tiny
farewells. They come as mustards seeds. Do you see them in a mulberry
tree? They slide down the needles. They come as growth on wolf trees,
the dead winking. They air the air. They come to forgive. They ask for
forgiveness. They come as hyphae. They come as hostages. They come as
clogged streets. They come in slow trains. They come as silver jaguars.
Burning bushes, doves, manna, the blood of horses' necks. They come as
purgatory souls. They chip off the wall. In loops and whorls. They want
to rent one line. They want to breakdown. They re-colonize. They come to
insulate us with snow. They come in giggles. They come in almonds. They
come to eye us, inside our panther skins. We bury them. They come in black
chadors. They rap on our door with churned-up grains, tides, whispers.
They come as drafts of juniper. They spread on the floor as a cross. They are
relics of grief and light. They perch on your branches like monk hedgehogs.
They come as juncos. They come in lekking crowds. They come in high-
strung beads and scatter into our vessels. They come in volcanic lavish.
They come as noble Odysseuses. They hover as hummingbirds, calculating
their rates of return. We bury them. They air the air. They are ubiquitous as
Tartar cheeks. They bilocate. They come as yellow secrets.

The Polish Language in Extreme and Intermediary States of "Siulpet": Miron Białoszewski's *Erroneous Emotions*

Kacper Bartczak

Translated by Krzysztof Majer

It has often been said that the poet stands guard over language—that is, language in general, but also when understood as a unified communication code. The notion of the lyrical poet as the high priest of this national temple ties into another idea, which is essential to the traditionally understood lyric: it is the poet's "I" that is being expressed. The speaking voice manifested in the poem will sooner or later refer to an entity that lies deeper than language and is known as the "subject." Reaching the essence of a community's code is traditionally linked with a reflective materialization of an authentic poetic "self."

Miron Białoszewski's work makes a smooth acceptance of the above notions difficult. As a reader situated more or less outside the critical corpus surrounding his poetry, I wish to strengthen the tale of the readerly astonishment that Białoszewski provokes. Moving between two languages, Polish and English, I find in Białoszewski an examiner of precisely such liminal, borderline states. Rather than explore areas such as language or subjectivity, the author exerts pressure on the boundaries of these notions, thus bringing them to a crisis. The news of the highly conditional existence of the subject—carried from theoretical frontiers and confirmed by the dramatic adventures undergone by the so-called "lyrical" subject in contemporary poetry—appears to be rather familiar. What about the language of the community, however? Does a poet who presents the arbitrary and unstable nature of the "I" increase the primacy of language? Is this so because, ultimately, everything is language? Having toppled the primacy of a central subjectivity, we cling to the principal role of language. Thus, language becomes a new space of transcendence. Or is this yet another erroneous emotion?

Białoszewski does not claim to be guarding language. Rather, if he does at all reach for the high metaphor of "guardianship," he immediately reduces its register, ascribing to himself the role of a watchman; even then, however, what he watches over is not language but reality. Could it be then that he is a metaphysical realist, desiring to reach things in their stabilities? Reality, then, in lieu of language?

Białoszewski's poetry books present a series of distortions operating on a variety of levels. This is well exemplified by the volume entitled *Mylne wzruszenia [Erroneous Emotions]*. The individuality, or even private separateness, implied by this book, already suggested in the cycle entitled *Leżenia [Lyings Down]*, enters in its second half into a relation with yet another cycle, *Zajścia [Occurrences]*. The transition seems alarmingly fluid and I am moved to wonder about the separateness established by *Lyings Down* if, all of a sudden, it enters into external communications with such ease. Another axis of conflict and tension is the language itself, albeit understood not as an abstract entity but as a particular code used by a community. Regardless of the intensity of poetic experiment, we still expect no difficulties in placing it within the space of the mother tongue. And yet *Erroneous Emotions* problematizes the identity of the code. Is this poet still speaking Polish to me? Am I entitled to assume so because I am always able to establish contact with him, despite the frequently horrendous distortions of all layers of the code which are, theoretically speaking, responsible for successful communication? Or does Białoszewski wish to separate himself to such an extent that he is constructing a language that is entirely private?

The possibility of an emergence of a "private language" derives from Cartesian deliberations on the nature of knowledge and cognition.[1] It was famously refuted by Ludwig Wittgenstein in his *Philosophical Investigations*. The intricate argument of this eccentric philosopher, whom Marjorie Perloff described as a philosopher-poet, can be seen as evidencing the fiasco of attempts at constructing a code of signs which would be available to an individual subject and simultaneously stable and iterative. The comments made in fragments 244-271 of *Philosophical Investigations* indicate that such attempts are either shattered by the impossibility of systematizing signs of an exclusively private code, or they resort to constructing signs in a manner which is typical of public language, i.e., the code of a given language community. In Wittgenstein's system, both language and subject are transferred to the external zone, into the field of scenes and interactions. In her book *Wittgenstein's Ladder*, Perloff indicates a proximity between the philosopher's ideas and the effects accomplished by other 20th-century experimenters with language, such as Gertrude Stein or Samuel Beckett.[2] In this way, Perloff was able to support her already well-established tale of the decline of traditional lyrical poetry, with its primacy of the expressive function, focused on the authenticity-seeking subject. Thus, the poet becomes interested in the language game, i.e. the pool of possible solutions appearing in grammar and cultural contexts.

The poet works with language, which—as the Viennese logician argued—is a strictly public matter. Language's signifying power, in the Wittgensteinian model, does not derive from mentalistically understood "meanings" which language "represents," but from the intersubjective sphere. The poet may become an explorer of these relationally (i.e., externally) played language games. Removing subjectivity to the far background or else abandoning it altogether, such a poet becomes a therapist of social discourses.[3] However, there is yet another possibility. Without returning to naïve beliefs about language as an entity essentially anchored in a subjective substance and without denying the communal origin of language, poetry may still inspire crises in the linguistic matter, almost detaching it from its maternal roots which guarantee meaning. The poetic experiment of the avant-garde returns us to the paradoxes of a private language and cognitive solipsism. This is the road which Białoszewski has very clearly chosen; the play between complete privacy of meanings and their public anchoring is particularly evident in *Erroneous Emotions*.

This is not to say that Białoszewski becomes utterly illegible. On the contrary, I suggest a reconsideration of the mechanisms which, despite such deformation, allow the reader to establish a contact of sorts with these poems—even to derive enjoyment from them. Let us ponder once again the origins of this ability to interact with such poems, with radical distortions, of which this volume—similarly to Białoszewski's other books—is full. Does it really suffice to say that we are safely within the boundaries of an area known, generally speaking, as language, and, strictly speaking, as the Polish language, the mother tongue? Are we satisfied with the hypothesis that a countable grammatical rule generates countless new linguistic usages, the identity and legibility of which are guaranteed by the durability of the rule? Is it sufficient to call upon the untamed generative power of language itself?

Let us then return for a moment to the Wittgensteinian linguistic tradition, in which reflection on the rule-eluding unpredictability of language is simultaneously an examination of the condition of the subject. An interesting contribution to the discussion of the consequences of Wittgenstein's late hypotheses on the non-essentialist nature of language can be found in the views of the American philosopher Donald Davidson. In his essay "A Nice Derangement of Epitaphs," Davidson analyzes the manner in which communication begins, progresses, and is successful despite the interlocutors' differences in attitude toward their linguistic code, which is both shared (they use one and the same national language) and dissimilar. The dissimilarity derives from Davidson's vision of language users as indefatigable and unpredictable creators of idiolects, and it is precisely these idiolectics that he values more, as a more significant feature of human "linguisticality" than the fact of sharing the so-called inherent linguistic competence, so beloved by metaphysicians such as Chomsky. The idiolect is always a few steps ahead of the latest dictionary, just as an individual trait is always imperceptible to a collective feature.

Davidson sees conversation as a complex ritual the participants of which gradually recognize each other. This recognition commences before the encounter; it is rooted in a set of unwritten and only partly conscious preliminary assumptions. Davidson describes them as "prior theory," which relates to the other interlocutor and the communicative situation.[4] The conversation itself is a process in which these initial assumptions are modified, progressing towards a singular impromptu translation of mutual differences. The crucial part of Davidson's model is his conviction that each successful communicative situation is singular/individual to the extent that it accomplishes unprecedented modifications in the prior theories of both participants. This means that communicative success does not rely on substantially understood linguistic competence, envisioned as a previously acquired apparatus. The reason for this—Davidson argues—is that one cannot foresee the idiolectic gestures of the other interlocutors and thus one must react spontaneously, using abilities which are considerably more general and total than the narrowly understood linguistic competence. The knowledge of a given language is in this case something much more extensive than the correct use of internalized grammar rules, lexicon, or other systematic layers of the code.

It is only this wider, greater, holistic capability that allows the overlap of mutual modifications, however transient they may be. Davidson describes this overlap as "passing theory." It becomes a state of mind, shared by both interlocutors, which does not completely derive from the set of prior assumptions and is therefore a product of this and no other event. In this sense, for Davidson, language is holistic: it belongs to a holistically understood "person," with their views and available arsenal of "sentences." Miscellaneous areas of this inventory are activated by a particular situation. In the crucial moment, according to Davidson, a capability is triggered which cannot be contained within the prior formal principle, and which, in the philosopher's words, meaning is derived by means of "wit, luck, wisdom from a private vocabulary and grammar." What comes into play, according to Davidson, is "knowledge of the ways people get their points across, and rules of thumb for figuring out what deviations from dictionary are most likely."[5] Thus, what we are dealing with here is a variety of instinct or general intelligence, which is more than merely "using language."

In the last analysis, Davidson sees communication and using language as an aspect of being in the world, a method of negotiating with the world. When we describe someone as knowing a certain language, for Davidson this statement means something else than an ordinary report on understanding vocabulary and grammatical structures. In order to understand words and structures one requires no more than a good handbook and a good dictionary; not so, Davidson claims, as regards actual use of language. He believes that to know a language means to be able to function in the world: "We may say that linguistic ability is the ability to converge on a passing theory from time to time . . . . But if we do say this, we should realize that we have abandoned not only the very ordinary notion of language, but we have erased the boundary between knowing a language and knowing our way around the world generally."[6]

What is the significance of the above disquisition for an analysis of Białoszewski's poetry? First and foremost, Davidson—a philosopher rooted in, among others, the Wittgensteinian tradition of enquiry—broadens the consequences of the hypothesis concerning the non-essentialist nature of language and solves the paradox of "privacy" attained in public language. Language is communal, public, and yet it lacks essence, which means that it is infinitely susceptible to idiosyncratic modulations of usage, without losing the ability to create and convey meanings. The crux of Davidson's argument is not a belief that everyone is a conscious artist of language, constantly producing a plethora of creative distortions, but the fact that communication will proceed despite sudden anomalies. Privacy and the inner life are born on the boundary between usage and its deformations, out of nonsystematic uses, albeit not ones developed in the seclusion of some retreat, but tried and tested in a communicative occurrence. An intense communicative occurrence, as Davidson describes it, leaves the interlocutor transformed; the arsenal of his "I" is enhanced by a new move/movement, or perhaps at this point merely an offset or a fissure, which nevertheless demands consideration. Rules are derivative records of past occurrences, of their success and frequency, and are no more than stopovers. They await *change*. Internality is precisely this change, an accomplishment and effect of the aforementioned modifications. Therefore, by allowing his poems to carry language to the limits of communicative capacity, the poet does not flee towards a solipsistic exclusion from the community's cognitive and communicative scope, but rather subjects language, as well as himself, to a certain test. What is tested is the possibility of internality as an extension of the public sphere, but also the possibility of a future.

That is all very well, someone might say, but Davidson's hypothesis is too radical, especially when he claims that language always undergoes such intense anomalization, which is assumed in the key stages of the argument. Davidson has frequently been criticized by other linguistic philosophers, who indicated—

correctly and quite soberly—that the bulk of human linguistic communication occurs along safe lines, which are formalized and which do not alter the rule, thus contradicting Davidson's key hypothesis. If, as Ian Hacking demonstrated in his tellingly titled essay "The Parody of Conversation," the hypothesis can be reduced to a conclusion that "each pair of interlocutors creates their own language,"[7] then the whole Davidsonian model may appear rather suspect. We will probably agree that the majority of communicative occurrences do not lead to such sophisticated effects and transpire without obstacles, running smoothly along the lines traced by prior rules and thus utilizing language at its highest stability, as an entity which we freely share with our interlocutors, without the need of resorting to interpretation, the indispensability of which Davidson so strongly argues.

Hacking's criticism allows us to comprehend the significance of Davidson's ideas for discussing poetry. Without attempting to settle this philosophical-linguistic debate, we may declare that what emerges from it is a notion of two varieties of linguistic encounters. In some cases everything transpires as usual, i.e., smoothly, predictably, non-interpretationally. However, there are also other types of communication, which we may label as *intense*. Here, sufficiently significant and extensive distortions can be observed to take place, though not enough to threaten contact itself, nor for its participants to suddenly drift beyond the breakwater of competence and the previously acquired principles which they have contributed to the situation. It is clearly the second model of encounter that is found in Białoszewski's work. Thus, we can now return to his poems without resorting to the two extreme views, which obscure the discussion of contemporary poetry. The former entreats us to see linguistic experimentation. As displaying attitudes of retreat from the world into the safe recesses of solipsism; the latter ignores the existence of the organism, in order to flaunt the importance of "language," i.e., an omnipotent sphere, which speaks of itself and through itself. Białoszewski's poetry points towards a different origin of the speaking voice.

Let us then treat Białoszewski's poems as intense communicative encounters, that is those in which—to call upon Hacking again—the participants always generate a code belonging solely to that particular occurrence. Intense encounters may transpire inside the self, thus bringing it to a sort of internal division, making the self a witness of its own monologues. Secondly, we may observe intense encounters taking place between interlocutors, outside the "I" but inside the poem, as is the case in *Occurrences*. Lastly, the third, the broadest, and the most general possibility is perceiving the poem as an interlocutor who behaves uncharacteristically, thus forcing the reader to perform flexible operations modifying his or her prior theory.

The tradition of linguistic inquiry represented by Wittgenstein and Davidson transposes the issue of meanings from mental interiors into externally perceived situations. The transposition consists in the fact that, abandoning the unverifiable recesses of the psyche, the cogitating substance with its intentional sphere, the examiner seeks linguistic effects in the correlation between utterances and external events in the world. This shift in perspective sheds light on a wider tendency in contemporary poetry; *Erroneous Emotions* is a brilliant exemplification of this very tendency.

Suddenly, rather than observers of reflections which can still be understood as "inner," we become field linguists who enter tribal territory. In *Occurrences* there is something of the strangeness, the logical marvel, the contextual surprise typical of the Wittgensteinian strategy of supplanting a fluent argument with a fragmentary procession of scenes that function as illustrations. In the bulk of *Occurrences* there is no stylizing intrusion into the linguistic layer itself. The sentences and words remain closer to a certain notion of ordinary uses, although evidently the primary effect accomplished in these pieces is to make the reader aware of how striking these uses are, how unusual this ordinariness becomes. Generally, we regard them as normal, meaning normative, as exerting no pressure on the rule. And yet Białoszewski's poems demonstrate the unusualness and deviation of these uses, although they never stray into incorrectness or a simple violation of the rule. The language of *Occurrences*, similarly to the language of the scenes depicted by Wittgenstein, is complete, even if illogical. It requires no definition, rule or correction; the linguistic scene itself is a correction.

One such occurrence appears in *Lyings Down*. The work entitled "Los? Co? Los?" ["Fate? What? Fate?"] functions primarily as an intercepted linguistic situation.[8] For the most part, the "poem" does not display any stylistic operations. The focus is the illogicality of the utterance, the dependence of meaning on a withdrawn general context, and an automatic repetitiveness of utterances. The interlocutors find various obstacles on their way and resort to worn-out linguistic habit. Communication occurs on a surface which, when suddenly taken out of context, appears almost fantastical. However, one senses that this is exactly what everyday linguistic interactions may look like. Even the shredded, sonically ragged remark of one of the interlocutors, who elides sounds and collapses entire words, appears to be a notation of phonological phenomena typical of logorrhea, which so often constitute our conversations. As in Wittgensteinian strategies, the language or the linguistic scene is perceived as something autonomous, functioning without the support of a description that could reduce the strangeness. This is precisely how we talk, how we work with language, distorting it and yet creating meanings and communicating.

The aesthetic force of *Occurrences* lies in these poems' being uprooted from larger contexts, which are purposefully omitted. In this manner the reader is reminded of the dependence of meanings on extensive areas of relations, only a fraction of which manifests itself directly in a given situation. An occurrence, a situational poem, is a temporary tying, a makeshift knot, which always indicates the rest of the net. The situational cluster contains traces of other situations, both past and future. The singularity / singleness / individuality / separateness of an occurrence is a coincidence of manifold factors, stemming both from the personalities of the participants and from the environment in which it occurs. The situation—i.e., the poem—is a "lump" ("zlep").[9] It is even difficult to speak of poems here; instead, we face a moving situational formation, which requires—as in Davidson's model—our readiness for quick adaptive maneuvers. We first glimpse it from the outside, as we see our interlocutors, with their entire set of mannerisms and tics; we must be ready for gestures and movements with which we have never dealt before. Establishing contact with our interlocutors, we use provisional compositions of various areas and skills.

In a way, Białoszewski's works subject language to the upheavals of life which defy attempts at codification. As a consequence, however, language is brought to the limits of its identity. In *Erroneous Emotions* sentences are derailed, the syntax is disjointed, words overlap with and miss one another, gaining new functions. Words, utterances, and syntactical units are pushed to their boundaries and beyond their ascribed grammatical categories. Grammatical classes of words shift, overlap, seem to shimmer. Linguistic uses become sonic signs (or signs in writing, where the poems rely on spelling, punctuation and verse distribution across the page), for which their ascribed grammatical category is merely a starting point. What we are dealing with here is a half-regulated sign, which resembles an animal of unstable taxonomy. Are we always certain about the animal's species? Do new species not appear? And if they do appear, is it because they have been "discovered," waiting, like some reality in itself, for someone to unveil and name them?

A lot of words, phrases, syntactic units inserted by Białoszewski in his poems would be utterly surprising to Polish interlocutors when used in an ordinary conversation. His usages sound almost foreign, yet reminiscent of something familiar. This quality, however, may not in itself prove the thesis of the disappearance of the stable national code. A careful examination of his lexical overlappings, sonic and syntactic distortions, neologisms, might show the actual working of grammatical rules that operate in normal linguistic discourse. Perhaps we could just talk about a caricature-like overproductiveness of these usages. Still, caricatured or not, these would be transformational rules derived from a stable corpus of a national code's grammar, in this case the Polish grammar. Thus, someone might argue, however foreign his usages might be, we do manage to interact with them because we, as Polish language users, activate the productive mode of the rules inherent in the language. In doing that, we stabilize the poetic distortion, bring it back home, and everybody is happy again, sound and safe in the house of the Polish mother tongue.

And yet, there remains a disquieting fact that some of the poems contain linguistic bits that are truly unrecognizable as language. These bits—and *Erroneous Emotion* is quite full of them—look like random spatters of print on the page, sound like accidental grunts. This is because Białoszewski is sometimes willing to present language with its attendant noise, the sheer background noise of meaningful message. Do we just say that that gets sorted out and the message proceeds to a safe decoding? Not quite, since the grunts, noises, stunted words are all reminiscent of real words, and they keep figuring in the entire sound system of the poem, bringing meanings to mind and keeping them in play. How does one decide which meanings to keep and which to reject? What is even worse, sometimes these noises coalesce in some sort of quasi-words, more reminiscent of real words than the bits of sheer noise, and yet resisting any stable lexical identification. This is the case with the word "siulpet," which appears first in the title of a separate poem, and then as part of a larger word-title in another poem. The poem "Siulpet" runs this nonce word through a series of lines, which act as contexts, each almost stabilizing the word and helping us spot its meaning, but never quite doing just that. In the end, the word remains a mystery. Nonexistent in the language, it remains untamed by the poem, trailing instead with a plethora of echoes and vestiges of meanings. Ok, someone will say, but "siulpet" is an extreme case, used only twice in the volume, and, as such an extremum, should not be treated as convincing argument. All inquiry eliminates extreme results and states. It seems then, that we can return to all these other usages by Białoszewski, which, although highly distortive and unstable, may be explicable by the application of the stable rule. Should this be the case, Białoszewski is giving us our good old Polish.

Things are not so easy though. The problem is that the distortive uses may be explained not by one, but by two or more chains of rules. Depending on the choice of the rule, we obtain one word or two words, noun or verb, two nouns or a prepositional phrase. The fact that most of these oddities can be treated to a grammatical explanation is in fact no help at all, since what is really needed is a kind of meta-rule that would help us decide which grammatical explication (already quite strained, even if recognizable and logical) to take. And such a meta-rule is exactly what we don't have.

Białoszewski's distortions often work like the famous duck-rabbit figure. Wittgenstein used it to discuss dependence of cognition on preconceived cultural patterns.[10] The smooth shifting between our seeing a duck or a rabbit is context-dependent. Such use of contexts is natural and easy in normal conversations. Such conversations are usually conducted under some degree of urgency. The interlocutors share conversational goals and will thus cooperate, when faced with each other's distortive linguistic gestures and malapropisms to narrow down the resulting indeterminacy. Ex post facto we could say that they cooperate to select just one set of grammatical rules and obtain relatively limited interpretation of an aberrant cluster. But only ex post facto. The question really remains how they arrive at such a narrowing down. Yes, the context is helpful but can we say that the interlocutors have conscious access to a regular inventory of grammatical rules? So we are just computers reaching for stable deep structures?

A poem by Białoszewski works as a conversational situation that is not driven by interpretive urgency. As we enter into communication with these poems, all interpretive possibilities, all rule-governed explanations, remain in play and keep resonating. In fact, we see them as such, exactly because of this density. We keep juggling them, and shuttling between them, until we see their reciprocal dependence. But if this is the case, then indeterminacy is kept in play, and we are back with "siulpet": the words and usages never cease to radiate their instability. "Siulpet" then is not a separate instance, but an extension of a common phenomenon: the indeterminacy operative in the poems.

The poems also make us aware of the fact that the stable grammatical explanation of a language oddity is only a secondary, post factum operation, a belated description. The rule-governed description comes later, when things have already quieted down, when everything is safe. But first, before that happens, there must be the recognition of the two or more competing facets of the phrase or syntactic fragment, the parallel possibilities of the aspectual coexistence of possibilities. There must be a flash of consciousness of the difference. The poems do not appeal to our knowledge of the rules. They appeal to a different capacity: the meta-capacity of seeing the duck, the rabbit, and whatever other form emerges at one and the same time. This capacity cannot be taught in the classroom. Only simple, normalized chains of explanation can, and this is called grammar. The other capacity is unteachable; some will call it linguistic instinct. But Białoszewski's activation of this capacity makes us aware that it is called poetry.

However, with this realization, we return to normal conversations. Białoszewski's poems, or, more broadly, avant-garde poetry, intensifies and generalizes a dynamic indeterminacy of each conversation. Even if, as we said earlier, the participants of normal conversations will narrow down ranges of possibilities, they will be more successful at that task if they are aware of these ranges. That is, if we want to have rich conversations—however urgent they may be—we would be well served by our capacity of recognizing the plural facets of our usages. And this is what they don't teach in schools; this is what you find in the poems. Thus poetry is an experimental field, a practice field. There are moments in practice when a good player attains a quality that exceeds mere instruction. A good tennis player's volley will always go beyond the practice repetitions prescribed by the rule. Something new occurs on the court. But Białoszewski (and Davidson) claim that, in the realm of human interactions, this novelty is always needed. You can't afford, as a human interlocutor, to be a mediocre player. And it is poetry, the kind of poetry that brings language to its near dissolution, that hones these special conversational capabilities. The term conversational, so understood, will combine aesthetics, language awareness, general intelligence, and all these holistically treated instincts, comprising the whole person that Davidson had in mind when he claims that we communicate with something much more than just "language."

In the end though, such comprehensive intelligence reaches far beyond any set of rules making up a national language. Białoszewski does not just speak Polish to me. The psycho-linguistic adjustments the reader negotiates in his poems, like the adjustments demanded by intense human encounters, do not leave the self untouched. The reconfigurations of prior expectations will produce relocations within the networks of the self. Thus what Białoszewski's poems communicate, or rather activate, is the capacity for internal changes, which does not just change the self, but change the national code.

Białoszewski does not stand guard over language; he stands guard over the future of the language.

NOTES

1 If, as Descartes believes, cognition and knowledge are products of an internal subject-observer, testing the certainty and clarity of "apparitions" marching in front of him in the projection rooms of the mind, then the possibility of doubting the authenticity of such projections appears, and, consequently, the possibility of solipsism, or even a construction of an entirely private language, i.e., one that is recognizable only by the internal observer. Such a construction would prove the existence of a world of unmediated experience, thus legitimizing an ideally "self-centered" subjectivity.

2 Marjorie Perloff, *Wittgenstein's Ladder*. (Chicago: U of Chicago P, 1996.)

3 This is a road taken, by a large number of contemporary US poets. According to Perloff, Wittgenstein's daring operations on thought and language constitute one of the major contexts in which these changes can be successfully considered.

4 Donald Davidson, "A Nice Derangement of Epitaphs", in *Truth, Language, and History* (Oxford: Clarendon Press, 2005), p. 101.

5 Davidson, op.cit. p. 107.

6 Ibid.

7 Ian Hacking, "The Parody of Conversation," in Ernest LePore, ed., *Truth and Interpretation: Perspectives on the Philosophy of Donald Davidson* (Oxford: Blackwell, 1986), 449.

8 Miron Białoszewski, *Mylne wzruszenia* (Warszawa: Państwowy Instytut Wydawniczy, 1961), p. 43.

9 "Zlep" is a Białoszewski neologism.

10 See Part II section xi of *Philosophical Investigations*.

Gallery II:

Erroneous Emotions

Seven Poems

Miron Białoszewski

happyend (1)

Translated by Katarzyna Szuster

it's drizzling mizzling
us sleeping us hand in hand dry
the goodtogether's
— — — — — — — —

when the risers get up
we're still nighting
and whee and window daily dry
—shu.it!
we're still nighting

happyend (2)

Translated by Katarzyna Szuster

stop fumbling in the bathroom
lie on the bed
I'm waiting for lovemaking
—is there any toothpaste left?
—yep
—and sssoap?
—schmope
and lovemaking? un expectedly
things again too much somehow today well unless oh wow

HOW TO APPROACH ONESELF?
from the perspective of mountain ash?
first through a pinhole
in a sad position
(yourself on the porch bed)
then I kept drilling this pinhole
right to the ash mountains and to myself
I was coming on until it came
              to this that they came
              and at self to oneself

Erroneous emotion

Translated by Katarzyna Szuster

if Whatsername didn't bring pills
the earth was shaking

Addie's walking in a coat
not him at all

tomorrow not Saturday

the street looks like a stree'
and isn't pleased with it

on and on

Białoszewskosaur is falling asleep

not pleased with it either

Green, therefore, it is

Translated by Katarzyna Szuster

You are . . . you are not . . .
do I believe in you or doubt
whatever you are made of—
     even if you
     were made of nothing
         —you're green—
         from moonlight glaze
         you winter landscape

         simply porcelain
         a little peopled
         and cold—
         with the ornaments of trees and mist
         on the brim
And when I know nothing about you
or the microvoid maggot
     that is eating you
or about calling you snow
         fringe of the town
         underside
         of the moonlit night
you can play me
the most beautiful part of unrest

We starfish

Translated by Katarzyna Szuster

It's not only
lost hair.

A deserted place
often hurts.

We multiply
when cut off
by longings.

—   —

We are starfish.

—.   —

Separated from nothing.
starlost.

Romance with a Concreteness

Translated by Katarzyna Jakubiak and Rick Hilles

and suddenly
love
for whom? for whom?

my legs bending me
in a direction
the opposite of kneeling
to a chair
first to it
I confess
and there is an emotion
and a bending together
and now it is you
          o chair
I love you
          chair
I love you
and it's a tragic love
because already there is
the lurking of the betrayed beyond the chair
it will spot me
it will seek me out   it will keep looking
it will find revenge

I have betrayed? . . . ?
I have betrayed:
    it's taking revenge
    it has looked out—beyond the chair—
the betrayed
rest of the world
it looks
its looks are not for me

A Dance on Mistakes Unpronounced

Translated by Katarzyna Szuster and Mark Tardi

Calm down, Białoszewski
you've been the first one happy today
(humor like rumor

                                        fell! oh
                                            rest
                                        unrest),
you're not the first one miserable
before you, after you, across time
                    millions
         monkeyllions
  like you
morph into
others, escape from monkeyllions
into monkeyllions
                          or if too many
urged
                    then something big,
because you want to be big,
so morph

Six Poems

Justyna Bargielska

a waltz in 4/4 time

Translated by Katarzyna Szuster

it's a waste to use it on a poem. i'll write you a letter about it:
at wind-up clocks time i felt like a prairie dog. i called
annie but she was in the phase amylase. i called my mom
but she was too old. i called. unluckily. the cat on the window
gave a sign to the vessels in the loop. the fiery sails fluttered.
before they fly away: you remember i was talking about carrying
the world and its environs on my shoulders. that now time will pucker
differently. in the furrows of days dirt crumbs i will kneel talk trash
about the war catalogs names for children. and how i'm afraid when
my neighbor pounds on cutlets (they won't open, they're dead)
i said: it's nothing. at nights sculpted high kind steps design
a sea-green crevice of light under the door. the hovercrafts
of his dreams land by my side all of them. you remember. remember?
psst: i might have been wrong. that's it. finally, i hope your days flex
in your hands now i'll be going
all beautiful and sleek

an invitation

Translated by Katarzyna Szuster

i speak of the iron border between me and you.
we swim across different tracks. here octopi
shipwrecks eyes everywhere. the same there
plus fragile differences that everybody takes
and examines alone. and if

he told? when i'm a god i understand that
it could disrupt but now i am a sunday
and i'd like to show you my school the wrists
eyelashes of my husband. you show me too.

Ophelia

Translated by Katarzyna Szuster

The redhead O. also sings other songs.
I dog her footsteps
with a microphone around the woods,
and her feet
inspire dryness into rustling,
and rustling into fires.

It's easy to say: I follow her,
but really, O. always falls behind
lingers over each tiny stick,
not burned all the way.

The redhead O. is accurate,
you might say—precise,
she uses adjectives
and dental floss.

The redhead O. is unbearable—
she lights hell for me
the same way she lights a match.

Mitsouko by Guerlain

Translated by Katarzyna Szuster

a dream of happiness with a Japanese man in a burned
manger: he's looking around the cinders. we need to find them
he says and arrange them a proper one. i'm pruning
water lilies because languages are assigned and his marbles
are rolling behind me now. let him brush aside the ashes with a
sharp counting rhyme. pruning. the day's becoming a black-and-
white photograph of itself.

Socio path

Translated by Katarzyna Szuster

A storm not really. And if let's go in a box of one-way mirrors
$\qquad\qquad\qquad\qquad\qquad$ from loop to loop?
In Finnish to wander—to walk from pool to pool. I've lost the language
$\qquad\qquad\qquad\qquad\qquad$ of birds and Finns
when I gave up stuttering. And let's go to sleep? When their breaths
$\qquad\qquad\qquad\qquad\qquad$ synchronize
they'll start filming the bed in which the boy from *Reading Rainbow*
I'll go from you through a hole with a finger in the wallpapers to six-graders'
$\qquad\qquad\qquad\qquad\qquad$ lockers?
And let's take off the rusty dress, no questions about who I'm looking for
between your pools? The wave cutter? A storm no. And chit-chat
$\qquad\qquad\qquad\qquad\qquad$ smash-up?
$\qquad\qquad$ And schreiberhau in sheets? And your in case—the Cap?

A poem starting with "I"

Translated by Katarzyna Szuster

Sometimes one is made of leatherette like these old schoolbags
and sometimes one is a chiropractor who'd never come back
because he'd sleep at The Holy Spirit's, on a heap of hot stones.
It's the first reprieve. One doesn't have to be a seamstress' daughter
to know that ektenia is a kind of garter, and this is the second reprieve.
violet, scarlet, mitosis, cracking grout, gasoline rainbows,
ankles stung by rabid pigweed:
and who says it's impossible to live?

St. Lucy, the patroness of blind fish, subatomic tablets
and kittens carefully licked out, puts us in twos in each pocket
and wanders. When she gets us in one piece over a domestic milky way
we'll know how to aim at each other's vile hearts from three miles
and it will be love, the hundred thousandth reprieve.

Three Poems

Miłosz Biedrzycki

[untitled]

Translated by Frank L. Vigoda

I am a night that doesn't want to end
so hot and dry my throat sticks
the soft walls coated by mucus by dust

I am the giant letters IŁAWA GŁÓWNA
the ashen glow of sodium lamps
the loud buzz of a fluorescent tube in the corridor

I am the mumbling of a hippie demanding
three thousand złotys for a cup of tea
because the pigs only just let him go

I am the pigs on the platform hunched in the wind
eyes red from lack of sleep
chins tucked in the collars of their uniforms

I am the iron-gray river under the bridge
I am the clatter of a train on the bridge's grid
I am a mercury vapor rising above the fields

I am the broken window a trip without a moral
I am the broken window that lets the fog
seep in, I am the clatter, the travel, the night

Five in the Morning, Cold

Translated by Frank L. Vigoda

how Warsaw sucks people up
like a giant vacuum cleaner—in Siedlce
I doze in the empty train to wake up with
a fat woman in a woolen beret on my

left and on my right, faces, gray faces,
tired faces, swollen from lack of sleep
faces swaying silently together with
the moving train. the stars

lazily and as if out of habit take
the last few steps of their contredanse
and pause waiting for the factory siren
of the sun. For a moment I feel

so terribly out of place, like a dandy
in my elegantly ripped jacket. and then
I think no, I am at work
right now, as I watch

[untitled]

Translated by Frank L. Vigoda

a precise procedure—the air, rough-hewn
from a dark stone, a newsstand
at the corner of St. Phillip's and Short St.,
closed at this hour, bright lights left on inside

a chat at the metal counter or a prostitutes'
picnic. one with her back turned alternates
a gulp of vodka from a glass bottle with a gulp
of cola from a plastic one. getting into

the mood for the night shift. this cocktail
mixes only in the throat, on the way down.
the drizzle stopped, damp cold still cuts to the bone

air, smell of wet stucco, flicker of street lamps
in puddles. all these images mix only in the throat,
on the way down. a frozen race.

Five Poems

Katarzyna Szuster

said oyster

       my mind is somewhere else
on the coffee table
where it gains perspective

let's pick a quarrel there

words just warp what's at stake
i'm tempted but i'm arbitrary
a shapeshifter and a lousy storyteller
and those cold mornings they
don't let go

       my mind is someplace else
on the bus stop bench
where it wins proportion

let's pick a quarrel there

from the desk of Żółwik

a start of surprise at how everything is
the usual way i'm scared of nothingness
but i'm scared more
of the dentist
all the things you don't have
an opinion on
like an old wiener dog running about
a cathedral
a waltz performed around a fat lady
you want to overtake

full of wonders
it's hardly enough—
i'm not a space open
semantically
soundless
of these two fruit i give you the whole one
i keep the bruised one
for myself

starched curtains for your visit

my skin
                less aesthetics on the catwalk
                contemplate it otherwise
                i drop clumsily
                somewhat tragic
                relief

                again

                the lightness that's not there
                the Empty empty space between
                my paraphrase and your exactitude

lemon muffin revelation song

my heart is pure and my axe is sharp
there is no other story i'd long more
to believe to know where we're lost
to feel the difference unrhythmically
spattered on your launching ramp
impalpable but beyond omission—
always generous
i can only grant you as much reprieve
as i'm keeping in store for me

riddle smugglers

to comprehend them
these feelings loitering
made of two parts—lesser and greater
on top

there's a film on their touch that says:
this is the e n d
of our field trip the policemen
are dancing and the benches are grinning
at the suicidal passersby
that they loved adventure stories
that turn out badly
and only so

such tinkering—you'd better not
cut on the cross
but you do
as you do what you want
you say: hand me my
scores the evening news
             is out of tune tonight

Gallery III:

Were & Whir

Nine Poems

Miron Biatoszewski

FROM **Calculus of Whims (Rachunek zachciankowy)**

Addition by Subtraction

Translated by Katarzyna Szuster and Mark Tardi

> letters
> you creep
> a scent
> sex
> luck
> a marvel
> thru:{ need
> a stream
> a squint
> breakfast
> a hop
> a jog
> as if you
> screeched

Whimsical Personality

Translated by Mark Tardi

today's I
today's most-possible-me
wants the immediacy of fulfillment
before sleeping into metomorrowness

Get Lost (Odczepić się)

Translated by Ela Kotkowska

FALSE TEETH

—**Straight away**
your look has improved.

FALSE TEETH ACADEMY

By turns they sit tight and slip out. Hold on! cram.
Off to a birthday party.
Wearing them.
Talking like through glass. I crackle.
Cutlet, tartlet. Rattle in my attic. As do the teeth.
A turn of the jaw. Which foreign part to chew,
and which to implant?
No one can tell. How could they? At first,
I didn't know any better,
either. It's only that the lesson is easier
to swallow if it's less of a bite.

COUNSEL CHOIR

— it will stop aching
— rise above it
— get used to it
— carry something
— read in it
— bite

Dreams with those teeth
are complicated
you need to spit something out
but can't

right away
confusion
people, meetings, sulking;
only one way out
to wake up
what was that about?
oh, just some teeth
what's more mine

— Stop wearing them to sleep
— I don't
— and when you eat?
— they get in the way
risky when reading
— so what are they for?
for lovemaking, no good, either
— to improve the view, for you
— is that all?
— that's all, on a desert island
I'd let it go

So all this selection, organ
radars, body parts
will always
serve
only

prospectively

What about skeletons?
in the pictures
they always have excellent teeth
in – ter – esting

toothless, what would they do?

NOTE

from: „Odczepić się"i inne wiersze opublikowane w latach 1976-1980.
Utwory zebrane, vol. 7. Warszawa: Państwowy Instytut Wydawniczy, 1994.
pp. 167-170.

Participle: Grammatic Play

Translated by Ela Kotkowska

CHARACTERS:

    Participle as Entering
    Participle as Exiting
    Participle as Doing What

There are three wire hats on a hanger. **Participle** *enters wearing one; exits wearing the second; and, wearing the third,* **Participle** *pryingly intrudes, instigates, interrogates. Entering, exiting are symbolic, and signify only the direction towards or from the back of the stage, which will later on get mixed up anyway.*

ENTERING *entering self-introductively*
    Entering
EXITING *entering and exiting self-introductively*
    Exiting
Exits.
DOING WHAT *as if self-introductively, and yet meddlesomely, instigatingly, and right away vanishingly*
    Doing what?
EXITING *entering*
    It's just me exiting
Exits.
DOING WHAT *addressing* EXITING
    so why first entering?
ENTERING *instigated by someone's entering*
    It's just me entering
Exits.
DOING WHAT *for a meddlesome moment addressing* ENTERING
    so why entering?
EXITING *instigated by someone's exiting*
    so why is Participle Entering entering against my Participle Exiting exiting?
Exits.
DOING WHAT *for a meddlesome moment addressing* EXITING
    so why is Participle Exiting entering against Participle Entering, even while saying it, doing exactly what?

ENTERING *entering, picking up on the instigation*

... doing what exactly not only against my Participle Entering
but even against Interrogative Participle Doing What in person

Exits.

DOING WHAT *for a meddlesome moment*

who against my Participle Doing What, without inquiring,
is doing what?

EXITING *entering as if taking revenge on both*

now deliberately, before my exiting, I'm entering, and doing what
Doing What!

DOING WHAT

who doing what as who to whom for what for Doing What?

Quickly switches hats.

EXITING

I am doing what? am I in any way entering entering?

EXITING *quicker and quicker*

I am doing what? am I in any way exiting exiting?

DOING WHAT

doing what? doing what? doing what? doing what? doing what?
doing what? entering—and doing what, exiting? exiting, and doing
what, entering, and doing what, exiting, and doing what, entering
exiting? exiting entering, and doing what, entering exiting ...

NOTE

From: *Teatr Osobny 1955-1963. Utwory Zebrane vol. 2.* Warszawa: Państwowy Instytut Wydawniczy,
1988, pp. 147-150.

considerations and deliberations (namysły i rozmysły)

Translated by Alissa Valles

a stroll's
too much
of a toll
a pipe drones
in my head
I'm out of it
already in bed
is it for good?

november's end
sea's beginning
. . .
what's that black glowing?
fanning?
dawn cawing
a she-crow

[SOPOT, NOVEMBER 23, 1980]

my head was a Jew
riding a tram
Germans, don't get off
just keep going on and on
so at least you don't move,
but now you can move—

aha—my pillow
aha—I woke up

Even Someone Else's Past Is Bad For You

Translated by Alissa Valles

not leaving this place
never traveling
to any other planets
unless they're here—
so if anything happens
pretend we don't know each other

Night
in the heart
of Wilanów
in yellow light
dark in the ditch
is that a drip?
a tap? no
a march . . . ? . . .
a night empty as a vast zero with a shadow
fixated on "no"
passes I watch
a water machine
on the grass
doesn't know what it's doing
and yet it knows

FROM **Added and Selected Poems**
(Wiersze wybrane i dobrane)

Translated by Monika Kocot

nothing happened
- - - - - - - -
I guess I'm standing
everywhere
only me

awful

* * *

Translated by Monika Kocot

sleeping cold
stirring up speech and breath
the world approaches

* * *

Translated by Ela Kotkowska

Wild carrots rose up
from the ground,
flew, fell.

A letter misspelled.

(Exhorting to crows)

Translated by Mark Tardi and Ilona Zineczko

BLACK WINTER
STREET NOT UNLIT
DAYBREAK
I stand
—and it's me
this stick
that twists around itself
the ravened sky
lengthily patiently and with fervor
chinese-like
from unfolding to folding
around and away
how much it wants
memory
my majesty
an ice floe
bass ackwards

FROM **(Variants of catching breath)**

Translated by Ilona Zineczko

of finality
by common finally
unserious
as if unreal
. . . none . . .

FROM **(American poems)**

Translated by Ilona Zineczko

in a strange country
in an unknown tongue
MEANINGS FLY BY
WHIRLING
wanting to
        crawl over
        me
        think me out
        and I say to myself:
        —you're losing . . .
        how animal-like
        slower
        quietly you go
        quietly you are

Five Poems

Monika Mosiewicz

zorbing

Translated by Miłosz Biedrzycki and Frank L. Vigoda

well, I tried this sport
and it makes me think of those orbs of light
in which we'd love to float,
all grace, effortlessly, always expanding
the realm they encompass,
the ever sharper peaks
in the thinning air, the stream
of light, delicate puffs on the neck, the hum
growing under the skull, horses dragging us
in all directions.

Ouuuuu! lipo!

Translated by Mark Tardi

Recall, say, binoculars with jellyfish and you feel like
Exploring *Mare crisium* or *Oceanus procellarum*. Or:
Neil Armstrong, and immediately you grow into
Imponderable indexings with all these
Arches and types from *Astrum atrum*.

They sense: testosterone implies impass

Raven, reverence won't make these one-trick ponies fly, so
Unseat their commentaries: diarrhea-tard . . . ooou!
Lipo out the flabby *gestalt*. This
Experiment ends with *weltschmerz*.
Solipsism a kind of metafucktual scandal!

> *eyebrow went, blood spent*
> *eyebrow went, blood spent*
> *eyebrow went, blood spent*
>
> *tra la la, tra la la*
>
> *eyebrow went, blood spent*
> *eyebrow went, blood spent*
> *eyebrow went, blood spent*

Winter garden party

Translated by Katarzyna Szuster and Mark Tardi

strawberries, oysters, furs, doves—
leaps: we are left in unknown rooms
saw: they have soaps with sunken scarabs.

Mirrors: Oh, we take these with us, alluring scarves
wrap the places we haven't entered yet,
but each has one of their own.

Yes: with raised head,
in a cool zenith we become lighter

Lucida intervalla

Translated by Mark Tardi

Gaps, inaccuracies, errors—
I look after everything, in order to remember:
when you turn a corner,
there's a bending of light

Alba

Translated by Miłosz Biedrzycki and Frank L. Vigoda

To talk to you, to part dark
surfaces, to install glass bricks,

Skylights, ornate crevices. to build
wide thoroughfares at the edge of town,

Multilane bypasses, blue launching sites
with golden hornets.

Bubbles of sizzling air twinkle overhead,
turn into cobalt polychromes.

To talk to you, saying: come on, dawn,
let's run

Four Poems

Kacper Bartczak

Narrow Poem

Translated by the author and Mark Tardi

I can hear between your gaps
I'm seeing some Nothing clicks for
me only unsettles I buy
maybe three rivets and move to
a rickety plot and a midget meadow
Or say a field and black
square Tacks of light in your eyes
deep metal
bending The sky

crumbles like asphalt
like a garden is cultivated here
I can already feel that somebody
Somebody dynamic who wants
good will drill holes
purchase breeze-blocks

You'll tighten up in yourself
A narrow janitor you
in a warehouse of freezers
Assess your inventory Outlook
not so good This mechanic of treats
will sweeten the swamp

Worm

Translated by the author and Mark Tardi

A sore throat stretches in me
your litany a periodic table
I'm a hard man at the age of
I'll pass everything along
to my wife All the best
I order a number six and stand
on my head Never say
that you don't need avowals
Indeed we need animals
in mucus Instead and away
Your Polish strikes me I'm treating
myself with your gap
Let its codes flow through me

Form of Exchange

Translated by the author and Mark Tardi

At dawn the houses stood so brilliant
well built for people
and produce Church spires
sewing markets into scenery The Black Forest

so historical Cleanly predatory
birds flew over it Trees healthy and
animals abundant between the power lines
and the quicksilver

of the Autobahn The air had this sharpness
and soundless trains gouged the gleaming landscape
into distances Pleasant for the eye
The grass green juicy Machines cutting

with a fragrant sonority
The birds' singing entirely
understandable Imagine
I went down to the street and met people

on a lawn They're eating olives salami and
barbeque Talked to each other completely
in German I understood everything *No really*
I really started to understand

Aura

Translated by the author and Mark Tardi

Behind every reality stands
its special effect You're going to the checkout
and it'll cost you Scanning through
an article gives you an ulcer
for weeks Finally somebody
gets it More responds You're not reading
the entirety because the sum speaks
between bar codes Buy a few more
scraps and you're left checked out

Nothing lands on you for long
like you're sand or rock and nothing
holds at the edges of a grey hour
Glossy or matte But the piece

I'm finding in me stretches
over square miles of parking lots
mounds of trash and far beyond
the limits of subjects delyrical
and economical All the best
from them For decimating ecstasy

I have decimating ecstasy From life
I got nerves of steel I shuck solace
from the greyest threads

Eight Poems

Aneta Kamińska

chapter 4.
week 2 month 6.

Translated by Katarzyna Szuster

you know after all how much i love
the polish
language *no i can't be ironic in german* you'll have to
sometime to vienna *you'll have to stay in poland* women never
no it's *men who don't* wine
tasting maybe
you have
I do have
what does it say
about us
the horoscope

(komm komm zu mir
come to me
come)

chapter 25, exit 2

Translated by Katarzyna Szuster

(out of admiration)

I

i dreamed
(dialing the number)
about you that
i didn't learn polish (he picked up some czech
traitor) you were shouting awfully i was
(types of connection direction)
afraid my entire (*to markus steiner what are you doing in poland* so so)
body was shaking (*what are you doing in poland* not too bad) and you
(*what are you doing in poland*) continuously (every day every day)
no it's a nightmare
(duration a number of units)
but fortunate
(the cost of your call)
i woke up
(in złotys
net)

2

writing
an email when do we have
(maturity)

3

next time

chapter 11.
two years later

Translated by Katarzyna Szuster

if not coffee then

the one
we buy is a blend of many (the prettiest) of different
(the most firm) only selected make up
exclusively (now with a knife) the finest brand steeped (in half
and again) of unusually
smooth
taste
(juice runs down your fingers) its aroma intense exceptionally lasting comes
from (it's sticky)
matures on
the highest (fluffy and milky)
the best conditions
to

and thick
and lick

me
(now or
 nothing)

(*orange mocha, cube cafe*)

discharge

Translated by Katarzyna Szuster

opening
myself
clean through
i **transpare** permeate monitor
the knocking from inside ringing pounding
(on and me)
i squeeze and study if they're **trembling** yet if
blinking atriums slamming and **moans** grinding and
bones something's
forcing its way through (happening hot and
foggy inside) in veins something
stirs slops
splashes across the eyes windows
(dark and tight
sanguineous and sanguinary)
not to think
what i am
from underneath

to concentrate
to diminish
to disappear

No virus found in the oncoming message.

discharge

Translated by Katarzyna Szuster

opening
myself
clean through
i **transpare** permeate monitor
the knocking from inside ringing **pounding**
(on and me)
i **squeeze** and study if they're trembling yet if
blinking atriums **slamming** and moans **grinding** and
bones **something's**
forcing its way through (happening hot and
foggy inside) in veins something
stirs **slops**
splashes across the eyes windows
(dark and tight
sanguineous and **sanguinary**)
not to think
what i am
from underneath

to concentrate
to diminish
to disappear

No virus found in the oncoming message.

self-portrait without lights

Translated by Katarzyna Szuster

in-the-darkly gropingly slyly
checking if still
i'm
by my side

self-portrait by a potter's wheel

Translated by Katarzyna Szuster

i—the shaper of lines
i—the verser of clay
a cluster plaster clings
and the wheel's—
been
angling

self-portrait in bits

Translated by Katarzyna Szuster

i ^{c}a $_{n}$'$_{t}$
$_{p}$^{i}ck $_{u}$p
$_{t}$$_{he}$ pi^{e}$_{c}$^{e}s

· NOTE

the last poems of nazar honczar written by aneta kamińska

ACKNOWLEDGMENTS

All poems are used with permission. Translations of Miron Białoszewski have been allowed courtesy of the Estate of Miron Białoszewski (all rights reserved).

Gallery I: The Salt of Structure—Miron Białoszewski

> "Of the Revolution of Things," "Study of a Key" and "My Jacobs of Exhaustion" are reprinted with permission from Miron Białoszewski, *The Revolution of Things*, translated by Andrzej Busza & Bogdan Czaykowski. (Washington, D.C.: Charioteer Press, 1974.)

> "Two Translations" ("Dwa Przekłady"), translated by Katarzyna Jakubiak & Rick Hilles, is from *Obroty rzeczy* [The Revolution of Things]. (Warsaw: PIW, 1956.)

> "Peelings" ("Obierzyny"), translated by Gabriel Gudding & Katarzyna Jakubiak, is from *Rachunek zachciankowy* [Calculus of Whims]. (Warsaw: PIW, 1959.)

Poems by Andrzej Sosnowski, translated by Rod Mengham, appear with permission of the author.

Poems by Przemysław Owczarek, translated by Katarzyna Szuster & Mark Tardi, are from *RDZA*. (Kraków: Wydawnictwo Zielona Sowa, 2007.)

Poems by Ewa Chruściel appear with permission of the author. "No na la" reprinted with permission from *Hot Metal Bridge*.

Gallery II: Erroneous Emotions – Miron Białoszewski

> "happyend" ("hepyent") and "Erroneous Emotion" ("Mylne wzruszenie"), translated by Katarzyna Szuster, are from *Mylne wzruszenia* [Erroneous Emotions]. (Warsaw: PIW, 1961.)

> "Green, therefore, it is" ("Zielony: więc jest") and "We starfish" ("My rozgwiazdy"), translated by Katarzyna Szuster, are from *Obroty rzeczy* [The Revolution of Things]. (Warsaw: PIW, 1956.)

> "Romance with a Concreteness" ("Romans z konkretem"), translated by Katarzyna Jakubiak & Rick Hilles, is from *Rachunek zachciankowy* [Calculus of Whims]. (Warsaw: PIW, 1959.)

> "Dance on Mistakes Unpronounced" ("Taniec na błędach ubezdźwięcznionych"), translated by Katarzyna Szuster & Mark Tardi, is from *Było i było* [Were and were]. (Warsaw: PIW, 1965.)

Poems by Justyna Bargielska, translated by Katarzyna Szuster, are from *Dating Sessions*. Kraków: Wydawnictwo Zielona Sowa, 2003; and China Shipping. (Kielce: Kserokopia, 2005.)

Poems by Miłosz Biedrzycki, translated by Frank L. Vigoda, appear with permission from the author.

Poems by Katarzyna Szuster appear with permission from the author.

Gallery III: Were & Whir—Miron Białoszewski

> "Addition by Subtraction" ("Niedopisanie") and "Whimsical Personality" ("Osobowość zachciankowa"), translated by Katarzyna Szuster & Mark Tardi, are from *Rachunek zachciankowy* [Calculus of Whims]. (Warsaw: PIW, 1959.)

> "False Teeth," translated by Ela Kotkowska, is from *Odczepić się i inne wiersze opublikowane w latach 1976-1980* [Get Lost and Other Poems]. *Collected Works*, vol. 7. (Warsaw: PIW, 1994.)

> Participle, translated by Ela Kotkowska, is from *Teatr Osobny* [Separate Theatre] 1955-1963. *Collected Works*, vol. 2. (Warsaw: PIW, 1988.)

Poems translated by Monika Kocot; Ela Kotkowska are from *Wiersze wybrane i dobrane* [Added and Selected Poems]. (Warsaw: Czytelnik, 1980.)

Excerpt from "Exhorting to Crows" ("Namawianie na wrony"), translated by Mark Tardi & Ilona Zineczko, is from *Obmapowanie Europy. AAAmeryka. Ostatnie wiersze.* [Mapping of Europe. AAAmerica. Last poems.] (Warsaw: PIW, 1988.)

Excerpts from "Variants of catching breath" ("Odmiany łapania tchu") and "American poems" ("[Wiersze amerykańskie]"), translated by Ilona Zineczko, is from *Obmapowanie Europy. AAAmeryka. Ostatnie wiersze.* [Mapping of Europe. AAAmerica. Last poems.] (Warsaw: PIW, 1988.)

Poems by Monika Mosiewicz, translated by Miłosz Biedrzycki & Frank L. Vigoda; and Katarzyna Szuster & Mark Tardi, are from *cosinus salsa.* (Kraków: Wydawnictwo Zielona Sowa, 2008.)

Poems by Kacper Bartczak, translated by the author & Mark Tardi, are from *Życie Świetnych Ludzi.* (Łódź: Wydawnictwo Kwadratura, 2009.)

Poems by Aneta Kamińska, translated by Katarzyna Szuster, appear with permission from the author.

poetry

A Tonalist Set,
guest edited by
Laura Moriarty

"Little Sigmund" by Hannah Barrett

A Tonalist Set

Laura Moriarty

What is A Tonalist? It is possible that this question can be answered by reading this set of poems and the essay by me, "A Tonalist Coda," also included here, in which I speculate about lyric, anti-lyric, musicality etc.? The Coda follows the long essay poem A Tonalist in the book of the same name due out from Nightboat at about the same time as this issue of Aufgabe. I want to express my appreciation to the editors of Aufgabe for presenting this A Tonalist Set.

Most of the poets in this selection have long been associated with the blog A Tonalist Notes or I have known them forever, often reading and occasionally teaching and writing about their work. Many writers whose work informs the notion of A Tonalist, but who are not included here, can be found online in a selection I put together for Jacket (Feb/March 2010 issue). All of these writers (and various others) comprise the community out of which I dreamed up the group, idea, or movement called A Tonalist. What they share is not so much a style as an attention to words and a belief, at least in the moment of the poem, that these words make a world—an "untethered island," as Myung Mi Kim writes. They, Taylor Brady notes, "Scribble in the wallow of a cosmic faith / then swallow up the sentence's dead end." I thank them for it.

Nonsound, The Musical

Rob Halpern

No song onsite these airs sing what things
Can't be needs forgotten grafted manes
To metal scored hews whose breath resides
In place where matter voided voices still

The things I've abolished beat down ears
With instruments plump dealers produce
Extracted breath by force returns tones
Sound silence dead in a cavity my mouth

Collects their parts in words bones graft
Lives undo deeds themselves struck out
Downed subjects don't matter by accord
Threat menace refuse no living sounds re

—sidues breath resides in anthem noise
Choppers ammo floods a sky not being
Sky and the sea's vast plains whose military
Sonics sew the ground what we produce

Trains ears on spectral sounds surround
Us systems sing in private mouths deeds
Force airs menace ears metal tones things
We've muted living hums blown bits into

Them being bone ash all our dead remains
Residual song refusing clings to breath
Wrecked mouths tubes absent horns beats

—a silence onsite of a music we'll never hear.

More Familiars

Patrick Durgin

It must have been something
to live in the age of painting,
before what occurred, when even
media gave way to what happened.

An equivalent perhaps:
that, short for in order
that, because confidence
and motivation were metaphysical then.

They call me Patrick.
It's my name. It has
my name on it. My
signature is a match.

Who forfeits this money
I earn with this endeavor
eats at this table and spills
the remainder; gratitude is,

in this scenario, like
taking nomenclature for language,
to syntax what my name is
to this sentence. A return to

the fold. But it's happened already.
Hanging one's head is like
turning to face destinations mingled,
a tailspin into its consenting wake.

Together again, two of us sling
a tree upright and bury it.
The tree splits lethargically.
Luminaries suck

and also-rans wheeze.
One of us unwraps their prosthetic.
Most of us are afraid to breathe.
In bridal white, disposable masks,

the entire head turns,
mouths hand guided at the knees
and traffic like water batched
around motions to the ground,

in sound-canceling headgear
trimming fallen leaves
from granite cubes
where to everyone all of it's apparent.

Everything depicted wanes,
and when anything magnified
persists, nothing is depicted.
I have no memory for it, either.

MORE FAMILIARS (CODA)

The hen in Guernica
The catalogue, the host
The leading leisure-service
Corporation, of course.

Androids in America
The pitch, the sympathy
The various hibernations
Antithetical, of course.

Vaporous in protest
The pump, the thrall
Secreting the ointments
Seditious, of course.

MORE FAMILIARS (SODA)

The culture languishes, like
Fizz . . . tickles your nose.
Of course I've had it in the ear
Before.

Norma Cole

Four brown birds
fly up into the false
pepper tree

conscious of
mist myself and
outside—when

does the past
begin?

      * * *

The night's
to imagine not

solve it then
home bed checks
second state

even space does
not repeat

its most welcome

self, standing, her
yellow backpack
waiting at a bus stop

waving at a little
boy in a floppy orange
hat running

    * * *

towards soldiers, one
a cabinet maker, the other a
barber—Adieu, mon étoile

layer of water
body of film
a high first floor

window from which
he jumped

Thunk

Andrew Joron

Sun, shun real relation.

You (all)
Revoke, re-
        evoke my name.

Manner to man, I
        o'er error roar

Your ore & ire.

To escape a scape of eyes
        at all scales, untune Night.

A why, a wire we
Are.

Filling feeling

You
        think & thank
You.

Being
Being the one

        unstable, unstatable
        state—

There
        O
Other—a throw through aether.

FROM **Journey to the Sun**

Brent Cunningham

DIVISION 2, SECTION 2

& we heard
a certain sound
unshielded & hurt
& tried to refuse it, yes,
but flects of sun
informed our eyes
& nerves et al

it's true you must study
it's true you must reason
coming ever nearer to THINGS
moving & burning & crying
bored & overbearing
it will never be easy
but what else were you doing

8 hours a night in shadow
they waited
stars & animals & literatures
starvation & practice cities
literally, politely, rapidly
DEMENTED
& now look at them
out in the malls
waving their hats

then I saw !
in a crater !
my replacement !

its body was brass & copper
& hard units of rubber
a torso like a frame

from far Atomic Seas
small wires, red & orange
& parts w/o decay
for all that was taken care of
quadrangals & rectangals
& brontosauri PETRIFIED
this really happened
yes, in America

hence the 3 classes of men
take their fix'd destinations
they are the 2 Contraries
& the Reasoning Negative

mark well my words; they have travelled through space

my legs became stone legs !
my arms became stone arms !
my arms commanded fingers !
my legs commanded feet !
& that is how !
by the Economy of Principles !

every desert
can & must be crossed
one edge in Origin
one edge in Number
one in the Purpose to Exist

if only to see
these bodies
to their deaths

The Voyage of the Lizopard

Alan Halsey

I

Spare seapiers prints in sepia.
Saints' farts collected by Mr Beddoes.
For "Gingulph" read "Fandigo" & vice versa.
Decimal code exactly ?ceded.

2

Unordinary, scratted, serrated
Sylvan, salvage, galvanize, saliva
(wraps round raptor in his right lure)

3

Mr Blemya saw a burnt arse elf
tail up & starkers
reminds him of a picture of Our Lady
he saw years ago
somewhere off the Edgeware Road.

4

So what about the crocodogs
and whatever became of
the lost works of Herodotus
they unearthed in Guiana?

5

Baffled in filths (unmapped)
where a quip of a quarrel started a fight
if it was a monster with cucumbers for horns
before it was scalped & scalloped or after.
If edible, not, but if not & so on.

6
"Read here" meaning
Stick to the recipe, again.
"A fox with his feet on backwards"
in the words of Mr Moros.
Snailish as proverbs and
cooks' alchemy I called it.
Without a name for God in their language
those locals telling how they slipped
off some Robin Hood planet
happy as happy ever was.

7
A single scruple of gold
two of saffron . . . "At Redbourn
and at the blood of Hales"
Mr Heywood wrote but we hadn't
left England expecting we'd
meet ourselves halfway out
halfway on the journey home

8
or find we'd been set up as badges.
Our little sunny faces popping up
like pumpkins or pamphlets
(item removed)
"as good as wrong and as empty"

See Above

Tyrone Williams

Indebted to the general
displacement of ground
                         sky horizon the
decimated ranks of one
thousand and one
                         Arabian midnights
conscripted into children
drowning in the Mirror
                         Loch of conscious-
ness can no longer be
said to –scend or –scend
                         turn –wise or –wise
Ezekiel's mis-
spoken wheel.
                         Persia aside . . .

frames the rabid
virgins-sirens
                         frothing up the Dead
Sea. Bound disaster
the horn of plenty
                         replenishes his
captive crew to say
nothing of the coffins-
                         coffers below: exhibit
A of case no.
ur- and Third
                         on permanent loan-
continuance to Franco-
Anglo-phone museums-
                         nations at competitive
rates unspelled out
being the given
                         groundlessness a-

cross which a pigeon-toed
bow-legged abomination—
                    Big Foot—
amortizes fe-
fi-fo-fum *tres-*

                    passer-by and by *bien*

The Same Complaint

Scott Inguito

Masking compulsion with connoisseurship,
talking, that shadow releasing signal-
anxiety, refugees in parking lots
can't help but kick the futbol
around. Something in there
that is ineducable, in here (points to chest); it's not a
political thing, man, it's a *thing* thing. What's the matter

with you, bound by the repetitive this and here, the
that and there, feedback that reinforces
the experience of our separateness, a grip lost to
crazed gnawings, no longer locative
of that poor chew of needful skinnies? Well?

Fines bat sweethearts blue for bathing
in univocity-bad girl, bad boy-not
because that that pleasure is bad
but because they can't produce a single one. Jealous?
I
try to run the possessed revel down. Soon
the dancing stops, streaked breasts
whirl and pour without ceasing
without an inventory of clues. It's as close
you can get to set things going under
a questionable sobriety, kindred to half-curses
of another morning. Another morning
slopes blank rays; put them on, any
of it, dozing, going thick-kissedly
into the act. Painting is a machine that cures.
Do I believe that? I believe it as much as
Lil' John does. Yeas~!

Green throated, ashy-kneed, you, you
bet only peyote buttons, ice-coldly, a
clump of medium drying sticky part
to sticky part, together making component clinches.
In the envelope the beginning of a new passion, the
butter and bread picking up the smell of the androgynous deity
during withdrawals from gender. Walk around and see all
the tools, love, hour to hour. These are the components of
our lives: speakers, tuner, derailler, amp, mixed dank, mixed hedonic
pourings as the mouth-wise scarify lime
rinds, salt, chile, and chicharrones.

Goddamn the same piece of plural stain in the carpet.
Too bad I can't find an audio system that
takes cassette tapes. This sitcom isn't
funny at all. The ideas are wrong and they stay wrong. Wait,
the line, "Long time no bro, Bro" wasn't bad. Yes, I liked
Suicidal Tendencies at one time, and wanted to
go the US Festival. Now the praise of idleness. I

have no plans for tonight.

Repetition As War By Identity

Standard Schaefer

"And yet it is possible to imagine an art in which the limitations
of reality would be minimized, in which the made and the unmade
would be indistinct, an art that would be instantaneously real, without
ghosts. And perhaps that art exists, under the name literature."

—Cesar Aira

Built on obviousness and silence suitcases full of smoking meat
In the high noon of endgames and hellos that like a moment of birth last
      for weeks
Irony is a provincial form of distance disabling wandering the circle looking
      for an exit
Pounding on the walls it cannot for a moment stop explaining
Redundancy poses as structure
Ambient shadows bisect a rough music
Existence, blind, throws a soft light on the lap of the imagination
Fish rise to take a cloud Dante reaches the San Fernando Valley and weeps
      in envy
The desert is pure composition
Silence escalates entropy and the priests create a language with which to
      kill pigeons
The repetition of entropy renders catastrophe stasis
Letters sliced sideways and struck through almost universal so thoroughly corrupt
So public and above logic as if language itself were the vessel of entropy
But identity doesn't victimize repetition because repetition is war by identity
And prophecy makes repetition the font bank gothic the page moleskin yellow
There must be, explains the stripper turning to cough, an ecology of alphabets
And folded sheets to metabolize the pervasive runs in the stocking,
The endless attempts at persuasion.
Whenever we dream them, we dream the unbuilt.

Here is my translation: Poetry is doubt in the absence of humility.

I have been hers, yours, ever since.

A Ruse Of Rule

Taylor Brady

Scribble in the wallow of a cosmic faith
then swallow up the sentence's dead end—

slight fogs the orphan teller's mirror
blabbed exacting logics from the naked *is*

that leg up gives a leg gives up on fenced checkpoints
louche admonishment your crosseyed drift

Post the ululated press-op
to resemble not a thing asleep
but at the wheel spun in river-mud
embarked on nothing doing gums
or rubbers rub the nap into a ball

This rerun was somebody's *more, please* from the corner booth's
charmed void exemplified in every lack of instance

the bulge of silhouette or two in elevation
and in section clasped—or grasped?—the politic long reach

defended marrying illegal to illegible an ethic's
acting practice named *improv* but pronounced *improve*

Always first, this mire of civil good

On Community:

Jocelyn Saidenberg

Or, our narrative of relevance.

On poetic communities, for we are the relevant.

Or, haven not haven.

We compel, conspire with ourselves, to reinforce inner walls, support frame, collective sum of individual ones, purchased at the loss of.

On community's law.

Community of our grief and anger, this is our drama, community drama, relived experience rather than of.

For whom is this the enemy?

Or, you did not arrive with all your parts intact, injured functioning more as backdrop.

Community hoards usages in the guise of hoarded techniques. Usages of us. This tendency is inherited, is our virtuosity with these techniques. Our operations are invested, true of the practice more true of our record of the practice.

Community, both necessary and elaborate, crowded with communication, furniture, and reporting, normal juxtaposed over and against the abnormal.

That community, that superior genius, that superior art of relation, total act of reminding, recalling, memorializing, memorizing.

Community report, recall, repeat, preserve, repeat.

This is the voice of history, preserve not create, recall, re-use, this is the voice of community, the memoranda of culture inscribed in the lived community. This makes us more urgent at the circumference, more relevance.

This is the act of community, continual act, of memorization, recall, repetition, a set of motor reflexes, throughout the entire body of the act, enlisted for the preservation of the body community, motor reflex provides us with an emotional release, a relief from anxiety and fear, all the extra injuries.

Or, the hypnotic pleasure of community.

Or, you are seized by disgust.

Our pleasure exploited as the instrument of our continual act, our body continuity, the latest memoranda to you, the lived.

Our community agents in place of causes, are in place of injured parts missing.

Or, you are a menace, haven for missing parts?

The agents are set in the doings, as actors, as colors, as things happening, events, things done, things occurring, both in the inner wall frame and on the circumferences, things relevance.

We are the syntax that supports the relevance, the act, the burden to carry along, the event. We vividly experience moments of doings and happenings linked by our injuries.

The we predominates over the I. Opinion predominates period.

Or, you.

Opinion as our instrument played to the tune of group identity, opinion becomes the community, its state of mind's becoming. Dealer in becoming rather than being with its many, rather than with its visible rather than the.

We sing our hurrying panorama of doings, becomings.

The hurry becomes us. You become us.

Sung into seduction into union with our doings and becomings, spelled by our own incantations, we sleep walk together, our complete emotional life, intact.

We, community, are the ghosts who think we are the mechanism that surrenders itself to performance, to becoming, to the situation, identities itself. Gripped and shattered, self to the claim, cleared to community.

FROM **Civil Bound**

Myung Mi Kim

praise | continents

in the museum of Public Actions

a sight oath

governs

parties to talk

heresy and particulars

remainder, appellate

||

ablative | trying at pitch

scolding wings removed, cuts flushed

choke canal

abuts agricultural, sunken medical

exacting dilation of the inner ear and its coastal timbres

| |

from atlas bulbs, a skull grows

ƒ n t r

rift immunology

hoof or fingerprint

| |

untethered island

strange fetched offices

brain blossom | pain's aspersion

this congregation   supernal

A Tonalist Coda

Laura Moriarty

> "Table manners are useless if there's nothing to eat. Poetry has to have passion for its food—either passion cooked up in tranquility or tranquility cooked up in passion. Eastern "poetry" has neither. We wait politely at the table and are served nothing but silverware."

—Jack Spicer, from "Dialogue of Eastern and Western Poetry"

i. SOME HISTORY

When, at a recent event, I first heard of a dialogue written on index cards by Jack Spicer and Robin Blaser with commentary by Robert Duncan, I was intrigued. I knew of Spicer's determination to keep his poetry in the West Coast, even specifically in San Francisco, of Duncan's complex relationship with publication and of Blaser's decamping for a Canadian West Coast presumably even more distant from the East than the Bay Area. Because the poetics of this circle of friends informs my own practice and that of the writers whose work I have thought of as A Tonalist, without their permission, engagement and occasionally without their knowledge, I wondered if these index cards would have anything to do with my thinking about A Tonalist and my intention to write about it here.

When I read the text (published in Miriam Nichols' *Even On Sunday: Essays, Readings and Archival Materials on the Poetry and Poetics of Robin Blaser*), I initially thought there was little that related to my sense of A Tonalist. This written conversation took place in 1956, when Spicer and Blaser were about thirty, Duncan a bit older. The cards were long part of Robert Duncan's papers at the Bancroft Library at UC Berkeley but only when Kevin Killian and Peter Gizzi discovered one card that had been separated from the bunch in a new set of Spicer's papers did the whole set of them see the light of day.

In this exchange, Spicer asserts a Western (West Coast) poetics by resisting what he believes to be an Eastern (East Coast) dominant poetics. The dialogue begins with Spicer: "Eastern poetry—there isn't any Eastern poetry—and besides, too many people read it." So the dominance is stated here as a readership monopoly. Eastern poetry is taking up too much of the mental real estate that Spicer imagines to be allotted to poetry. Duncan and Blaser question Spicer's sense of Eastern poetry, pointing out that many poets who would fall under the "Eastern" category actually live in the West and vice versa. Duncan and Blaser each also then ascribe value to poets they assume Spicer would term Eastern and whose poetics they don't share but seem to respect. Spicer eschews such civility. His counter arguments are more passionate than logical and he seems gleefully aware of it, as for example in this response to several assertions by Blaser and Duncan that there might be some value in reading "Eastern poets:" "There's not one under forty that does anything. They just rhyme and pick their noses." As Kevin points out in the essay that accompanied the publication of the piece, the writing on these index cards, is an effort to reproduce the vivacity of table talk. The project falls slightly flat, but is interesting in the context of what other texts show to exist at this point in their poetics and for what follows both in their friendship and in their other work.

On closer consideration I realized that, in several ways, I had found exactly what I was looking for in this exchange, both as historical information about the roots of A Tonalist and as a good example of what A Tonalist is exactly not about. In this conversation, Spicer asserts a group identity, shared by his interlocutors who, in turn and in spite of their concurrence with the poetics proposed by Spicer, point out the contradictions generated by any such assertion. Duncan refers to the kind of work they value as Vitalist, an interesting name for the writing he values, but one that clearly didn't last. From a contemporary perspective, I see the term as an interesting alternative to "experimental."

As I reread it, their argument finally began to seem useful to me, even emblematic, partly because of the connection between Spicer/Duncan/Blaser poetics and those of A Tonalist, but also because it is group formation in action. Spicer's assertion against table manners without sustenance can be read as a diatribe against craft or technique for its own sake and against work that aims to fulfill expectations rather than outraging them or that is written to be part of literature (part of the curriculum) rather than to be something that will not easily fit into the canon. There is a lot to hate there, but Spicer was a great hater and, while A Tonalist may take exception to some of his objections, we are sympathetic. But of greater interest is how, in this exchange, one can watch group formation include contradictions, inconsistencies, refutations and assertions, as well as personal relationships that, importantly, often form the basis of all else.

A Tonalist is not a style but an attitude or perhaps a context. It is not a set of techniques. The surface(s) of work that might be called A Tonalist are not superficially similar. A Tonalist proposes an anti-lyric whose viability relates to the history of lyric poetry by resisting as much as enacting it. The table manners are bad. The tranquility being cooked up comes from emptiness. And passion, as everyone knows, means suffering. In A Tonalist the lyric "I" is complicated rather than celebrated. There is doubt. There is, as Kafka said, hope, but not for us. Perhaps that is a lot to ask of a poetics – that it write itself right out of or up against the canon or the idea of literature, that it shoot itself in the foot. The sense of dissatisfaction or self-destruction, not with the person but with the writing subject, is rife.

Such a poetics need not, in fact does not, have a location. Back in the day, however, Jack Spicer loved to assert California as being important to his poetics, to his group and to his enterprise as a writer. Famously he refused to allow his work to be published outside of the Bay Area. I don't share this orientation, which seems part consciously mad poetic jingoism and partly sour grapes, but the locations he often celebrated are the ones I have lived in for most of my life. I have often walked in his mental and actual footprints. However, the idea that place influences the writing of a group of people who are intensely connected to each other and to it, interested me when me when I began writing A Tonalist and continues to be a notion, perhaps a legend.

The only place directly associated with A Tonalist is a blog called A Tonalist Notes which, like any group blog, includes individuals from a number of locations and has readers from all around. This nonplace follows an earlier site called *non* that was A Tonalist before I had invented the term (like much else mentioned here).

The effect of place is not easily discerned. Perhaps those who are attracted to a place and then stay there to make and take part in the milieu have some things in common with it and themselves. For example, is there a heritage among New York City writers of New York School thinking and writing – use of lists, speech, other elements? I feel if we were in a bar together I could convince you that there is. The notion that a poetics can be connected to a place is always difficult to prove, even if , as in the case of the New York School, it might seem apparent on the face of it.

The Bay Area attributes I have identified from Spicer's time that seem to me to relate to A Tonalist today are a sense of elegy and of utopianism (or more usually dystopianism). Elegy was claimed by Kenneth Rexroth and others as being characteristic of the Bay Area in particular. In his book, *San Francisco Renaissance*, Michael Davidson quotes Duncan's letter to Rexroth agreeing that elegy is the thing that could connect such different poets as himself and William Everson. Rexroth planned to make a Bay Area anthology with the idea of elegy in mind but he never did. Many, including Richard Candida Smith in his *Utopia and Dissent: Art, Poetry and Politics in California*, have noted the utopianism here. For example, the painter Jay DeFeo, a contemporary of Spicer, Duncan and Blaser, refused to attend Dorothy Miller's prestigious Sixteen Americans show in New

York, though the inclusion of her work in it was both an honor and a potentially important moment in her career. This was a gesture of Bay Area hubris that would have warmed Spicer's heart had he known of it.

But that was then. A Tonalist is not about place, not limited to a particular place but, like the Duncan/Spicer circle and others before it, A Tonalist is made of, found among, an extended group of people who share an acquaintance. They sometimes have a connection to the Bay Area (and to me) but it might be tenuous. As a young art student I was told that Bay Area painters differed from their New York counterparts in that they were more figurative, more attached to the human form. It was a commonplace of the time. When later I became aware of a questioning of lyric practice in the poetry community of the 80s, I felt that my own attention to lyric, despite the resistance to an unquestioned celebration of voice, craft and bourgeois beauty among other resistances I shared with its detractors, constituted a parallel gesture with that old figurative impulse. The desire to retain the possibilities of lyric was something that I shared most intensely with Jerry Estrin and later with Norma Cole. Some people write lyric poetry because they just want to and think it is great. Some write it though they think it is impossible. The latter are A Tonalists.

On a visit to New York in 2003 I read with Pamela Lu at the Bowery Poetry Club. That reading was, I believe, my first from A Tonalist, which, at the time, I think I was still calling Tonalism. At a restaurant afterwards, I commented that there was, in old Tonalist landscapes, a quality of California light that seemed familiar to me and that I wished to get to in what I was writing. Pam Lu was interested and immediately wanted me to say more about what I could mean by that. I did but felt she was unsatisfied with my answer. Let me try again. Tonalism interested me from the moment I first heard of it in art history classes or maybe I just saw it as an intriguing footnote in the required reading. It is a kind of landscape painting in which the technique is dark and there is emphasis on a mysterious or even a spiritual quality. Though it seems anti-modernist the painters who identified that way or took up the style were very much aware of what was going on in the art world. Some painted Impressionist paintings along with their Tonalist efforts. Some didn't use the word in relation to their work but were later included in Tonalist exhibitions. One such show occurred in 1995 at the Oakland Museum. It was called Twilight and Reverie. The phrase says a lot. What appealed to me about Tonalism was not only the dark intimate landscapes of local scenes but my perception that it was an orientation irresistibly taken up by people who could have gone to (or stayed in) Paris and become one of the ten thousand Impressionists said to have been there at the time. They knew better and did it anyway. Xavier Martinez went to Paris to study, made a success of it and then left a promising continental career to return to San Francisco.

Tonalism was local and yet national. Part of its influence is from the 19th century Barbizon school in France and it has been associated with the work of James Abbott McNeill Whistler and yet it is, like Whistler, American. The paintings, by Martinez, Gottardo Piazzoni and others, look to me like the old California I still see around me. This Bohemian California was in a dialog with the European art world in a way that was knowledgeable yet provincial. The local utopianism took on an ancient Greek form that set the stage for Isadora Duncan, as well as for Robert Duncan. There is a connection between Tonalism and my sense of A Tonalist, but the writers whose work I find to be A Tonalist would probably find that they had little interest in that old style of painting, though I might be able to make a case for why it connects.

Obsessing more about my exchange with Pam Lu, I realize that the *Ambient Parking Lot* atmosphere of the South Bay, so accurately evoked by her own prose of that title, works for me as a modern equivalent of a particularly Cailfornian landscape. Her approach avoids the prettiness of those old paintings but Pam Lu's Bay Area is not the one of Piazzoni's pillars or Arthur and Lucia Matthews' Isadora-like dancing girls. Her description is deadpan. It sometimes is the content. Foreground and background blend. There are shadows. This brings up the connected point that A Tonalist can be prose. In fact, much of the poem *A Tonalist* is essay or memoir. Much of my own current writing (including this?) is fiction. A Tonalist prose seeks to complicate while it explicates but in a useful, even a utilitarian, way. Pam Lu's own words, from an excerpt of *The Second to Last Country*, published in a chapbook by A Rest Press on the occasion of our reading, are a good example of a prose redolent of the particular magic of the South Bay

> How can I possibly express, that which is nearly impossible to locate in human expression, namely, the terrible fondness and affection I feel for the sights, sounds, smells, tastes and textures of my favorite sit-down diner chain, or the specific ache I experience upon recognizing the perpendicular dark blue street signs with white gothic lettering that mark the arteries of certain friendly and welcoming subdivision housing tracts?

Pam goes on, in this excerpt, to point out that such imperial architecture is "infinitely portable" and can be found "anywhere in the world." It's not that she is describing California here, though she probably is, or that she is making a landscape, but the tense, emotive frame of her observation makes this text seem A Tonalist to me. The value placed on what is not usually valued despite or even because of the awareness of negative qualities in this phenomenon, this form, this expression of modern life is not totally unlike the relationship I would expect an A Tonalist to have with lyric or with having a writing practice at all. It is the quality of "despite."An atmosphere of doubt, honesty and awareness of all the drawbacks exists within the context of a determination (that is also strangely pleasure-driven) to go there anyway.

Here it seems appropriate to mention Jen Hofer and Patrick Durgin, formerly of the Bay Area (Jen was born here), but currently located in LA and Chicago. In their collaborative book, *The Route*, they have cultivated a way of thinking about (among a number of other things) place, displacement and the exchanges that are possible among people—themselves, their correspondents and interlocutors—who have poetics and affection in common but not location. There is self-consciousness in *The Route* of not being written in a particular location (or a particular genre) but locating the work in a place that is always literally on the way. They write, in a letter to me, of the conventions of correspondence found in my own *Self-Destruction* and the ramifications of taking the possibilities of their exchange to heart:

> We've been thinking about a way that locations intuit themselves into being when actual geographic distance is sustained. But what if that distance is unverifiable? ...What kind of knowing is insinuated in the discursive address of epistles? And of whom? So this is how we find ourselves reading the "Convention" poems, although they are clearly implicated in a lyric, maybe a tonalist enterprise as well as an epistolary one.
>
> Jen Hofer and Patrick Durgin, *The Route*, Atelos

Like Spicer, Jen and Patrick use letters to each other and others to find the route. The route here consists of finding a way to move forward in writing that honors the doubts, resistances, provisos, rules and illusions these two writers have accumulated from Iowa, Buffalo, the Bay Area, Mexico, Minnesota, Chicago and many points in between, including a lot of reading and arguing and a massive amount of real life. Their nexus of relationships is international and multi-genre. It is inclusive, personal and timely.

Like the atopia, if I can call it that, created by Jen and Patrick in their book and unlike the "West Coast" poetics asserted by Spicer in the index card conversation, A Tonalist is not defined by hatred of other poets or groups. It does not seek to disclude but values contradiction and compromise. The word bastardization occurs to me—to be declared fatherless and without legitimacy. To be of irregular or dubious origin, not genuine—to be no better than one should be, to have a dubious future and the air of being part of and yet separate from the situation.

Is that A Tonalist? Am I the only A Tonalist or can the word be usefully applied to or appropriated by others? If it is useful, it is because the writing and writers in question, question. They are permeable to, by and in the context of others.

Here I want to bring up the poetry map I once found at the American Poetry Archives when I first went to work there. The Archives is part of the Poetry Center at SF State and is comprised almost entirely of sound and moving images of poets reading. There isn't really a map or diagram collection, but nevertheless I found this map, apparently drawn by past archives workers and reflecting a distinctly 70s and early 80s view of the Bay Area poetry world. As I recall, there was nothing surprising to me in it. I had more or less the same map in my head. Language poetry was there, along with New Narrative and I think the Kearny Street workshop poets, the Women's Writers Union, Beats, of course, Bolinas people and many other varieties of writers and writing. Since then, that imagined map has changed and changed again. Map technology itself is not what it was. The most basic terms of the relationship between writer and reader are in flux. Is A Tonalist anti-lyric poetry written in a way that questions the very fact of its being poetry and attempts to break down the self while attempting also to assist the threatened person? Spicer again: "The self is no longer real." Is that (this) a manifesto or just another false proposition?

2. SOME PRESENCES

One's intimate community of interlocutors changes a lot over one's lifetime. There are many writers who have remained central to my own thinking and then there are the writers and other artists who are central to their thinking. It's like a phone tree. I have hesitated in this essay to implicate Norma Cole in the formation of A Tonalist. When I first thought up A Tonalist partly in response to my own feelings about the stroke she suffered in 2002, I asked Norma a question—something like did it make sense to speak of our work in that way. In some way, the question was a way to focus on what we did together. We were close, traveling and experiencig holidays and big events. Norma was with me when Jerry Estrin died. It was she who closed his eyes. At the time of my proposing A Tonalist, she was still in the hospital. I have written before about the incident and recently Robin Tremblay-McGraw, in an interview in XPoetics, asked Norma to characterize the agreement, the "yes" I have claimed. Norma responded

My "yes" then meant I could muse about something that was not involved with my having a stroke. I was in the hospital, couldn't talk, walk or use the right side of my body. It was such a relief to see Laura, hear what she was thinking about—and I am always interested in the armatures people think about or towards.

I had been involved with thinking about Schoenberg, listening to his work. Reading about Schoenberg's "Pierrot Lunaire," and also about the Committee of Mothers of Russian Soldiers, I then wrote a little "song," a passacaglia to/for both:

I saw shells...
... that were bigger than I was."
Journalist, Chechnya, 8 March, 1995

Rhythms are precise, the
intervals approximate

Night, passacaglia
black butterflies
in front of the sun
killing memory

Night is scored for
Soldiers mothers
Come in trains to take
Them home

Worldstruck, with an instrument
Night, gift and theft
                **(Contrafact, Potes & Poets Press, 1996).

Possibly it's an "a tonalist" poem avant la lettre.

Exactly. Norma's response characterizes most A Tonalist practice at this point and probably forever because anyone who is A Tonalist would share Norma's resistance to being limited to being in a group. It is also appropriate that she mentions Schoenberg because atonalism with its connection to John Cage was also important to me as a writer and is part of why I adopted the term. The reference to music (and to *Silence*) in the " tone" part of A Tonalist emphasizes the existence of tone in multiple disciplines. Tone suggests musicality and can also relate to accent, emphasis, force, inflection, intonation, resonance and a range of color terms such as hue, shade, tinge, tint and value. When "A" is added you have of all of the above, but separated as you are by an eternal gap, you are left with a quality of being astringent, flat, dystopian.

Cage's comments on and practice of art in *Silence* and *A Year From Monday* dazzled me as a young poet in the 70s. The way the text includes both commentary and examples of work and yet also stands to one side of the fact of Cage's practice which was, after all, music, was completely enabling and entirely confusing to me. I felt his books were meant to be workbooks of a way of living. Not a blueprint but, as with Spicer, a set of propositions or admonitions.

I wrote "A Tonalist Rules" early in the life of the blog, A Tonalist Notes. Both the poem and the blog were a way to provide and cultivate responses to imaginary and actual questions about what A Tonalist was. The poem is actually a part of a collection of pieces called *Divination*, valuing as it does the gamesmanship and sense of risk that characterize the pieces in that book.

A tonalist rules
For the game
When we are unafraid
Narrative coincides with meaning
Flatly in love with
Rhetorical continuity interrupted
Only to be taken back up
Like two things in one
Beauty for example
The present and past enter into
A prosody of unfinished gesture
Against formal predictability
Synopsis is predicament
Irony mitigated by shamelessness
Lack of value for the conspicuous
Turning mentioned earlier
Of fate into history
Unable to be made
Unfashionable as the fact
Of particularity
When prediction becomes
Love of that
Chance

In response to the poem and a lot of discussion at Small Press Distribution where Brent Cunningham and I have worked together for ten years, he has commented, in the A Tonalist blog, "I am A tonalist, not the tonalist, problematically neither untonal or tonal." He goes on to write,

> Grounded in situational practice: that is, there are no a priori determinations regarding specific use of style, technique, form, order. Importantly, this is not a lack of aesthetic theory. In a sense it is theory theorizing upon theory. The indeterminate is never, here, transcendentally indeterminate: rather it maintains a connection to the determinate of its being claimed in the first place. Just as the unknowable is only and merely something a person may come to know, this indeterminate is something that may very well be tethered to a forthcoming determination.

> So this non-declaration of the A tonalist, however wavery, is hence meaningful.

This was a time of much amusing ranting among us at work, in emails, at readings and elsewhere. I became aware that Standard Schaefer was interested in the possibilities of argument present in A Tonalist. Standard's musicality and awareness of politics along with an almost *noir* sense of negativity, caused him to relate easily to the A Tonalist ideas being put forward then. In relation to Brent's post and to my poem, he wrote:

> On the micro-level, to be an A Tonalist might mean to carve out a space where many small gestures, musicalities, and coincidences can be legitimated within your own work... Or maybe it produces thought or vision but not knowledge or certainty. There is no shared style and no efforts to legitimate the differences and similarities between us.

> On the molar level, there are perhaps affinities within the various works and writers that cannot represent A Tonalism. There is no reason to represent it. If I come out of or work in a tradition that is against representation, I might seriously consider myself unrepresentable.

Sometimes I am on the verge of thinking A Tonalist entirely a fiction. Then I find that a younger writer has produced a text or made a gesture that I recognize as entirely A Tonalist and then I again think that the kind of writing or writer that I think of as A Tonalist exists. This always seems amazing to me. Because I am now working in fiction I am aware that the idea of A Tonalist is like a fiction imposed on reality. In my life, it is a strangely affectionate, intimate term that serves as a point of agreement and understanding among friends—when it is mentioned, which is almost never.

An important influence on and source of A Tonalist thinking, the English writer Alan Halsey brings into the A Tonalist mix a group of writers he has published and drunk with for the last few decades. Alan's prodigious output as a writer, visual artist and publisher enlivens this English pod of A Tonalist activity which includes the work of Geraldine Monk and other individuals who, in Alan's work, are occasionally identified as Logoclasts. There is a parallel between the idea of A Tonalist and Logoclast which can both be defined as comprising readers (writers) who arrive at either of the terms and, feeling both relieved and revealed, agree to them, before simply going on. Alan took the word from Gregory Vincent St Thomasino's *Logoclosody Manifesto* in which St. Thomasino comments, enigmatically, "The mind knows the word in the figure of its substance." St Thomasino includes Alan Halsey's work in a short list of Logoclast phenomena. Alan's use of the term in his writing is evocative because it seems to refer to his use of synonyms, antonyms and other Logoclastic moves to amuse the reader while focusing attention on the surface of the language in a way that belies the interesting points being made. Like many, these A Tonalists don't, as far as I know, regard themselves as such.

Alan's "On Poetic," (written between 1980 and 1982) appeared in the A Tonalist Notes blog in 2006. As it was written long before the time of A Tonalist, it is clearly, to use Norma's term, "a tonalist, *avant la lettre*." "On Poetic" is more (hypnotic?) suggestion than manifesto. Beginning with the use of the word "Poetic" rather than "Poetics," these directives articulate a way of thinking that reduces to the essential. Alan suggests and demonstrates that concision in language can work toward a satisfying compression of thought. The last of these fifteen suggestions, or dicta, on poetic, characteristically invokes the broad concept of "Imagination," then connects it to specific actions in language and, of course, in doing this it presents itself as an example of the desired outcome.

> Thought at the maximum degree—Imagination, in Blake's sense, the opposite of Fancy. And this comes down to the merest technicalities: e.g. the rightful precedence of noun over adjective—that adjectives are the tools of Fancy, their abundance a blur—whereas poetic risks with its precision the rough-edge of meaning, turns that pressure on the word: appears to pass into nonsense and pass back. In-turns, and proceeds out of language; creating what it means; meaning just what it creates.

"On Poetic" suggests not a style or technique but a criteria, a working model or set of admonitions, not, as with Spicer, against God. Rather these recommendations are *for* finding the poem entirely within the logic (the logos) of the words in it. It seems necessary here to include an earlier admonition—for me this is the most A Tonalist moment in "On Poetic"—to remind us what the compression invoked is not about:

> The demand for precision is too easily presented as reductive, a mere paring-down. 'One thing at a time'—whereas poetic always says two-things-at-once.

A Tonalist might add meanings beyond two and, if these impacted meanings create difficulty, if you laugh at them instead of with them, so much the better. It is typical of A Tonalist to see the humor in the line or situation and take it seriously (or not) anyway. This kind of behavior in a poem relates to the "Irony mitigated by shamelessness" mentioned above. As Alan points out in his most recent book, *Term as in Aftermath*, in an eponymously titled poem which begins "THEMPYRE. The literal said it. No use"—"Satire will always be your friend."

Occasionally I notice that younger writers mention A Tonalist, usually in relation to me but occasionally to refer to a gesture in writing that might also be called anti-lyric. "Anti-lyric" much as with "A Tonalist," can be thought of as a gesture in poetry that includes the thing it is resisting. Before or, it must be, during the writing of *The Route*, Patrick participated in A Tonalist Notes, posting in response to my blogging about his earlier book *Color Music*. This work of Patrick's was for me foundational to my idea of A Tonalist, allowing me to know for sure that A Tonalist was not just me and friends in my generation of writers but was identifiable in new work. *Color Music* wasn't written as an A Tonalist text, as by definition it is not actually possible to do that, but was composed as a way to figure out what to do next. Well after the book was written and published, Patrick wrote in the A Tonalist Notes blog:

> I become a tonalist on my lunch hour today. Thank you for having me.

> But, dear Martian, what I do is to make things, and this making is not about new things made but about the process and its desires in achieving appositives, whose plurality entails alienating devices as much as synthesis. In other words, the music is the desire for song which is somewhat unresolved or at least infinitely mutable—i.e., any sound I can produce and present as a thing made can be and recycled. So, synthesis doesn't merely suggest an ongoing process based in intermittent instances of unity.

Viz. apposite positions, you, said Martian, may wish to ask why this seemingly redundant process should occur at all. You may, in fact, employ a battlefield metaphor to invoke my neglect of efficacy or practicality in considering myself a maker. [Why do we assume that interstellar contexts will brook warfare at all? And we do.] Why? To participate categorically is the desire that has nothing to do with ambition. And, isn't A Tonalism emphatically post-ambition? Or, are there only a tonalists?

3. Our Commonality

A Tonalist was always a way of looking at writing in retrospect. In some cases the work was in the moment as work by myself or friends or people unknown to me whose work I admire or who happened to read the blog and get it. In other cases, it was by people who are dead, as my first husband Jerry Estrin, who died in 1993, or by others longer gone. As mentioned above, a moment of particularly intense motivation occurred when Norma Cole had a stroke almost a decade after Jerry's death. When that happened and it wasn't clear what the outcome would be, I became aware of wanting to have a way to speak about our writing and that of others whose work we valued. In a way, A Tonalist began simply as an expression of love. "Our Commonality," to use Jerry Estrin's title of a piece he wrote not long before his death, is our mortality and our willingness to witness each other's actions in relation to it. Perhaps our common task is to go as far into this witnessing as possible while retaining the ability to come back. Or maybe we don't come back. In a way, A Tonalist has always been a thinking about physicality and death, in relation to some of the work that I write and read and am surrounded by. An interrogation and framing of what we think in relation to each other.

That was in the spring of 2003. I wrote much of A Tonalist in the next few years, arguing for the poetics while and by enacting them. *Self-Destruction* came out in 2004. I was trying to complete my science fiction novel *Ultravioleta* which appeared in 2006. Ideally, I should include the publications history of several friends here. At times their books seem to prove the point and influence me more than mine do. During all this, I started another collection of short pieces called *Divination*, now almost complete. My relationships with younger writers increased in intensity and in number, both in teaching and in the poetry scene. Working as I do at a Bay Area poetry destination for locals and visitors alike, I seem to have many lunches with poets, not to mention long chats in the warehouse. I don't believe I have ever suggested that anyone be A Tonalist even when it was obvious that they were. Okay, maybe once. It rarely comes up. When it occasionally does come up I see it more as an opportunity to ask questions than to answer them.

The A Tonalist Notes blog, begun in 2005, was, as mentioned above, an experiment to find out if there actually was anything to this A Tonalist idea I had been writing into for a couple of years. A Tonalist Notes has always been a group blog though, with some exceptions, joining it has been more a symbolic action for most writers than an agreement to post comments. Some discussion occurred, as much in the world as in the blog, but I was never eager to characterize A Tonalist with any specificity and it wasn't a technique or a style so it remained a possibility. With some amusement but little surprise, I noticed a distinct aversion to being called A Tonalist among most of the writers whose work I regarded as A Tonalist. The older ones had perhaps been bruised by the poetry wars (in which people were included or discluded in groups to their distress, epithets were hurled, relationships strained, accusations made etc.) or they were independent or were already calling themselves something else. The younger people seemed to have a bit of all of the above and maybe they also wanted to keep all of their options open. Andrew Joron regards himself as a Surrealist but contributes to the A Tonalist blog. When I told Renee Gladman of A Tonalist at a teahouse in New York, she wondered if my work actually fit into the poetics I was describing (though she claims now not to remember this exchange). I very much enjoyed Renee's suspicion but think that my poetics do fit into the idea of A Tonalist. Lately I seem to be writing strangely linear fiction but lyric, or anti-lyric, is something that will remain part of my writing practice, even though I know better.

Some of the people mentioned above are part of the nonsite collective, where Kevin Killian's talk about the Spicer archives and the index cards took place. The collective is both a website and an event series taking place at multiple venues in San Francisco. I am not aware that they regard themselves as A Tonalist but I have written about various members of the nonsite collective (Taylor Brady, Rob Halpern and Jocelyn Saidenberg) in the A Tonalist blog and they have signed up as contributors. I regard these nuanced and yet passionate positions fondly and without insistence. My sense of A Tonalist was always tinged with a certain hilarity. If, at this or at any later point, you feel that you are being put on, fictionalized or in some way compromised, but continue to read anyway, you probably are an A Tonalist.

"Our Rage" is just another poem in *Divination*. In a way, the title is a trick or a puzzle but in another way it refers to the rage that exists in the texts and contexts we are in. Perhaps our age is the one in which negativity can be invoked as a way of encouraging access to the work. It is a new terrifying view of success. Does the emptiness of the houses below suggest that we are the audience Brent Cunningham invokes and that we dwell in the negative, shadowy, doubtful, open, vexed, private and yet public fullness intimated by A Tonalist? When I try to write about A Tonalist my efforts quickly devolve into poetry, often not even my own. So be it. Should I include more names here? Better not. End, instead, by replacing Spicer's trope of inedible silverware with Brent's cake from his book *Bird & Forest*.

> But there comes the terrifying aspect, which we have avoided. As the man finishes, he turns to his private darkness, identifying his desire. He speaks it inwardly. Over and over he will be asked what was his wish, but can never divulge it. Thus he sees no authority touches him, no other soul, except by the whim of human need.

> What really happens? What happens in the material itself?

> The audience accepts the cake, eating it resentfully or cautiously. His year becomes them, and they are content.

> How merry we are when the cake fills and becomes us. Never does anyone ask what it means to "become" a cake. What was the cake before, and what are we?

> But it has made them satisfied, finally very comfortable. With his life dispersed among them, they go back to their empty houses.

poetry

Edited by
E. Tracy Grinnell,
Paul Foster Johnson
& Julian T. Brolaski

With contributing editors
Jen Hofer & Nathalie Stephens

"Duchess d' Badminton" by Hannah Barrett

Bleat

Anne Shaw

a lisp, a lung, a fuse, a book
a throttle song, a snare—

A fuse of lung. A lisping book.
How they expulse. Constrict.

A slip, a bottle job, a bird
a rusty breed, a wheel.

Where slipper-birds sit hidden in the trees.
Chirrup. Chirrup. Cheap. Cheap.

The air assumes its *mis-en-place place.*

As if the shriven rivers thrice
parsed. Minced tongues

to make me pie. Make cheep
illegible prose.

A substance mixed
in water. We call "solution,"
cannot separate.

Apothecary scope
refracts

whose medicine
or sun

a corpse theocracy
set down in sheets

Two Poems

Julia Bloch

Welcome Abroad

I had a feeling of wanting to walk
the way I was told to walk.

But everyone worries and rents
and swivels as little machines.

After the first haircut the left side looks
OK but the right side kind of looks like shit.

I had a feeling of wanting to protect my joint.
A sea bird is moving north on one leg, another

aimed at his tail feathers like a bullet, it is hard
to forget these things unless it isn't.

Bonnard's nude happened in the past, she is
on the bed, with the red threads,

she was once owned by Stein,
and all the museum's a future feeling.

Level

For Sarah Dowling

In a view from the train,
as if the mixture of trees organized the water,
or a face over the surface of it,

or a new set of structures in the water.
One object hinges into another
and we know that is like ethicality,

if only from a long view, even in truest winter.
There may be this view from a train,
or the cooling effects of a train in winter

inflecting sight, like an altered tree,
and filtered distance that fashions
new structures, fibrous or laminate.

I did hear on the radio about a "bad little cloud," I did
"click here to like this." Then I watched the spilling among the trees.

Waker Erasure

Geoffrey Olsen

all unawakening wakers

   left reprieve
   glint under pavement

wince

        hero's tactile tacit
stapled to fridge
aghast at blooming

      it tints red
      all does

all hiding in aftertaste
blooms last gust

fixed er
faked

flings down tempo
lasting cloth

      the frames sheet spread over
          under
      aggrieved surface when

naming comes in
each piece tints

& undoes, litters

clutters, fragments
  piece is open
mash

  after intake
    after grounding
pieces where shard
pressured over

so many angles
pasting synth
mass a

building
shift over
draws

        hasp
    all creeping tempos
carefully displayed

erasure underneath the
front threaded
undoing

        taste fabric
weaved overlay, dis

          sense face
                behind

the hint in what takes from inked the wince in

all conundrums socius garbled from shred

characters again
the wakers feint altered

who is
    is here?

among these fakers
hyped blinding light
docile slash

un healing flows off precipice

city un shifting blows
        with uptake & induction,
paces
calibrates if wakers
   fills

enter
condition
crease

might apprehend lines
a hardened, felt to,
wafts

present
what ammunition
generates

depths receding said
    layers
foliage barriers inexplicable
layers multiple
becoming over
here & this

    wakens limit
rustles

residual
thin papered

refuse it alters
some
a plastic husk

each action. let's begin
again fettered under
track wastes
symptoms faux paneling

altered tips these
   fibers, noise

or do, doing
or sleep, one day

illusory onto death
or repeated beginning
             what of
responsibility layers

fragmenting armor above
eases repetition narrow
tracks of tan housing

Noah Eli Gordon

Ghastly form,

we are as human and in need of salvation as any other people. This drives the Source wild with anger. To cover the cost of attendance, to list one's impressive lovers, to wear a little blue linen dress, these will not still its mystery, replace the mirage of imagination with that of memory, the time a bullet takes to travel a dozen feet with its true vast and complex architecture—for the Source builds towers of smoke with the stuff of our lives, the anonymous, unwritten music that comes from beating, scraping, and shaking naturally sonorous materials.

Crossing a river and healing a leper. Collecting a great crowd. Its principles are no mask for indolence. It doesn't dare appear to be dead. It will never simply burst into fragments which might lodge haphazardly among the branches around you. If you have a solitary life on a forested country estate, consider it more appealing than the corrupting pleasures of fashionable society and drive your jeep into a canal, conscious of your own facial expression, which, in comparison, seems a failed prototype.

Any fool can climb a tree, render with bare precision the caution with which one communicates an impersonal wilderness, but, in doing so, has to fashion and refine an impressive armory of weapons, leaving them aside to enter battle unarmed. Although our militant culture is suspicious of it, a delightful sense of freedom is then at once achieved. Piano lessons, French, drawing—in the Source one is forever bashing one's head against obdurate reality.

Amid the general chorus of praise, with a mixture of admiration and murmurs of disapproval, the terrible thing is not death, but to cease living.

The Source operates as though over a wide field, one which reflects no restrictions imposed on drama but that of the dramatic itself—the country in spring or the city in high carnival. You cannot capture the intensity and immediateness of the first experience, but you take pleasure in reliving something of the same feeling within the Source.

Suddenly its wild note of praise dotes upon another face, a pure state of consciousness, original unmanifest sound. Is this how one tends to adjust divine prophecy to one's preoccupation with the horror of event never having been properly communicated? There are doubtless origins to it but the Source cares nothing for the method of its presentation. A bucket of blue mud from a newly dug well is, after all, only more dirt.

Pines, pigeons, air, earth, the consequences of the hunter—how else attack the causes of suffering? This greedy sort of sturdy idleness is represented as dissolute to the last degree. A book written by a doctor ordinarily includes some talk of a cure. To string a rosary of precious gems, to elevate from a state of barbarism, to remember being pious in one's childhood, rising in the night, addicted to devotion and abstinence, admitting to being, to being overcome, to being overcome by a different kind of infantry—desire.

The first flash of candles tells all, or if not, enough and more.

The Source is to be taken in very small doses. It has no youthful enthusiasm for revolutionary deeds because it is the earliest form of social organization to drive tawny lions from the stalls, letting them loose upon all masterpieces at the Metropolitan Museum, weeping and wailing and lamenting, feeling that they had solved the problems of balance and control. "You're no miner," the Source says in disgust. In the end, hiding in emerald sleeves of perfumed silk and smashing rocks in your path gets you no joy.

No costume or destination will explain the errand the apparent scenes of domestic bliss enveloped. One considers only the evidence that is most readily available: the barn, the old, rusted machinery, the pigs, and the fields. How long dawn is in coming. How it places you in your own land. How everything else makes sense in terms of both life and gun. Innovation never brought the original obsolescence. Released from the drudgery of real work, without which a life successfully dedicated to metaphysical inquiry is practically impossible, human thought at its best is concerned with the intersection of points and straight lines—the only map of the Source ever envisioned. We are, in it, the source we seek, which becomes our real burden: we have a proposition which in being thought is thought as necessary.

Two Poems

Elizabeth Zuba

Ted Mitchum's locked up

There ought to be a night
metronome in the clover
meting out fault lines

under a flashlight
small anguishes

however slowly
shimmer on the beam's
uneven terrain

with only the paving stones
giving it shape
some echoing

I answer but eternity
is still unaccounted for, clover

and to talk of miracles
is to talk of a botched universe

the first visible color a bullied O
my hand at my eye
spontaneously reddened.

Two planted feet: lapsed blur of a body swaying

make basin light a tunnel entrance
wintered leaves like men

pound the ground in mourning
is a tension as motionless as the grieving rabbits
you have seen them

and not much else
becomes a destination

even the telephone poles string themselves up
a low sun chord

hum pigeons in sagging rows

we bend into one another
a resignation our heads and heavy medallions

near as I can tell
you bring all your needs

drop from our necks their medallion feet
just dangling there midair

it's frightening
"pigeons," say the rabbits, " pigeons."

Petasos

Filip Marinovich

I like to wear my Petasos (traveller's hat of Hermes, with or without wings)
when I travel. Where am I going? I would like to announce
I do not know. I want to go on a short journey
Back to the Hotel Bon Journée
or was it Bon Séjour and stay there and play
with the bodies of my two friends,
J and K. They are both alive, why do I call them
Bodies? I do not know this also. Also I eat aloe plants
for lunch and my divine name is—NO—I'm serving Hermes,
so I don't know it or it is a secret—guess.
Guess. I will thieve you of your spawn, Civilization,
so you will learn a lesson about
conserving the planet's natural resources. Yes?
Yes. Also I drink much water because I need it pure
To cool down my hot-head nature. Do you have a nature?
You can light a lilac soy scent-candle, place it on a handheld mirror
or handheld camera lens, take a shower and find out

To what end. To your rear end and mine, this toast, to mind-
fullness, lest mindlessness be inclined to steal the white wine
out of your head and your calm with it. This is a guess, do you
suffer from these problems—this is a guest pouring red
Wine on the carpet by the fireplace in your mansion
because you asked him what he does for a living before you offered
him free hospitality. You cannot do this to a guest, it violates the la-
W of Zeus, protector of Guests on High, guardian of
Civilization. Gandhi was right, it would be a good idea
Both Western and Eastern. And if those two could join together,
clasp hands and dancing save the planet with Romance
you might hear a secret recipe for Rice Krispie Treats
from a mollusk oracle inside a jetty as Atlantic crashes

down on it, Atlantic Ocean where two nuclear submarines collid-
Ed this week. Supposedly no radioactivity leaked. But would they
tell if it did? Decidedly not. Why raise panic when
so much is steak, what's for dinner, the burnt end of a cow
what did you expect, Rump Enlightenment? I feel that when
you touch my rump and say "Ah, that's what you want, yes, ass play"
covering it with both hands and language makes the heat even
intenser throughout the bodymind. But you're sick with cold this week,
I hope you heal quickly. I wear my Petasos (Traveller's Hat of Hermes,
with or without wings) down over my left eye to shield Sun's rays

when I emerge from Underworld bearing a fantastic red
popsicle for the Gods and when they eat it they live on
immunized against death Nothing can kill the Gods and for this I love them
we are Weak Weak Weak without the belief DEMOCRACY human-shaped
is immortal in the Universe, otherwise, thinking our actions
consequenceless, we shovel garbage into rivers
the rest of our short lives. River's foaming blue hand will reach
Us and snap our necks. We like when
River does it while we're coming. River
denies us this pleasure and snaps our wig shelves
for sacrificial fire and red wine libations and
incoming naked aliens kinder to guests than we ever were
when we hammered together gallows
welcoming Xenos with rope.

FROM **Lunatic, Act III**

Paolo Javier

19

[Music—slice and dice the thing one pays to wipe one's ways.

GOOD GRIEF comes, as does A MALLARD DUCK.

Hinder sending ANGER to the THREE GODFATHERS and GODMOTHERS.

Thought angling willy-nilly until ANGER cunningly mangles an apron.
Post a position, silly, in the liquor cabinet. Allow ANGER to lick it up, the
liquor, and there the door opens.

The Likud Party annihilation of why marrying, singing a larger portrait of
LOLA MARIA.

Too tubby, ANGER and THE THREE GODFATHERS and GODMOTHERS at the
magic tableau pairing off.

Sing the looming litter of otters.

Others, lay out a gut ninny MAJOR TOM, DIONYSUS and LUNÁTIC dwell upon.

ANGER manages to cook to "Iraq, Iraq" as everyone sings the mess.

Tick it off now SURMISE NEW MALE and A SWINGER BUSTER.]

A SWINGER BUSTER.
Niggle it so rind, silly, from "Iraq, Iraq."
Anger heckles nilly-willy, wrong so only
which we are.

SURMISE NEW MALE.
      How nations are made
to distinguish Anger
from satin.

A SWINGER BUSTER.
      Minoan ark, hand-crafted by
the yolk of a pale face, Anger and
Major Tom.

MAJOR TOM.
Mama, it's Lunátic.

      [SURMISE NEW MALE makes a curt gesture. Aside from A SWINGER
      A SWINGER BUSTER.]

SURMISE NEW MALE.
Gawking morning, your plane of existence.

DIONYSUS.
      Anger really
drinks it all down,
doesn't he?

SURMISE NEW MALE.
Hinder the bailiff!

MAJOR TOM.
      Anger's love so big
he's young and in need of
saving, why wage now
your able magic?

      [A SWINGER BUSTER stands, punting the liquor cabinet.

      Magic simulation of the whispering wail of maintained hands.

      Lavish the outside as A SWINGER BUSTER crucified.]

SURMISE NEW MALE.
      Gusts of candor the layman
of religion would mug a manager,
ganging up on him like a cause.

DIONYSUS.
Serrated Catholic discourse rings upcoming told ballots.

SURMISE NEW MALE.
In a tutu?

[A SWINGER BUSTER *makes the sign of the cross.*]

SURMISE NEW MALE.
   May comes, a book that
bullets zing past. It hinders too
much beauty that our hearing
listens intently.

DIONYSUS.
I think, dear one, that is old gossip.

SURMISE NEW MALE.
It's best that we prank each other now in the hour
to proceed with all of Anger's difficult naming.
Once I sever the relationship among our children,
word of it will spread like wildfire in these parts.
It will taste sweet as a slice of mocha piyanuno.

DIONYSUS.
Buster . . .

[A SWINGER BUSTER *takes out his own garlic juice mix spray.*

ALLEGORY *measures this image in kilos.*

Enter JACOBY, GLORY.]

ALLEGORY.
Page hindering ache naked page pigs ill-
gotten Dada rat tinkers with mine
Anger gagged a gong like that.

JACOBY.
Allegory, quit dilly-dallying. Your
vital ego longs fr it, so too will the
fragrance of crushed garlic dissipate
into the armor of your banter.

GLORY.
Apparently he kinda collects it wholesale!

> [Map a bucket of longing since A SWINGER BUSTER sold a liter of ration,
>
> already paring away at what is there to narrate in rings.
>
> Titillation among the usurped pageantry, ANGER tattles.]

SURMISE NEW MALE.
Your godmothers and godfathers, child—where are they?

DIONYSUS.
      But I yawn.
Mining a beauty that now only they wage for.
Allows them to see past the seen, instead of
blaming other items that naming will wail about.

> [I lavish A SWINGER BUSTER into his bottle of butter.]

A SWINGER BUSTER.
There is no bottle of butter. Hey, what if I told
you it's your heat that humidifies this bottle.

LUNÁTIC.
Annoying!

A SWINGER BUSTER.
This is the bottle of butter ripped for the purpose
to whomever. A Swinger proceeds
from this place of living.

> [SUBALTERN-I picks apart DIONYSUS and LUNÁTIC.]

SURMISE NEW MALE.
More isn't knowing Anger's pinprick of healing.
Here we are for your very own protection.

LUNÁTIC.
Naked insults you carry over to me!

[*Again, LUNÁTIC lunges for the bottle.*]

DIONYSUS.
Lunátic!

SURMISE NEW MALE.
A Swinger! A Swinger! Truly!

DIONYSUS.
You came here simply to insult the eunuch
and the entire clan whom we shall inherit.
Leave us!

A SWINGER BUSTER.
Aching to harm you!

DIONYSUS.
Here is your bottle back. Move!

[*DIONYSUS will strip LUNÁTIC of the bottle.*

*LOOSE SUITS IN BANGKOK filled with carefree dalliances for the
sake of speed. They will recover the bottle in spite of bullets passing
magic through. Make a gut call now that the canyon opens hands in the
tree of sources.*

Care free.]

Laura Elrick

migration through
time of meaning
layering
      it's
dilapidated
guarantor of goes
comes
sediment like
heavy gets
heavy gets   prismatic
again   migration
misdirection
my
direction
again migration
it
my words
migration   layering
sediment
as if sediment like
sediment
through time lodged

in that geology
in that geology is
of terms
a geology of terms
a geology
like geology
the place gets
named gets
heavier?
gets more
dense? terms
gorge

the terms have gorged
get
more
get more prismatic
text
time speech
dirt
the layers
waterways
fallen layers i
spit up spit
it
up
I spit up spit
sediment
like migrating

sediment
and clarity
like clarity migrating
sediment like
migrating
clarity
prismatic
sediment migrant
migrant clarity
prisms heavy
prisms
heavy
heavy light

the king
is dead

the king
is dead POP!

the king
is dead

as speech I
speaks this violent
saying
the violence
of saying the
violence of saying
saying anything
vs the saying nothing
violence the violence
of saying of
not
saying violence
is the saying not saying
is the nothing violence
something violence
is saying
anything
if
nothing is said is it
violence
if
nothing
is violence
violence is
is

this

is
this
anything or
nothing violence
is
this violence
anything or nothing
violence

Traje a casa estas piedras y las dejé en el suelo,
fuera del mar aquellas que rodaban
con su canto de invierno entre la espuma,
y aquellas que elegí de la montaña
por su color, su forma o su silencio.
Las traje a casa y las dejé en el suelo,
como piedras.

—Héctor Viel Temperley

Intervene

Dolores Dorantes and Rodrigo Flores

Intervenir **Translated by Jen Hofer**

I brought these stones home and placed them on the floor,
removed from the sea those that spun
with their winter song amidst the spray,
and those I chose from the mountain
for their color, their shape or their silence.
I brought them home and placed them on the floor,
like stones.

—Héctor Viel Temperley

Y

VAS

PASAS

CAMINAS

DESHEBRAS

POSIBILIDAD

ARMATUCORAZÓN

TUABANDONONUEVO

FRÍOPARALLEVARCON

MIBOCATUCORAZÓNFRÍO

colabora, interviene, diariamente en el cuerpo del

CADÁVERHÚMEDODETUCUERPO

misericordioso, del poney, de tu patria, tu máquina oficial

BAJOLAFOSADELOBELIAS me emboza

MEAMASYLACENIZAYENELDO

diariamente, entre preguntas, SOFOCAS

DIARIAMENTE para dejarte

pensar en los metales DIME

QUEMATESÓLO

PÍDEMEUNA

BIEN pon

FRÍAY

abajo

AND

YOUGO

YOUPASS

YOUWALK

YOUSHRED

POSSIBILITY

ARMYOURHEART

YOURNEWABANDON

COLDTOGOWITH

MYMOUTHYOURHEARTCOLD

collaborate, intervene, every day in the body of

HUMIDDAMPCADAVEROFYOURBODY

compassionate, of the shetland, of your homeland, your official machine

BENEATHGRAVEOFLOBELIAS muzzles me

YOULOVEMEANDTHEASHTHEDILL

every day, among questions, YOUSUFFOCATE

EVERYDAY to leave you let you

think about metals TELLME

BURNYOURSELFONLY

ORDERMEONE

GOODAND put

COLDAND

below

nada:
una pila sin fondo
un maestro que di
un amor que tuve
un asesinato de ti
estuve nada tensa
nada:
tus piernas en mí
en mi tierra, cursi
lobelia sin vestido
estuve nada torso
nada:
he de hacerte la u
he de vivirte cada
amor que me diste
he de quemarte el
abismo del pasado

nothing:
a bottomless tank
a teacher I gave
a love I possessed
a murder of you
nothing in me tense
nothing:
your legs in me
on my land, sappy
lobelia with no dress
nothing in me torso
nothing:
I have to make you the u
I have to live you each
love you gave me
I have to burn you the
abyss of the past

Y

A Ú N

A H O R A

Q U I E R E S

D E E L L I R I O

L A V E R D A D ? D I

forma compacta, acero brillante,

brasa perfecta, el amor que me diste,

AND

YET

NOW

YOUWANT

DELILYLIRIUM

THETRUTH? IGAVE

compact form, brilliant steel,

perfect ember, the love you gave me,

Una flor sobre el agua
Una gota en el fondo
De corazón cayendo me gustabas, amor

Una institución
para darte
Un Maestro
para dirigir tu corazón
Un pozo

Un muelle
donde tu corazón se salva
Un muelle
donde zarpa tu corazón

Un museo
que exhibe mi ladrido

A flower atop the water
A drop in the depths
With falling heart I liked you, love

An institution
to give you
A Teacher
to direct your heart
A well

A dock
where your heart is saved
A dock
where your heart anchors

A museum
that displays my barking

A

U N A

T I N T A

A M I U R N A

Y A M I F O R M A

G U S T A B A S V E R

G U S T A S C O R A Z Ó N

ládrame, cómeme, dame tus formas,

D A R M E E S T E C I L I N D R O

ahora exhíbeme C O N M I C E N I Z A S

E N T U B U R Ó P O N M E U N A L L A G A

A L C E N T R O D E L A M E S A sobre el frutero

Y U N A F L O R E S T Á S Ó L O U N F O N D O de

TO

AN

INK

INMYURN

ANDMYFORM

YOULIKEDTOSEE

YOULIKEOHHEART

to bark at me, eat me, give me your forms,

TOGIVEMETHISCYLINDER

now display me WITHMYASHES

ONYOURDRESSERPUTMEAWOUND

INTHEMIDDLEOFTHETABLE *on the fruit dish*

ANDAFLOWERISJUSTBACKGROUND *for*

A mi urna
A mi museo
A mi ladrido
A mi dolor
A mi fondo

vengo

Desde un país de ceniza
Desde un océano de sangre
Desde otra ciudad inconclusa
Desde mi cabeza desierta
Desde la boca sin los dientes

Y tú

me das dureza
Me invitas una ciudad que se levanta
Me pones el buró que falta
Me siembras un florero
Me entregas un pulso

No tengo

la mano
La lengua
La identidad ni la palabra
El amor ni la mente
La guerra profunda
El animo

Quiero

andar en otro cuerpo
Masticar con los dientes
Agarrar con tu mano
Matar sobre el buró
Acabar
y acabarme

To my urn
To my museum
To my barking
To my pain
To my depth

I come

From a country of ash
From an ocean of blood
From another unfinished city
From my deserted head
From the mouth without teeth

And you

give me hardness
You offer me a city rising up
You give me the missing dresser
You sow me a vase of flowers
You deliver me a pulse

I don't have

hand
Tongue
Identity nor word
Love nor mind
Profound war
The spirit

I want

to move in another body
To chew with the teeth
To grasp with your hand
To kill atop the dresser
To finish
and to finish myself

FROM **Wardrobe**

C.J. Martin

A case in point, stepping forward, full of loose weak fans
like sexual parts towards purity, always of a petrified kind, rounded up here.
Vision, which is given to <u>see</u>, we cannot justifiably, of a shop window,
an algebraic formula. Shedding clothes in tribute, cloth or paper enclosures
(plate 39).—To look <u>through</u> it, or dirt, underwent evenings off <u>from</u> it.
Meticulous concern, act on movements as a cosmetic, try to make glamorous,
saw everything else was quivering. (Room of the room, meadow of the field.)
Whole sensible suits, criticism. Then conditions: a very small space
rolled-up sleeves, direct lens, which is a type of arduous refusal work.
A risky go, distinct, they all go through. Water of artifice, a pair of nylons.
Interpretive layer of wardrobe. Group reaction (that it goes through indifference)
seen numbering through networks—& one's capacity for real horror
who didn't envision, as appendages to labels, to move around in it w/ need.
"'At home' w/ atrocity imagery." All the things defined, subject to (now) uses,
over walls, images at home—"sensitivity clarity."
Brief description, what really was it.

              * * *

Memorized convulsive machinery, collectivity coat, afflict us here.
Evidently enjoying, nothing more than, what ends it might.
Think about it a lot. Abused in all kinds sought-for (block'd view of it all).

Come in like you are, you might be handed a piece of paper.
Large stone cavity, exactly cut out (direct treatment), never to complain.
So blur upon, & so love them—& body magnetism, charm sound
that becomes movement, a thing, or stationary, w/o curb or bit.
So get wisdom, give the real thing, ready $. "b/c of the nature
of what is sufficient" ^Work of some sort^ instead the meanest choose
to stay w/ you. (Bell ringer, becoming now amplitude.) Learned think,
bracket after, decoratively infinitely, thinks it's labor.

* * *

Boredom in tandem, forms designed to contain it: painted collar specialty,
plaster separation exertion. Meticulous whole rolled up interpretive description
(Breezy intrepid. On-the-go. For freshening up What Happened,
Livens up, & of what is sufficient just little roots, save-time registers.
Sorely lifted overcoat, securely (like us) undressed in the dark hall
of a cinema (encounters not wholly historical). Replace w/ compulsion,
misdeed machinery, scot-free something. More lively paralysis, & it is a waste.
So much provoking, is there more. Going to be, pronouncing it perfectly:
"Loud & no cataract." There is more fever, the singular contraction is fainting.

Two Poems

Rob Cook

A Cockroach's Revision of History and Sorrow

We never said anything.
Like the hermit crabs,
we never corrupted the air.
We listened only to what didn't move,
our women using us
for a better calculation
of the ground after it was
deserted
and hacked into
for its oil satellites
and missing moons.

We refused
the humiliation of sleep,
that dark empire when our mouths reached
down to our socks,
the most ambitious
sorrows in cockroach history,
the ones that lived
because they slept
in the reminder of a human
who said
its name was "me"
which meant its own part of the sunrise
and later "nothing"
meaning more accountable than
what preceded it,
a storm civilization that's been
reached

i.e., as a whisper will tell you
when someone causes
it harm:
the wrong microbe,

a freezing dimension
arrived at by children
made of nickel and weather changes,

wrong or belonging
to a different silence,

more than one pouty physique staining the subatomic sunlight.

The Humidity Project

Always the same deserted summer where somebody loved by instinct. Always the same neighborhood cop tugging down the claws of a plum tree and the blinking lungs of a streetlamp. Always the same humidity while the mailman uses real estate flyers to soak up the sweat in his head, and a fawn that stays after midnight when nobody knows it's there, looking for the lost sunlight, the missing honey bees. A house at the side of a road not on any map. Lit windows. The inside of someone's mind seen from a passing car. Clouds caught on a weathervane at Mrs. Finley's and the rain that crawls into bed with her.

* * *

Always the same canned bean families drinking from shovels at Fifteen Minute Lake, and the same heat where a boy swims farther and deeper until he's no longer one of us. Always the same starlight as evidence of other torches at the back of our cave. And then this one town alone in the gutter. "We live on a piece of scrap paper," a mayor once said. Men buying weaker men with trivial pieces of moonlight. Always that same money determination. Proof of water elsewhere. Endangered messiah campaigns. Nobody goes there anymore, except as further manipulations of greed. Animals conducting missions into the crop circles. Animals invented by children and the fear of a christian winter.

* * *

"You might call me a friend, or a man who looks like a friend," a salesman will say, someone who belongs to a survival project, a predictable misunderstanding. Someone selling a book against the encroaching dark matter. A book that breathes on its own. Insects who have to suffer as words all over again. The salesman opens to a page where he's already bled, and does something quiet with his voice. He doesn't talk about the pages where nothing lives, the pages whose lack of bleeding troubles him.

The earthquakes with names now copy themselves inside the sandcastles and the bodies of mud children. Anything can be learned or acquired. Names and video tracking skills and storms on the piano. A boy who sings just like the devil, but without darkness. The weather continues to spread underground. What happened to the people who were good because they said they were good? This morning there was nobody left in their sheets, the grasses did not move, but there was talk, you could see it in the satellite dish, and the boredom that approached each flower as a different intelligence, a mirage, a bruise not yet collected, and in the lightning that still slithered between the torn open sacks of buffalo.

Six Poems

Nada Gordon

Please Usufruct To Me

This evening, I am so livid just like beavers in the mystery . . .
Suddenly my eyes seem so much jawbone to come . . . But, without humming . . .

Baby, every time I look into the wax lip mouth,
Is your image that reflects in my heebie-jeebies,
Should I say "gross" to the tricks in the inspiring machine?
Words of love are just as the seared in the hardness of lover,
Flying up hard to heathens.
Lay my vehemence to the yeasty horizon,
Baby, Please come blistering to me.
I come in my mouth, breathe in tears of lassi,
Please, leer at my hump,
I shall waiting for you at the end of the wrong number.

My Dexadrine, I am so wistful like amber in the rumpus

O starling, say it scratchy to me,
Scratch your lowing hands out beneath the bless of love,
Were there lies on desertion?
Through the screen, I look upon the lies,
My überman, you are so b-rated just like a raging under,
Where all the buds are bound to be humiliated,
One doubt underneath your bootsteps that flustered and fly away,
As your tears had bring the diary into lissome pretension,
I . . . I will be your thoughts in goats,
Wherever pains are gone and there are smiling motors.

Is Nourish a Noisy Quarrel?

Is nourish a noisy quarrel?
Mature size of a foxes?
What are some dialogues that show irony?
Why grooming is important in aviation?
What is the voice of the girl the lovely?
What did Mary Wollstoncraft argue for?
How do you use being?
What is the definition of a boyfriend?
Who wrote an elegy?
What is the phobia of being nervous?
Where do clown tiger came from?
What is smooth interpersonal relations?
Pictures of different relations between living things?
How love become?

I need your prurient lantern

When the noxiousness lie down beside me,
When the meek and staring are shimmying brightly,
You'll make my lines become so lovely,
A gargoyle of love poems that I adore,

Don't you know that I am a 'pataphysicist?
Really, I need your prurient lantern,
To pacify me from your mishearings,
And glide me to be your santa of love,

Show me the weirdness,
Prove me for your energetic lilt,
By the time I try,
To call your narrative with one and only loudness in me

Don't Listen to Me

Darling, I am hebephrenic. Please . . . Please for the sake of levitation, come blearily to me

Whenever the mundanity still not enough to search a lien in my head,
I'll weep here until my tag clouds run dry,
If the skink won't live in the winsome forest anymore,
I'll jump in a weird arrangement with you, my curator,
Wherever the swallow from the deepest handwringing that ever exist,
Could it be one single lisp that thrown away from our organs?
I . . . I wish I can answer that,
Although my hands can reach the white sound and hold it tinkling
It seems only your semantics that left,
Baby please don't lurch at me . . .

Ovaltine Love Feeling
or
The Beauty of Love

The beauty of love that I feel in mimic of eyes' slippage
Into the "cubistic environment" of my soul
As if my body ripped the experienced chaos of everyday life
By the deepest of love's neglected child.

Understanding love as a more fundamental set of dualisms
Translate life into a visual corollary of a word trap:
A perfect feeling like an echo chamber.
There's nothing impossible: I work with ephemera.
I walk with passion, oar buckets, shovels, etc.
Try to stand with the power of love and artichoke suppers.

Have you waiting for my damn thing or my big star-studded names?
And say love words in language as a damnation of human sensibility into the
blinder mouths of politicans?

FROM **Most Popular**

Dustin Williamson

36 hours in Baghdad
With monaural executive
Receiving re-enlightenment shock therapy
Where, yes, looks do matter
When students fall ill, and illness is likely cause
Or growing up Buckley
Declaring express written consent
And the pursuit of haplessness
Pay bouncing blackish nearly
Slouching toward brackish seltzer

—

At the end of the universe we blew it
That's what rich freaks do, freaky shit
Shelters drunk doctor
Abject in corner office
Panel crouton: moody for nothing
Receiving re-enlightenment shock therapy
Geithner, not only an overseer, but a member
The banality of Evel Knievel
Pays flu toll stealing New Mexico
Declaring express written consent

—

At the end the universe we blew it
Over the Caucuses, spectators switch parties
Tiny hominids with no place on the family tree
That's what rich freaks do, freaky shit
The horizon in talks for a ride home
Basic boned, elastic strength and show tunes
Man chooses meat over girlfriend
Shelters drunk doctor
Abject in corner office

Man chooses meat over girlfriend
At the end of the universe we blew it
For a vice president's secret vise finger lock
It may be cheap but it's also tasty
Let's hear it for bees
Without cafeteria trays, colleagues find cologne
Lose the scent of Arlo's specter
A tortured sexual compromise
The horizon in talks for a ride home
Lost in the Greater Recession

—

Man chooses meat over girlfriend
Heavy petting the lord for logos
Ultimate frisbee takes off
At the end of the universe we blew it
New jerks by pornography's old masters
Unable to discern the trap's playfulness
Let's hear it for the bees
For a vice president's secret vise finger lock
The off-brand presidency
It may be cheap, but it's also tasty

—

David Brooks, the modern
Man chooses meat over girlfriend
Ultimate Frisbee takes off
Heavy petting the lord for logos
An affordable salvation
At the end of the universe we blew it
36 hours in Baghdad
Glowed in college, hurled on a hurdle
Put on wasting list, braised Manhattan ire
After 341 years, words falling off the phonemes

David Brooks, the modern
36 hours in Baghdad
Lighting torches at late lunch
Man chooses meat over girlfriend
Defecting to faith
After 341 years, words falling off the phonemes
Teaching Germany's Jewish history
Ultimate Frisbee takes off
At the end of the universe we blew it
Joe Biden, the flu and you

—

David Brooks, the modern
Homegrown Dutch master
Corrosive to character actors
36 hours in Baghdad
On a real estate bender
As a tennis professional I'm a pragmatist
In my first 100 days
Defecting to faith
Lighting torches at late lunch
Man chooses meat over girlfriend

Three Poems

Linnea Ogden

Untitled

The city's view of us
before a party
everyone lit up on Scotch
and wasabi. Night wrapped
in graffiti from
the hospital next door, inhabitants
no longer writing,
borrowed concrete diggers
at rest. Skipping rocks
across high tide, a beach that smells
of bloodmeal. What is
the best way of getting back.
We empty the compost, where something
must have percolated
to be correct. The sun's low angle
stripped of nutrients. What is a boss.
What is a room. Mild radiators
make their contribution. I drop a telltale
drop of water on the gridpaper.
We pass well-behaved
homeless dogs, walk diminished
by a sullen moon.

Legume Family

The small empire of diploma
Latin handed over

The need to traffic in words *all day*

People show up who know themselves
not new friends

Those punks

I move to the compost side of the garden
Uprooting junk trees

To have no effect at all
is the necessity of being reasonable

We do have bean plants
with bright yellow blossom chains

Our little wolves that made it

Is Crucial Is Not

Supposing the passenger had a preference

Don't we draw lines between looking,
basically free

And feeling, not basically free, an objective towards
being wrong about that

Face to the wall, the way you might win is immune
to visual observations

You had exactly the question

I was thinking beyond early
morning, a moment you had all my evidence

Every terrible effect you speculate

Another burden

I was going to say this morning the concept

We raised the question of major participants

I can tell what could be asked
windows up or down

Not required to answer

Liz Phair

Vincent Katz

This stuff's tasting better and better
long time since I've seen Al.
Liz Phair requests, lining the side.
The bread and butter are coming.

It's against critique at forded win

everything is in its time oblique

awarding Officer Hyde prolapse member of the

bride formalities revised
historically demanded
but rebuffed verb

My point has been consistent:
win, win, win.

Orange legging, quaint
      wot? armlength
      bundles, out

from under it, slow
loading logic
      appraises

domino lunchbag diamond
cassette porterhouse vocabulary

I go on, without pause.
I am unending, pure.
I am alive and lift
into the moment, funneling,
fueling tapped off the hook
assembled, forgotten lapse

dink in poet dish, be live
for one driven up airways
desolate doughnut in privacy,
a sanded whole bottom rounded

I am so focused on Glen
one in a number burger
precise at one merge wrist
protagonist hemlock Wheatie tie

ungorged hunger stroked
midneck under lies, strawberry
pie December brain until olive
purchase command sink peanuts

so much weight because of
fraudulent sign storefront
exotica extended from a whiff
waves of hysteria hitting high

I am forced to endure
gracelessness more than any
other person alive. When
they want to "let it out"
they come to me.

Tonight I want to tip my head
into a vat of molten lead
In case I want to unravel
from that point under to the

Weaseled pet carver id
synchronized spaghetti.
a foreign hum.
confetti.
a petty officer, Howard Brayson,
had been seen, face down in
the "Schucklies."
ribbons of despair.
old vacuum cleaners,
typewriters.

got along.
mended.
a bright comet had braided

the sizzle has left us
we lie, burning, on a
        lead shore,
uncowed, ready to
do religion, all the
branches and sects

By the time Emily returned
Brad had undressed and was
standing facing her. She came in
with a joyful air of insouciance—
in her own world.
Jolted out of yet!

The Hotel Roger
simply stood
benevolent
uncreaky
a waiting
command
more waiting

dog-size to
plummet
word   cost
detail
at prism
fortune
milk
precedent
deaths

humdrum rotisserie
beloved shank

left reading
brooding in

a Chinese
sandal
soap shot
in your drawing:

an oak
justifying
beer cylinder
pre-line prog
reg- rage
tumult

in breaking in, the rider
know the saddle;
sadly jogging
eyes waterless

limb
attuned
brick
aside
reft
"Yes, in Mugstown, Potter
              Reaves."
Old lieback.
Part five.

I couldn't get up off bed
flesh insensate to sheets
everything is achievable:
coffee in the morning to
straighten your cells, air
conditioner on full, today
is Tuesday, so Liz Phair
new album can be purchased
chink in a dip, splayed on
stone, emit light 34 St.

A slew of ecstasies
falling down a sluice
of barbed response.

Chloë Sevigny demurs,
through the "direction."
He hates when she does
that, which I love, because
it means he'll be back.
Aborted overtures,
Mexican alleviator,
abridged sighs,
shut-ins.
Aloft,
misted
aloof
tenisphere
your sky
pressed

inward at abutting pickle
Potsdam . . . I've heard it
uttered Red White's a liar
unless you're told stuff ya

Oh, Christ, Eddie, I'm all
right for next shudder
prayer a yellow leaf
exterior revamping still

Writing while you smoke
is a dangerous flail
while you spoke less so
soak not at all Friday

weathergram secured in
last wedding's up and will-
in'ness t'be brought finest
grand fling for the tie fore

jump into folly, intend
time angle unsettled exhale
don't like what you see
can't get anything done at all

FROM **Ethel's Dream**

Kate Schapira

Ethel spent the indoors marrying the front of the garment to the back of
the garment,
       "devoted her life to Mama and Mama allowed it."
                         In the grim
devotional city, a mother and her two children got more relational, their
relations more frugal. They were made of bandages and tubing. They were
tucked back under a crumbling sink. After she died the brother and sister
had no one to tend but one another.
             "They adored one another, Ben and
Ethel."
      Trinkets and oligarchies ranged,
                  "you couldn't tell"
                          one muscle from
another.
      "They cut the legs off. Nothing was ever left in its original form."

Each born with a purpose of parts when first the salt, then the water
separated, leaving soap and grease. Divisive voices, occasional visions
through the windows or abandoned in the hallways. Books continued to
enter. He died. Traffic increased the streets.

An individual voice distracts the regimen, twitches a thread from around. Leave your voice on the mat. Hunger unwinding into sufficiency, robbing herself little by little, keratin becoming.

"I tried to cut her toenails but they were too hard."

Food is of necessity of the body. Newspapers too seemed to increase themselves like manna, faith that sustenance would be provided. Appearances became tastes: how much a molecule looks like a complicated seam, is sounded as a zipper keeping body and soul together. Aware of her tongue in her mouth like soft, tanned leather, a shoe made specially every leaner tailored year. She was cheap. She was purely. Taking in, she was in. Almost like being entirely empty, keeping pores as tight, the entrances as small. Faintness partook of her skeleton. Tissue by accident. Bred in the issueless bone. Humming outside herself or shell. She found she couldn't swallow.

"She walked out like a lady."

Ethel siren of a prosperous dreamland, Ethel chatelaine, parasite, Ethel handed down.

"There wasn't one that wasn't chipped."

"The apartment didn't reflect her elegance"

anymore, inked margins closed, set up

"little set-ups,"

horrible, necessary order gleaming with dust. A bird of parings living on

"bananas I used to buy and leave at her door by the ten pounds. Cases of yogurt—they didn't eat normally. Knox gelatin. Jewish social services finally called me because she was walking around knocking on people's doors and saying she was hungry,"

saving for her imminence where she found it, floor to ceiling. Whipstitch refuge into elegance. Refuse the willing room. Thrift is just enough hunger to maintain life, as much preventative as will cover the blade. To keep a bird alive, a figure. The stupid body changes just enough to knock on doors, clamors, whispers. Sugars, proteins, attach themselves, strands pulled from the hem to pattern that holds itself up.

"The kids adored her. When we visited her and they went out walking, she would ignore the red lights. She just put up her hand and stopped the traffic. And they'd follow after her like the Pied Piper."

Shell color the stamp machine not any shell you've ever seen. Evidence of the thing you see first, entering. Folded into shame, if any, like a star, no shank, silk. Alone in the apartment with the apartment stamp on her hand tremor returned, moving. Plumbing shook authentic like a work of art. Noise gloved and tracked her black plastic and brown paper avenues, huge vases full of greens,

        "Rhododendrons and leaves like that, in huge pots that she would paint black. She painted everything black."

                        Heyday

mixes with decline. Stacks up with the folded news. The button came in parts: a shape, a little batting, backing cloth to needle, metal to form the bulge, to embody. Grid gathered into stars or panicked sprawls. Paris: involution of spirits. Sanskrit: the first last language. Same silk. Self same. The fabric

      "shredded"

                from button to button when my mother touched it. The only way she could be perfectly sure returned and never left returning. Corner snipped from the lining. Once pressed, she couldn't separate color, new use, continued use, new use.

Un nom, un singulier, un autre

I

Tous les noms ont pour moi la profondeur du miel

—**Pierre Oster**

Je le dis propre étrange apaisant singulier
Je le dis vigilant
Il ne m'appartient pas
Il me désigne d'un sentier
Me décrit feuille et rumeur
Il me résume
Histoire et voix
Me tient me traîne m'entraîne me soutient
Il m'accroît et m'étreint
Il me hausse m'enlace
Ou me demande une attention
Il est le requérant l'exigeant le fragile
Et le vivace
Qui éclôt et se noue
À chaque geste
Rompt le temps
Réclame
S'efface
Renaît
Seul et nombreux
Je le dis
Je le renie parfois
La laisse au clou
Je lui reviens
Je le détache

FROM **A thousand paces in the garden also go around the world**

Michel van Schendel

extrait de <u>Mille pas dans le jardin font aussi le tour du monde</u>
Translated by Nathalie Stephens

A name, a singular, an other

I

> For me every name is as deep as honey
>
> **—Pierre Oster**

I say it proper strange appeasing singular
I say it vigilant
It isn't mine
It designates me from a roadway
Describes me leaf and rumor
It summarises me
History and voices
Holds me pulls me draws me supports me
It grows me and holds me
It raises me enlaces me
Or demands attention
It is the applicant the demanding the fragile
and the vivacious
That burgeons and binds itself
To each gesture
Ruptures time
Claims
Self-effaces
Is reborn
Alone and many
I say it
I deny it sometimes
Hang it up
Return to it
Remove it

2

mon nom
je le dirais
s'il était à moi

—Mohammed Dib

Une usure peut-être
Une pièce rapportée
Sur l'échine

Du nom même il est privé
Le sien ne compte pas
On le lui prête il le porte
On le prête à d'autres
Il le porte avec eux
Il le porte sur le dos
Butin taxable
Le prêt porte intérêt
Celui qui porte le nom prêté
Doit payer le poids
Du nom prêteur
Doit payer le poids
Du nom prêté
Il le porte en gage
Le tire le traîne
L'use
On l'échange en chiffres

Celui qui n'a pas de nom
N'a qu'un chiffre à donner
Celui qui n'a pas de nom
S'est fait voler son nom
Celui qui n'a pas de nom
N'avait que prête-nom
Le chiffre est retiré
Quand celui qui n'a pas de nom
Ne touche plus pitance
Ne peut payer
Le nom qu'il n'a plus

2

                                            my name
                                     I would speak it
                                        if it were mine

                                   —Mohammed Dib

Usury perhaps
A patch
On the spine

Of the very name he is deprived
His own doesn't count
It is lent to him he carries it
It is lent to others
He carries it with them
He carries it on his back
Taxable spoils
The loan carries interest
The one who carries the lent name
Must pay the weight
Of the lender name
Must pay the weight
Of the lent name
He makes the pledge
Pulls it draws it
Uses it
It is exchanged against numbers

The one who has no name
Has but a number to give
The one who has no name
Had his name stolen
The one who has no name
Had but a loan-name
The number is withdrawn
When the one who has no name
No longer makes a pittance
Cannot afford
The name he no longer has

3

Je le dis commun je le dis assembleur
Végétaux et chair
Lueur grège de l'œil
Soir beige des rues
Crépi des murs et lierre
Les oiseaux les ciseaux le papier
Les cheveux et la main un arbre de Judée
Un amour à la fenêtre
L'entretien de la chaussée
Un crêpe sur le banc
La parole d'un ami
La mort aile battante d'une rose à l'oreille
Je le dis commun de leurs aspérités
Je le dis assembleur de leurs étonnements

3

I say it common I say it gatherer
Vegetal and flesh
Raw color of the eye
Beige evening of streets
Spackle of walls and vine
Birds scissors paper
Hair and hand a tree of Judah
A love at the window
The maintenance of the road
Crêpe on a bench
A friend's word
The death wings flapping of a rose to the ear
I say it common with their asperities
I say it gatherer of their amazements

4

Je le dis ancien je le dis nouveau
Ancien comme un coffre de cuivre empli de voiles
Nouveau qu'entre deux rues l'on vient de murmurer
Et qui le soir nous quittera
Je le dis sur un radeau
À la dérive
Je le dis en haut de l'arbre
Que l'on abat
Je le crois mort je le clame vivant
Il vient à mon secours
Il adoucit la voix
Je le dis en haut des murs
Que l'on détruit
Il est là il vient à ma voix
Je le dis dans les sentiers
Il nomme les pierres les brindilles
Je le dis à l'atelier
Près de la broche brisée
Je le dis à l'école
À hauteur des bancs cassés
Je le dis à mi-voix
Si je crains de me taire
Je le dis chaque fois
Qu'un ami vient me voir

4

I say it ancient I say it new
Ancient like a copper trunk full of veils
New which between two streets has just been whispered
And which come evening will leave us
I say it on a raft
Adrift
I say it high in a tree
That is felled
I think it dead I proclaim it living
It comes to my aid
It softens the voice
I say it atop the walls
That are destroyed
It is there it comes to my voice
I say it on the roadways
It names stones and branches
I say it in the workshop
Near the broken skewer
I say it at school
Atop the broken benches
I say it in a low voice
If I am afraid of being quiet
I say it each time
A friend comes to see me

5

Et je dis tous les autres
Que l'on n'ose nommer
Que l'on n'ose plus offrir aux arbres
Ils traînent
On se les passe
Ils sont usés comme une école
Dont on ne se souvient plus

Et je dis tous les autres
Qui ont servi n'ont plus servi
Et je dis tous les autres
Qui n'ont servi qu'à essuyer
Les pieds les plâtres les débris
Et je dis tous les autres
Qui peut-être serviront
Comme autant de chenilles
Laissées vides le soir
Mangeuses le jour
Demain volant
Hâtant leur mort

Je les nomme
Les étale
Brins
Chahutés d'éclats
Ramas
Je les ajourne et les tempère
Les relève
Ciel blanc de nos mots

5

And I say all the others
That dare not be named
That are no longer offered to trees
They linger
We pass them around
They are used like a school
No one remembers anymore

And I say all the others
That were useful fell out of use
And I say all the others
Which served only to wipe
The feet the plasters the debris
And I say all the others
That may perhaps serve
As so many doghouses
Left empty over night
Eaters of day
Tomorrow in flight
Hurrying their death

I name them
Spread them out
Specks
Jostled by shards
Accruals
I adjourn and temper them
Raise them again
White sky of our words

Un regard

I

rien n'est dit qui ne voie clair
rien ne repose qui n'ouvre l'œil

2

Le regard est une parole qui déshabille le monde et l'invente.

Les peintres le savent, les peintres l'enseignent.

Le regard est un espace ouvert. Rien ne vit par le trou de la
serrure. Le regard est une respiration. Et une construction
de l'air, l'aménagement d'une demeure sans mures, je m'y
installe, nous nous déployons.

Nul besoin de le raconter. Vous l'avez entrevu, maintenant
regardez. Alors vous l'accueillez, vous le comprenez.

A gaze

1

nothing is said that doesn't see clearly
nothing is resting that doesn't open the eye

2

The gaze is a word that undresses the world and invents it.

Painters know it, painters teach it.

The gaze is an open space. Nothing lives through the
keyhole. The gaze is a respiration. And a construction of air,
the arrangement of a dwelling without walls, I settle there,
we spread out.

No need to tell it. You glimpsed it, now look. Then you
welcome it, you comprehend it.

3 Comprendre Entendre

J'entends l'image avant de la voir,
Je l'entends quand je la regarde,
Je la regarde avant de la voir,
Je la regarde, je l'entends.
J'apprends ainsi à la voir.

4 Comprendre Voir

Je ne vois pas la même image,
L'ombre entendue, l'ombre épelée,
M'enseigne à voir l'enseigne et le nu.
Et je vois une autre image.
Elle me frappe, elle frappe l'œil.
Elle vit dans l'œil, elle est de l'œil.
Elle ne vit pas ailleurs,
Vient de l'œil quand il est différent.
Veau, maison, cuiller, plume, étang
Ne sont pas des images,
Ne font pas des liens.
Une image et un lien, le noue.
Une image est un nombre, une intelligence.

3 COMPREHEND HEAR

I hear the image before seeing it,
I hear it when I look at it,
I look at it before seeing it,
I look at it, I hear it.
I learn to see it thus.

4 COMPREHEND SEE

I don't see the same image,
The heard shadow, the spelled shadow,
Teach myself to see the sign and the naked.
And I see an other image.
It hits me, it hits my eye.
It lives in the eye, it is of the eye.
It lives nowhere else,
Comes from the eye when it is different.
Calf, house, spoon, feather, pond
Are not images,
Do not make ties.
An image is a tie, binds it.
An image is a number, an intelligence.

5

Au loin, voir au loin.

À distance, une colonne. À distance, une fenêtre et une
porte. Un nuage traverse la porte. Au-delà du pilier, la
maison semble désolée. Des gens ont fui, viennent de fuir.
La colonne paraît s'effriter.

Au loin, une misère. Et c'est l'arbre qui s'abat.

Au loin, une route. Une cohorte d'hommes, de bêtes,
de charrettes. La marche est lente. Les avions viennent,
piquent. Les fossés vont se remplir, ferraille et sang.

À distance, on irait à distance. On se réfugierait dans la
montagne.

Au loin, la ville était tranquille. Les gens ont compris qu'elle
ne le serait pus, beaucoup l'ont compris. Ils étaient habitués.
Ils ne le seront plus. Ils ne l'ont pas voulu. On l'a voulu pour
eux. Le soir, ils se tairont. Ils craindront le bruit.

À distance, dans l'incertain de nos pas. On imaginerait
là-bas l'évidence des fleurs. On supposerait qu'il reste des
brumes, des passages. On échapperait à ce qui n'a pas de
nom, à la destruction même de ce qui n'a pas de nom. On
se tromperait. À distance, l'illusion est flouée. Ce qui n'a pas
de nom est un homme détruit, ce qui n'a pas de nom existe
flétri. On n'échappe pas à ce qui n'a pas de nom. Ce qui
n'a pas de nom nous détruit, voici, en plein visage au sol.
L'illusion est le fantôme d'un fil.

5

Afar, seeing afar.

In the distance, a column. In the distance, a window and a door. A cloud traverses the door. Beyond the pillar, the house seems regretful. People have fled, have just fled. The column appears to be crumbling.

Afar, a misery. And it's the tree that falls.

Afar, a road. A cohort of men, of beasts, of carts. The pace is slow. The airplanes come, dive. The trenches will fill, metal and blood.

In the distance, we would go in the distance. We would seek refuge in the mountain.

Afar, the city was calm. The people understood that it wouldn't be anymore, many understood it. They were used to it. They wouldn't be anymore. They didn't want for it. It was wanted for by others. In the evening, they will be quiet. They will fear the noise.

In the distance, in the uncertainty of our steps. We would imagine over there the obviousness of flowers. We would presume that there were still mists, passages. We would escape what has no name, the destruction itself of what has no name. We would be mistaken. In the distance, the illusion is swindled. What has no name is a destroyed man, what has no name exists withered. There is no escaping what has no name. What has no name destroys us, here, in the face against the ground. Illusion is the ghost of a thread.

6

Au loin, de loin nous approchons. Au loin auprès je te voix.
Je viens de loin, je viens auprès. Au loin je te vois, auprès je
te vois. Je t'aime, auprès et de loin.

Nous irions au loin. Au loin, pour voir auprès.

Et pour tenir.

Un monde, un nombre

I

le monde un monde
parmi tant
détaché attaché dépecé
ranimé effeuillé vif mort ardent
un monde les mondes les pluies
vont s'achevant vont mourant
leur nombre n'a pas de fin
chacun d'eux dans sa longue vie
approche à l'écarté de l'infini du nombre

6

Afar, from afar we approach. Afar close by I see you. I come from afar, I come close. Afar I see you, close I see you. I love you, close and afar.

We would go afar. Afar, to see close.

And to hold.

A world, a number

I

the world a world
amid many
detached attached dismembered
revived leaved livid dead ardent
a world worlds rains
go ending go dying
their number has no end
each in its long life
approaches apart the infinity of number

2

Le monde est petit comme un oiseau blessé.

*

Le monde est l'établi du matin, la promesse des outils. Tu y passes la journée, tu reviens épuisé.

*

Une ombre et l'or à l'horizon. Les pavés se taisent, le sang caille.

*

Le monde existe comme un frémissement de peau dans l'amour.

*

Le monde et l'étrange, l'absent, l'abstrait de leur absence, leur attrait. Mais des mondes, les mondes, plusieurs et singulier, forme et visage, leur présence, chair et fumée. Ils parlent. Je les prends en main, je les entends, nommés et sans nom.

Ainsi parlait, ainsi voyait et dessinait l'ami Gérard : "Je te prends en main," son encre chinoise le disait. Ce monde avait des mains qui tenaient un miroir. Et le miroir inventait le monde. Il ne le happait pas, ne le soumettait pas. Le miroir et les mains apprenaient à l'incliner.

2

The world is as small as a wounded bird.

*

The world is the workbench of morning, the promise of
tools. You spend your day there, you come back exhausted.

*

A shadow and gold on the horizon. The cobbles fall silent,
the blood coagulates.

*

The world exists like a shiver of skin in love.

*

The world and strangeness, absence, abstraction of their
absence, their appeal. But of worlds, the worlds, several and
singular, form and face, their presence, flesh and smoke.
They speak. I take them into my own hands, I hear them,
named and without name.

Thus spoke, thus saw and drew the friend Gérard: "I take
you into my own hands," his Chinese ink said so. This world
had hands that held a mirror. And the mirror invented the
world. It did not swallow it, did not submit it. The mirror
and the hands learned to tilt it.

3

Rues, ruines, murs, mains et ongles, mondes,
Les attachant, les détachant,
Coupant, minant, rongeant,
Longeant et unissant
Rues, murs et ruines, mondes,
Têtes et mains, un autre monde,
Une blessure, une tuerie, un silence, une autre porte.
Elle s'ouvre sur les ruines,
Elle s'ouvre sur la fin des ruines,
Leur abandon.
Les mains ont fait la porte,
Les mains ont ouvert la porte,
Bec et ongles l'ont taillée.
D'autres ongles ont taillé d'autres portes,
D'autres mains ont ouvert ailleurs d'autres portes,
De fer et de bois, de roseau et de lin,
De sang.
Des mains se sont pendues aux poutres,
Ont tenté d'ouvrir les trappes, les soutes,
Ont tenté d'apporter l'air.
Des mains ont été prises,
Des mains ont été liées, encagées,
Il était défendu
De rien ouvrir, de rien apporter,
Elles avaient délivré le défendu,
Elles ont été saisies, démises,
On les a désailées.

Rues, murs et ruines, mondes,
Têtes et mains, un autre monde,
Des mains se sont trompées de portes,
Elles ouvraient sur le vide,
Des gens se pressaient
Derrière la porte ouverte,
Des gens n'ont pu se rattraper,
Le chambranle n'a pas résisté,
Ils ont glissé, ils ont chuté,
Ils sont tombés de haut, de très haut,

3

Roads, ruins, walls, hands and nails, worlds,
Attaching, detaching them,
Cutting, mining, biting,
Bordering and uniting
Roads, walls and ruins, worlds,
Heads and hands, another world,
A wound, a killing, a silence, another door.
It opens onto the ruins.
it opens onto the end of ruins,
Their abandon.
The hands made the door,
The hands opened the door,
Beak and nails trimmed it.
Other nails trimmed other doors,
Other hands opened elsewhere other doors,
Of metal and wood, of reed and linen,
Of blood.
Hands hanged themselves from the beams,
Tried to open trap doors, holds,
Tried to let air in.
Hands were caught,
Hands were tied, caged,
It was forbidden
To open anything, to bring anything,
They had delivered the forbidden,
They were seized, dislocated,
They were unwinged.

Roads, walls and ruins, worlds,
Heads and hands, another world,
Hands mistook doors,
They opened onto emptiness,
People hurried
Behind the open door,
People could not catch up,
The frame did not resist,
They slid, they fell,
They fell from high, from very high,

Et parfois de moins haut, ils se sont écrasés.
D'autres ont pu tenir la rampe, ont reflué,
Ont descendu l'escalier, l'ont dévissé,
Sont sortis dans la rue, ont démonté les murs,
Rues, murs et ruine, ils ont
Fermé les portes, ils ont
Fermé le monde ; ils ont
Coupé des têtes,
Ils disaient qu'elles ne comptaient pas,
Ils disaient sauver le monde ;
Ils étaient le monde, ils le disaient,
Eux seuls étaient le monde,
Et le monde était insatiable et malheureux,
Le monde appelait un sacrifice ;
Ils se sont pris la main, leur propre main,
L'un sa gauche, l'autre sa droite,
Ils l'ont coupée, ils ont chanté,
Braillards de sang,
Ils ont chanté leur gloire,
Ils ont saigné ;
Ils sauvaient le monde en se sauvant,
Ils le croyaient.
Ils ne sont pas allés loin,
La rue était en ruine,
Ils avaient perdu leur sang,
Ils sont tombés, ils se sont affalés
À quelques pas, parmi les détritus.

Rues et mondes, mains et ruines,
D'autres gens ont descendu l'escalier,
Ne l'ont pas dévissé, n'ont pas cassé les murs,
Ont quitté le trottoir, ont marché plus loin,
Des gens ont cherché d'autres portes.
Ont essayé leurs mains, ont fait glisser le pêne.
Quelques portes sont dures,
Comme des murs de pierre,
Quelques portes ne cèdent pas, quelques autres bâillent.
Ils ont ouvert l'entrebâillé,
Ils ont regardé,
Ils ont laissé ouvert au vent,

And sometimes less high, they were crushed.
Others could grab hold of the rail, surged back,
Went down the stairs, unscrewed it,
Went out into the street, dismantled the walls,
Roads, walls and ruin, they
Closed the doors, they
Closed the world; they
Severed heads,
They said they didn't count,
They said they were saving the world;
They were the world, they said so,
They alone were the world,
And the world was insatiable and miserable,
The world was asking for a sacrifice;
They held hands, their own hands,
One the left hand, the other the right,
They cut it, they sang,
Bawlers of blood,
They sang their glory,
They bled;
They were taking the world by taking off,
They believed it.
They didn't get far,
The road was in ruin,
They had lost their blood,
They fell, they collapsed
Several steps away, among the detritus.

Roads and worlds, hands and ruins,
Others went down the stairs,
Didn't unscrew it, didn't break the walls,
Left the sidewalk, walked further,
People sought other doors,
Tried their hands, slid the bolt across.
Some doors are hard,
Like walls of stone,
Some doors don't give way, some others yawn.
They opened the one that was ajar,
They looked,
They left it open to the wind,

Ils sont partir,
Ils ont cherché, ne savaient pas
Quelle porte, quel mur.
Ils ont erré,
Ils ont fini par trouver
Les uns la lourde à deux battants,
D'autres la poterne ou la bâtarde,
Quelques-uns la barrière
De bois tendre, douce à la gâche,
L'ont poussée, ont affermi leurs mains sur le portail,
Ont huilé les gonds de la poterne.

Ils ont ouvert, ils ont vu
Un champ de lunes,
Une forêt de bras armés,
Là-bas des champs de ruines,
Puis, encore au-delà,
D'autres mains, nombreuses, délicates,
Poser des pierres, des planches, des toits,
Percer des fenêtres,
Accompagner le vent, gréer le vent,
Rentrer le blé, les outils, les enfants ;
Ils ont vu des gens se parler, semer la rue,
Ils les ont vu battre ensemble le pavé, lever le grain,
Ils ont vu des gens affronter d'autres gens
Qui barraient le passage, portaient un voile ;
Ils ont vu un grand soleil et des maisons reposées,
Et ils ont vu par-dessous le voile et par-dessous les yeux
Des défenses, des interdictions, des armes, des lames,
Des maîtres déclarer des interdits de rue,
Que la rue était à eux, les maîtres, comme une lubie de lune,
Que les pas et les rêves sont leur chose qui vaut cher,
Et que la voie nul ne l'emprunte hormis le maître.
Ils ont vu, alors ils ont vu avancer, passer au-delà
Les maçons du vent, semeurs de rue, les passeurs,
Rues et ruines, mains et mondes,
Derrière eux armes et lames tombées, les maîtres courbés,
La voie est libre, une marée est passée, les grilles n'ont pas tenu,
Les barrières sont cassées, tordues, une marée de gens libres
Au-delà de la rue, l'arrimant à leur voix,

They left,
They searched, did not know
Which door, which wall.
They wandered,
They ended up finding
Some of them the heavy double door,
Others the postern or the side door,
Some of them the fence
Of soft wood, tender to the strike,
Pushed it, reinforced their hands on the gate,
Oiled the hinges of the postern.

They opened, they saw
A field of moons,
A forest of fortified arms,
There in the fields of ruins,
Then, even further,
In other hands, many, delicate,
Laying stones, planks, roofs,
Piercing windows,
Accompanying the wind, rigging the wind,
Bringing in the wheat, the tools, the children;
They saw people speaking to one another, sewing the street,
They saw them stomping around together, raising the grain,
They saw people confront other people
Who were blocking the way, wearing a veil;
They saw a bright sun and rested houses,
And they saw beneath the veil and beneath the eyes
Defenses, proscriptions, weapons, blades,
Masters declaring street bans,
That the street was theirs, the masters, like a hair-brained moon,
That the steps and the dreams are their pricey thing,
And that the way is open only to the master.
They saw, so they saw moving ahead, passing beyond
The masons of the wind, sewers of street, passers,
Roads and ruins, hands and worlds,
Beyond them fallen weapons and blades, bent masters,
The way is free, a tide came through, the gates didn't hold up,
The fences broke, were twisted, a tide of free people
Beyond the street, mooring them to their voices,

Venant, allant, venant vers eux, vers ceux qui voient,
Les voient venir, grandir, les voient gronder, entendent rime,
Entendent et voient une ligne, un buisson, la forêt
Venir, montagne d'hommes, l'eau roule on ne sait où,
Ne crie pas, ne décime pas, dévale, ouvre, vient.

Ceux qui les voient ne savent quoi,
Ne savent qui,
Les voient sans voir, entendent peu, ne se dégrisent,
Entendent mal, devinent et glissent, qui vient là ?
Glissent l'œil au ciel, certains partent
Quêter le vent, certains hésitent,
Risquent l'oreille aux Huns, restent, sait-on quoi ?
Ce sera la foraine, la fête, sinon grand-peur,
D'où viennent-ils ? De lune ou de l'usine, du temps, ce n'est pas dit;
Le mal de voir, celui d'attendre, on va, on est là,
Le temps de s'égarer, le dos aux ruines,
Rues et murs, mains et ongles
Qui se brisent, la fête ne vient pas, les branches cassent,
On n'attend plus, un arbre cache l'un, l'autre une fumée,
Un toit, non, une porte trouvée là,
On s'en va,
On fuit.
Est-ce une fuite ?
On dodeline.

Chercher la rampe, une porte vers la digue,
Une autre porte, monter,
La digue est là contre la rue,
Tient les portes, monter, aller aux vannes, garder le vent,
Respirer, je m'apaise, tu t'apaises, étions-nous là ?
Ils craignent la ruée,
Ils redoutent le repos.
Les voici repartis,
Boitillant,
En contrebas des portes,
Vers d'autres portes.

Coming, going, coming toward them, toward those who see,
See them coming, growing, see them grumbling, hear rhyme,
Hear and see a line, a bush, the forest
Coming, mountain of men, the water runs who knows where,
Don't cry out, don't decimate, hurtle, open, come.

Those who see don't know what, don't know whom,
See them without seeing, hear little, don't sober themselves,
Hear poorly, guess and slide, who goes there?
Slide the eye to the sky, some leave
In search of the wind, others hesitate,
Risk their ear to the Huns, remain, do we know what?
It will be the fairground, festivity, else terror,
Where do they come from? From moon or factory, from time, it isn't said;
The malady of seeing, that of hearing, we go, we are there,
Time to go astray, back to the ruins,
Roads and walls, hands and nails
That break, the festivities don't come, the branches break,
We don't wait anymore, a tree catches the one, the other a smoke,
A roof, no, a door found there,
We leave,
We escape.
Is it an escape?
We nod.

Search for the rail, a door toward the sea wall,
Another door, climb,
The sea wall is there against the road,
Holds the doors, climbs, goes to the floodgates, holds the wind,
Breathe, I calm down, you calm down, were we there?
They feared the rush,
They dread repose.
Here they are having left again,
Limping,
Below the doors,
Toward other doors.

The Memory Group

Martine Bellen

Brewing tea, falling in love—delusional
states of transition—a brief stay in life, then
traversing into nonlife or adjusting the
flight patterns of an airplane. The light
patterns of a candle clarify the origins of
memory.
Stilling a tadpole
Beside a knot of frogs.

The Memory Group meets every Sunday
To untravel the universe, mind's
Scholar system, its cameralike ability to isolate
Language as a function in the still-frame editing tool.

How candlelight fluctuates mood,
Unconscious optics
Extend bodily limits
Lily pond limits—
A projector throwing light across water's skin,
Enframing conditions for potential, or a cattail that expectorates
Seeds on the pond, stifles the pond with too much life.

Each participant of the Memory Group participates
On Sundays in creating a provisional reality
Of which she is provisionally aware
Is inseparable from that which she creates.

The Memory Group coordinates the coordinates of one memory,
Forgotten points of forgiveness

Remember two flutes made from the wing bones of a mute swan
What has been done, *before*

Giving occurred

For giving
After

The ability to choose the correct meaning
Of an action appropriate to a particular social situation
That arises out of dependency on the observer's
Perception and the provisional Sundays of those
With whom the observer interacts
Exemplifies a functioning memory.

        Point: If one substance comprises everything:
        /pond/breath/a star's flame
        Or shivers a window
        Agency
        Vacancy
        Contrail

Focus not on substance but on fractioning bodies,
The formula for the production of emotion
(back in the day before emotion was mass-produced).

At the last Memory Group meeting, a member declared the group
Is fading. Declining attendance and aging
Participants is heralding its quietus,
So it seems the memory that the group is living
Is a dead one to be put out in the memory dump,
        After all, it's through memory that the past clings to us:
Think of starlight light-years from its source
Think of the frog
That's no longer a polliwog
A flute carved from a hollow bone of griffin
Subduing soil and sky with its song

The Group's lifetime illusion flashes before its eyes.
        It experiences and forgets, forgives, lives/

Her north opens with a whisper you see
Wind, will-o'-the-wisps. You see,
Her mouth
Struggles receptive
You see

Cave's fading hallucinations, in the mind-darkness
The grid overlying cave's chakras

     A man refuses to leave the terminal
disease. Recombination of numberless
horizons—Sunrise/-set. No guarantee he'll
see the in-flight movie with his Memory
Group that has gathered around him. He
awaits word on the time of departure. This is
not a narrative. One step leads not to the
next, but to a dense forest; fugitives find
shade there, awakening and fluid. Forms
sustained within the form world, unsustained
in an atmosphere that won't contain form
and when he falls in love [dies] the story no
longer follows
Procedures but investigates surrender,
murder, [Here is where
it turns into a murder mystery.
Everyone wanting to know whodunit,
waiting to learn their true identity
[provisional]. Translated
As relational self to isolate alien,
Ritualistic instruments (magic's music) or
the phenomena of close distance.

A Discourse on Gender in Eden

Edric Mesmer

out of respect for which
one says one need not change one's mind

made more readily available in the self-help
Socratic learning
of a critically sanctioned theory: that Adam
nearly matters, and Eve, Eve a smattering;
and through various vantages,
a temporal query (in italics) phenomenological

apple. The overlaying linearities arise
pathologizing
a single mention, in passim,
whereas the polis
holds, and all things Mom and Dad tag
and recur as fad

in the burgeoning garden
of sartorial leashings . . . Who wouldn't
remain vested a ways from dissidence?
as children prefigure matter
in a pattern less linear
or at least more so obfuscated that we needn't

make our vocab locus
to our cascading significance.
For the reason "so long that no one
individual is specified as
the 'father of the'" thus etiologically non-
customized conclusion,

facilitates flood; not
of the bitten but of
the unbuttoning that may ensue;
so stress is cognized ibid:

William, Julie; Bill, and Susie,
in the media-free collage. Glibness marks.

Subsuming euphoria,
resultant in absence
of ivy and of chickadee,
or preternaturally singular door-
steps never
for grace of exit;

can the hypothesis Oedipally
cross-manifest? Must the tropic
menagerie be flora, be
reified? to some vainglory?
Evidence that
transplantation of old stock

is hazard-friendly, is unbacked;
likewise, the common model
of the extraordinary
trained along a field of
ordinary trellis,
framing. The manners

of appearance, an adequate
lack, and dialogic pronouncement
foregrounding all quandary
of quotidian powder-blues—Hue
meandering the fresh-cut
ruts of shapen worry: 1)

In the kinship of scaping technics; 2)
within the shaped legality
of discursive shame; or, 3) the communal
shapeliness of evangelical re-
furbishing; and, 4) in the favor
disallowing a familiarity

taken into account
in the changeling personae of

these—as French theorists have it—
trauma fees;
cool in their raucous consensus
of "doing battle" in district

with skimpy map to pass
as skirts the question:
this too a moody anti-
stance, instead forging [Kristeva's]
firebranded stigmata
[ha-ha-ha]!

Fixation a construct—
a concept, a condition as air-conditioning
cached in the googling nebula
of desirous cursive. A bal-
loon pantomimes the panel-
to-panel like-aged and –minded kith

of nether natal brands; pattering Frisian
in the polyglot
abscess of reasses-
sment, punishable by quest.
The "hot topic" of progress-blocking, secondarily
betrayed in trade

of largely non-irreversible verbage:
toxins, that "other politics" of forgiveness
wriggling passed a jury struck
for the therapeutically-accommodating
forget—putting-off
in the fall, analogy, lends, meanwhile,

a virile consumerism of such an age.
At once freed from
realms of labor
and popular in the crucial sexing,
to play a little for the hier-
arch and the dollar,

let alone agency. Glows-in-the-dark?
Impossible without the day's trawl,
ubiquitous if collusive,
evidenced in the tumescent
despite cost, and the bright-to-dim
slipknot of disastrous circum.

Antiauthoritative, nor academe...Hefty
puberty of the abovementioned "not
only" but indeterminate adherence to
an acronym for chiaroscuro in
phenotypic "fit in" in the very
alien signal especial-

ly where the tidal
keeps, at flux, at bay
—and not all tides (desiring the phasal)
—not tides at all (phasing desirous)
in a surgery of origin—
spontaneous protocol—

to leave off consent at
discontent, of premising
the moment-to-moment
flak jacket
sanctioned by a trifold behalf:
Consanguineously?

The heather loathe
to present an un-
wavering appliqué
of *parens patriae*,
from onslaught to too late—currying
exemplars

of a gravure nature:
the typings tout, an is-
suance wastrels, and all-around
functions festoon; lest the likeliest proceed
to institution, whereby
addenda would be prescient.

So serious as to warrant
between both the problematic
and noncomplacent. A refusal
limiting best wishes
transfuses a murky stasis
in the bias of strata . . . Let

merit, fantasy, be
the dichotomous basis
demarcating a horizon doubled
for shore. And underlying
favor, enacted by headiness
of informed daylights

by a moonless night went dire
and later than, neighbor-
hooding an ostracized af-
firmative; formation in such envious
familial and at-risk
presuppositions

in most studies dys-
phorically citing
but no more rigidly
citing, although non-
constituent, citing
western-bound hark: "[I]f

inherent,
then
inherited;
and thus
inheritable,"
stigma confers...

Variance is a public pace—
"So where to next?"
Often a desire to correct
a correct desire; tool
fully articulate
"'the etiquette.'" Tiny

bubbles. Commonly
confused in the commons amid
a plethora of co-
morbidities; to prepare for unknown
encounter—to become so.
And to policymake in the

turmoil of narrative
foils, the unique
ultimately to traject a
"more likely" libido,
spiraling the Punnet; momentous
as a negative-negative in logic

procuring effeminate
footnote, as well as to inter or endure
at large, the phasic cures of query
in the twinned referrals
of youthful epistemology and,
as it pertains, one's own

non-retrospective study
of 'cognition. In statistical answering;
in their mothers' sons' questionnaires,
associative with bravado,
and almost exclusively without the shaming privilege
only, until noticeable samples

compare peers with neither
clinical nor feared
lacks of opposite focus, in alliance descended, and by desire
found, and disavowed from naming
may come to resemble silent loci.

Champion Mill

Jasmine Dreame Wagner

Variations on a field, Missoula, MT

there is a buoyancy to ice unencoded
there is a buoyant blossom in spectacle
no part comes naturally part is work
and the days work and the aphids
the telomeres and tentative wrist
a glass quality in them now
a glass quality in the snow
a windshield embedded with spectacles
bedazzled quotients of ice
a windshield withstands elements
blue windshield supplants a sky
hazed red with rumor smoky
clavicles of turbines
cavities design

hooks in the shoulder of a byway
old rumor unproved appendix
a buoyancy in the shifting gear
gearshift of manual transmission
in tape loop lupine cellophane
rumor backpedals down the highway
but what of drift of hint in shag and
what of green flies and what of redux
platinum sparkplugs and what of harts
of speculative fiction spooks coils kisses
and what of domain walls and monopoles
and what of the trowel used to contuse
this water to describe dance
as curve of pursuit

a surface of a sphere is an approximation
a wily chaotic hoop of flagpole
a chimney stovepipe gyroscope caduceus
a shipboard compass computer
simulation a rotating plate of dust
and what of tibia of china and what lust
and what of siamese we
all a bit live a bit must
the brass quality of the gimbal
the brass quality of dusk
and what of radar
analogous to duel
of turbulence
of rust

somewhere a landfill with its callus
of cold beryllium
measured wind with foil fan
rebar skewed to violet
somewhere a window painted pink
closed its ear
archaic torso of a mill
decorated like a war veteran
its red and yellow tags
black tape lip
mouth ajar lets
weather in
what would a geologist do
with a heart like this

blue is symptom of a deeper malady
two kinds of blue   mesozoic pleiocene
neither intuitive neither dream
neither metacentric boundaries key
the violet blacklit landscape painting
its *nova totius terrarum orbis geographica*
its glittery theater of snowglobe
their fasciate obligate cartomancy
their theater of key with velvet rope
theater of scree of bruise of
wild unknowing wild
blackberry made bronze
by scarcity made barb wire
unable to uncrow

in deconstructing a minor key
in a popular book on an ancient world
from the hoover dam to cape canaveral
where do these stairs actually go
and why do black holes radiate energy
and why does this energy imply heat
and heat imply body and body
imply loss and why does slow loss
of heat suggest we evaporate slowly
and who does the black hole really love
and where does this aqueduct flow
and where do we store the silent
films no one screens anymore
and the end music why is it silver

go to field a periphery
go to a field with a friend
pass caricature paintings
past weed acrylic flint
and lay on your back arms spread
and lay in the black stink of park
earth convex against your harp
dirt flexed under mars
go without javelin corn or lens
and go without trial goal or fence
without the batsman will insist
without the batter will insist
and will assist
and will assist

what percent tungsten
                           percent lead
what lock shale of yellowcake
thread beams too damp to burn
pitch like a tent
somewhere a lack of firewood
strikes a blue match
somewhere a satellite seals
its mind cell by cell retires
its blueshift
sinks
in a drift
o what longing for drift
if there were no drift

Three Poems

Craig Watson

Radio Faucet

there's no introduction just that absence they call the river
but it's our mistake to touch any profits unsullied by a
universal force who loves our consciousness so much that
helplessness means passion and obedience bestows every
life with earth's weight to shed so a tourist is also a thief in
pursuit of a wandering cow across the abacus of antiquity or
whatever it is they say to get in here without having to pay
the tributes to those master business plans which built the
second society on three words affiliate acquire repeat which
have come down to us now as spray powder oil so if I'm
not home by Thursday you can call the kill box and leave a
penny for the next wave to parse and spend

Hurdy Gurdy Porn Sonnet

Walked out into prosperity
Sex drive harp nerve
Mind-over-matter
So what do you want from me
Tomorrow was too late
To get a monkey off
Sing songs and dance
Don't ask whomsoever
Ask my "self"
Conscious judgment
Rightness next to service
Love dries on a grin
No difference otherwise
Except not now again

A Dead Man's Last Pistol Shot

Hey, you reapers
Is there time for one more?
The species as a whole
Never looked better.

In order to find victims
One must first imagine them.
But who persuaded consciousness
That beauty relieves misery?

Apology is the animal
That doesn't clean itself,
Every point of self-reference
Inseparable from own contradiction.

If you want to eat my peaches
Put your foot on my larynx
Mercy never wanted to be a song
And silence never wins.

Three Poems

Tomaž Šalamun

Translated by Michael Thomas Taren and the author

[untitled]

He stared. Another bar. He stared. A puddle.
Heavy. Platinum. Another bar. He

stared. Silent piece of cotton wool. The moon
sands lime. The moon leads lime.

Mares emit smoke among granite cubes where
moss grows. There's a dome. There're

table-wares. There're sins. There's a Czech cottage.
There's a dragon. He dives. The dragon

dives. There're too many elements. There's
silverware. He stared. Another bar. He

stared. He was drunk. He was drunk. Did he give
a canvas cover? He had a cartridge clip. He had

cut through sandals. He stared. Another bar. He
stared. With a cap the diptych dies. I lunch.

[untitled]

Translated by Michael Thomas Taren and the author

Someone with a blue garlic—ricochet—
soaps the doorman. Should we
help him?

All corpses falling
under my bunker
will be called

asslicks.

Let a Revolutionary Fist

Translated by Christopher Merrill and the author

Let a revolutionary fist
smash
the belly
of the latent fascism of the white race—
the stars.
Let the mind, the genitals
and the heart
of the astral garden
be blown apart.
I'm stopping the bloodthirsty machine.
Only I—
a man with the destiny
in my own hands—
can crush the intrigues
of the Eros of the planets.
Only I—
a man with a destiny
in my own hands—
can reject the passion of
gold and alchemy,
the fatal blindness, and
him, the innocent god
of my own face,
Hermes Trismegistos—
the criminal.

Two Poems

Lee Norton

Passage Rite

I have walked where
but away to here
which I find a laden hollow

with the grass titters
and the language is doubtful
or feral, the full stop

slid away or grew thorns.
Edward: is a tinsel
proposition, all gaud

and bauble, all covered in symbol

and hollow. I quakes
in the fire its mirror.
a strange suggestion of weather

on the air. where from
is unclear, the sky's
too black of mood

hides the hour's color.
old and unable, I remember
that night, and Edward:

our neither knelt to naming

itself, smithied against sameness.
we returned with dawn
attending us, and purpose.

The Generative Gesture

goeth before the fall.
here we suddenly are, because

I said so. the air is sharp
but lacking in things

to throw. an instantaneous century
bubbles. eat what you must, sleep

where you must, but leave no trace,
the math would say, if it had

voices. we have the tools
to leave. we have deaf thumbs.

the generative gesture goeth and
there we fall. approach

with caution.
the air is sharp

and shouldered, but lacking starlings.
vigor jumpstarts the sky.

FROM **Enumeration of colonies**

Ellen Baxt

Teenagers elected hope, from our state, humility or work,
but he turned out like the rest. Plastic cups in the gutter,
promising they'll leave.

Circus is a celebration.

The baby is newly elected, promising, like the rest. Throw our
state. Nothing will change. Humility will rest you, grieving.
The newspaper reports candles. I and a toddler, hungry for.
Teenagers are caught. Candles encircle this critique. Some
are saying, What business do I have. Teenagers, fire, a home
filled with lights, reports the newspaper.

I, filled with lights, watches the lion, hungry, maul. This is
elastic. Cups in the gutter, leaving.

"Circus is the celebration of living potential."

I didn't mean to love, but suddenly singular—muscular,
unfalling, breathing the sway, a long time, repossible.

Patience was observed
Females, cases, a hundred in
these landfills
Fishing was seen among fishing so
it was vindicated, balled-up
Concern of
          concern of
Colonies of nets
An increase vindicated fishing because
among reported cases, females—
public patients, individual health.
Landfills saw hundreds floating by
Jim Churnside reported concern.
Still, where the nets are females were observed
increasing concern
balled up, fishing in landfills
Nets are old, increasing floating
bodies of bodies of water
The public individual is patient
must be reported. At least a hundred
concerns floating in landfills, but it was still
fairly efficient fishing.

Two Poems

Stefani Barber

I lost everything in the last fire

I was buffeted, where the water parts red,
or the earth is brought to heal, or the blood
that connects is given free passage and feeds
this thing, or sucks it dry from loving too much.
a place where they worshipped.

this must be where they part ways. One
took an east turn & suddenly my outfit
made no sense. It was to a different
epoch. & folding again inside of
that old part, this time, of a people
you never would have known. Not even
knowing now. So obviously you are

distancing. Tracing their outlines & with
your magic mind, draw a feeling, context.
no matter what gives you away. The salt
in your tongue, or ripples dancing deep.
what it cost to converse, & whom to thank.

tonight I dared to imagine myself
in the shower, the response outside,
an unknown herd, to do their homage,
distanced—repositioned
within the chaos—

hers was the image missing—from the wall,
inked into the skin, the back of a jacket—
was pride & boasting, was refuge in the desert
was a people defined, a language to write
oneself into, then wait for recognition—
from the very earth—among this to cast
one's fate. Splash of rose consecrates

because the day will come when even those words
will fail you

part the crowd, the script just under your breath.
find a clearing there on the platform. your eyes
the broadcast

as the palmeras
against a darkening bruise
given shape by the shadows of
the desert hills—you ride the road
that led to its insistence.

the party is behind you now.
as though you escaped with secrets
clutching them to your chest while you
trace the outlines of a new perspective—
a peace disturbed

to believe at the end of that road—
communion perhaps, born out of a trance
the desert inspired—another night's oblivion
marked by the pressure of teeth
& a new bruise surfacing

but knowing the other is not imagining.
between the desert & this other place
exist only miles of stark terrain whose sky
seems to slip without complication
between the impossibly colored moods

a person's thin, inked flesh, a message
to all who knew it. *Enact your reverence*
except: *this one thing.* the audacity,
you wanted to say, was in approaching
that door at all, the vanquishing fear
that kept you from it.

"good girl, just tyid"
a little ghetto never hurt nobody
a place she called "the cut"
crept in the edges of a slow smile
something from a memory you created
the moment of its happening
disquiet: sweetness of the impulse
the false words to placate & get me home
everything about this is wrong

this—this air is just
a texture of something unseen

the broad chords you heard sailing
through the aisles of the bodega
were carried by something mournful
you saw in the taut skin of an arm.
insistence of this submission to it
would not release you

a mathematics of familiarity,
how to fill the space

I was glad when he left the train
so I could stop asking myself these questions

she said, "it's capitulation"
was intended to appear as freedom
to the ladies of a wild street mob—
such displays in inclement weather
claiming victory in a losing game

the ruins they leave littered with mines
become hunting grounds
or a place to girlishly wander

pinch the flower or take in
that peculiar angle of light
& texture of the fall
I think maybe I won't want to leave

the blood rises, and hunger grows

you couldn't even leave the house.
that was the cycle.

her response contained not a single word:
some sort of kiss.

I am daring you to touch me,
you who are divine

[untitled]

early in their journey they had reason to believe. The pueblo tossed fruit towards the sky, caught by the passengers on top of the train, who shouted grateful gracias in return.

later the fruit became rocks hurled with hatred at the boxcars full of cowards who dared dream of north. She thought she had found a protector. She was the unlikely survivor.

in this rain anything would melt. But this one night, it would not have mattered. I memorized everything I could. Memory would return me to you. This undercurrent unknowing.

distended harmonies to drive them onward. As in a dreamless night, the waking day becomes refuge. The one time you would risk the breach, your sad & certain fate, it was small.

you refused, and image of the dead man became lullaby. The constant slamming. Conformity to it the cure & vaccine, but it won't quit the formation, reduce to mud.

give me of something that dark, to light a candle against. There to murmur under those car stereos & cigarettes, the only word you'll hear. A cascade. Wasn't nothing to fear.

they made only one small promise to each other. Behind those few words, it was infinite, understood. Not the hope they sang of. When they didn't sing. That was from the others.

in this way they built the road, also by keeping quiet. She did. She ran away. More than halfway there, chose to fashion a new.

does this look like something they put on tv? Do they really touch like that?

to approach like that, cleansed—but marked somehow. A folded map because it is reassuring. Indecipherable. What everyone knows. No shelter on that road.

Two Poems

Craig Cotter

For Carrie Preston, During Lunch

I bought a blue plastic toy airplane for your landing strip.

Man who was said Shu Mai to says,
" . . . and 15 million goes to me.
Bonus is pretty good, 15 percent . . . "

I want most of the language spoken on the street   [Williams]
to shut up.

"You make me feel like a prostitute,"
Victor says.
                I think this is a good feeling for him.
At least there's poetry in Ocean Seafood
(pocket FCH, backpack Koch)

(Hi Ron Padgett!!)
and only one wants it the rest
commerce and pleasing.

Forgot my flip-flops,
put out my hand, no ashtray.   [O'Hara]

11/9/05, 3/3/06, 8/27/06

on hamlin beach

homage to frank o'hara and
influenced by french poets i haven't read yet

alex ate a cheeseburger in four bites
long fingers white and clean—

showed their girlfriends their dicks wanted only pussy
by attacking us (flat stomachs, defined pecs, tanned!)

i released your bare foot
you moved toward them

—no, let's go.

drove my '69 monte carlo
to the next parking lot.

you massaged my neck.
o'hara's addictions
never hurt him
mine have made me
nearly straight
so i'm in rehab
of my mind
in north hollywood
with clouds.

2 kids from el salvador threaten me
cuz they like me like 2 puerto ricans
threatened o'hara because they were attracted to him.

rent is better than mortgage
because the clouds have stopped.
i have met four best minds.

with the earth
not moving
i spent the earthquake money
on javier.

the representative of the church
my parents forced me to attend
banned My Sweet Lord from the guitar mass
once a chick told him the radio version
included the Hare Krishna Mantra—
i was 10
then i Knew.

rent is better than mortgage
clouds have stopped moving against santa susana mountains
paul asks
will animals be in your afterlife?

when i die
i ask all vehicles
in los angeles
to stop for a time—
even the president's motorcade
(to see that there's not always danger).
hate to use the energy
to burn me
please put me on a pike
in the angeles national forest
for the animals and microbes.
my executor
may sell the rights
to a filmmaker to document
these stages of nature.
follow my goddamn Wishes!

and take my europe money
and give it to a whore!

Two Poems

Cal Freeman

EA Abbot's Book on Summer

Who can iron the pop machine
down to two dimensions?
EA Abbot. Edwin Abbot Abbot,
Abbot Abbot can. The cylinder
of the pop can is a trophy.
Could he place the image
on a beach towel? Abbot, Lord knows.

We remember the pop machine's glow
in the evening. Did the farm lose its depth
when the world got dark?
Only in his story. In the object barn,
the roof still loomed eight feet above
the rafters. In Abbot's book the light never varied.

EA Abbot rolled the barn down to an octagon.
It became a royal object in our memory,
a polymathic shade that housed its horses proudly.
Horses had no depth in Abbot Abbot's work.
His horses were presented as squares.
His women appeared as bisections when they rode.
We'd share our cigarettes near the glowing pop machine.
We'd share Skoal bandits and spit tobacco juice into cups.

In the oft-disputed text of that summer,
the crickets in the dust would sound like "Abbot Abbot Abbot,"
which is identical to the way the frogs croaked.
The gate hinges closing on the pasture horses
would also sound like "Abbot."

The lightning those August nights
looked like people, like our doppelgänger selves,
the ones that make shapes of the weather.
The thunder sounded: Edwin Abbot Abbot.
The rain on the aluminum barn roof: Abbot Abbot
until the recitation of the name became
not incantation of the two-dimensional, but praise. In the dark
of the stormy night, we could not find the house.
The direction of the falling rain,
impossible to tell.

An EA Abbot Primer

What the readers long for
They should not. They already have it.
They learn this lesson often after longing.
Whoso charges the knight,
Charges the knight, and the sleek dish
Of his horse's face stays intact.
They already have the sleek face
Of the horse, the tens of pounds of armor.

But get them to say *horse*, write *knight*,
And what they are in the process of losing
Flattens. What they have has
Fallen to the erasure of a word.
Say *square*, then *conditions*
Of the horse: colic, etc.
I write the words "Conditions of the square."

Loss comes to namehood,
The polygonal language of the cursed,
Angles as obtuse as the structure
Will allow. Walkers unaware
Of a sharp corner come to peril.
The pain that they associate with walking
Is simply the awareness that they can't.

But I cannot either.
Walkers all become dead weight,
Anchors with eyes that fathom zero depth.
The lines of their existence strung
To points of zero space.
Flies, knowing nothing,
Eat the ink and learn of nothing more,
Eat the dry ink and become it.

In the knotty groves of the dead,
In groves where *horse* is buried,
Resurrection is a process of winnowing
Down. Here are the lines
They have drawn themselves by living.
Here the hexagons put upon them,
Here the squares that they have always been.

AEROPUERTO. Primera impresión: descortesía y conflicto de culturas. El hombre tirando la valija por el dispositivo de control con rayo láser. La mala forma de los verbos MODALES dicen cultura (me siento latino)—¿y a él? **Registro**: indio, no tiene modales. Y me pego la cabeza 20 veces. Mi modal político y correcto me revienta el coco, por imbécil, por no poder ver al otro. **Joselyn. 1era impresión** (no puedo hacer de madre—dice.)
lo que no se puede se afirmará durante todo el Evento de Poetas.
La imposibilidad ¿será una falta? Acaso posibilidad de permanecer
esperando sin que venga alguien
¿o sin poder ir al encuentro?
Santiago es inhóspita al alba rota
Rota de fisura en la calle extraña cuando un árbol desconocido en la plaza
es mi verdugo:)
nadie persiste, ni el anónimo de esa travesti
ni mucho menos la noche blanca

se asocia, se asocia, **sea.socia: a**.socia cuatro veces la ausencia

me quemó las ganas el amor me hartó el tráfico la bohemia
cinta enferma de un indio, otro, otro satura este
amordaza
y hace escarnio a veces siento intuyo peligro de un sentido corrupto cierto
lenguaje canjeado de absurdos
pero siempre cree en el absurdo racionalmente
busca motivos, panes para creer
y suena a **crickcrickcrick**
crickergri

grillo abierto a Pinocho en enorme nariz falolograda.

FROM Ah.Me.RICH.Ah: Your Exchange Value

Virginia Lucas

de <u>Amé.RICA, tu valor de cambio</u> **Translated by Jen Hofer and Dolores Dorantes**

Santiago de Chile 10, 12

AIRPORT. First impression: rudeness and culture clash. A man heaving a suitcase onto the laser x-ray security machine. Poor conjugation of verbs MANNERS speak to culture (I feel Latino)—and him?
I note: *indio*, has no manners. And I beat my head 20 times. My political and correct manner busts my noggin open, because I'm an idiot, because I can't see the other.
Joselyn. 1st impression (I can't make like I'm a mother—she says.)
what cannot be done will be asserted throughout the Poets' Event.
Impossibility—can it be a lack? The possibility perhaps to remain waiting without anyone's arriving
—or without being able to go to the gathering?
Santiago is inhospitable at the broken dawn
Broken along fissures in the odd street when an unknown tree in the plaza is my executioner:)
no one persists, not even that anonymous tranny
much less the pale night

associates, associates, **as.so.she.hates a.**sociates four times the absence

burnt up my desires love had it up to here the traffic the sick
bohemian conveyor belt of an *indio*, an other, an other saturates this
gag
and gathers scorn sometimes I feel I intuit danger of a corrupt sense a
certain language
exchange of absurdities
but believes always in the absurd rationally
seeks motives, bread so as to believe
and sounds like **crickcrickcrick**
crickercri

cricket open to Pinocchio in enormous nose phallussuccess.

RAINCOOP

No soy quien escribe porque escribir es desaparecer.

—**Héctor Hernández Montecinos**

modo diáfano
los amigos de antes van a desaparecer, los amigos de siempre van a desaparecer
la escritura va a desaparecer la escritura -------tt-------tt---tttt-------- -- -la
lógica escrita antes hace doler otra vez, el paro nacional de transporte----------
----la línea de ómnibus,[1] la línea se me subió a la cabeza   –

-

-

-

- rampa se sube o se baja si escribo la chica a mi lado quiere enamorarse y
  la mosca en mi pierna también yo no quiero más que - -- ------tt---------
  ttt------------ttt--------- --- ----------tt--   --- --- --- --- --- ---ps ps ps ps ps
  ps tus ojitos claros-- ------------tt   -
- siempre seguí el sendero, siempre quise volver a mi casa de luz y de
  moscas el tranqui escenario deslumbrante y la mudanza Haciendo balde
  haciendo silencio- - - - - - - - - pero *ps.ps.ps.ps* tus ojos como moscas
  ps.ps.ps.ps concentraditos es de mosquitos no de mosca ruidosa, es de
  picadura eso de: *el silencio es una raya en tu trasero*
- porque también es una rampa.
a veces la sonrisa vertical confundida en un verso como sable lanza
un cartel allá, analogía quiso decirme: sigue pensando en la lógica causal del
tiempo
línea temporal enseñó mi abuela en la escuela rural línea el cable de tu lámpara
y decirte acá acá acá acá está la línea centrípeta que gané entrando en tu colita
por tu centro ojival línea torcida doblada mi mano entra en tiempo circular
))))):) ¿y qué mirás?

tonal
lector
lecteta
(tres líneas atrás
la caravana (casi redonda) por la traficada tela india a bocinazos la muerte la
muerte por la calle se festejaba la Injusticia en nombre de pensar pensar la
analogía de la raya de tu pantalón te corrés (las muertitas a golpes, las moscas,
las madrecitas, tener ojitos y decir) me corriste despacito en procesión, las
luces, los gritos y el muerto, y el cementerio y el papel del diario en el suelo

RAINCOOP

I am not the person writing because to write is to disappear.

—**Héctor Hernández Montecinos**

diaphanous mode

friends from before will disappear, tried and true friends will disappear writing
will disappear writing -------tt-------tt---tttt-------- -- -written logic before it
causes pain again, the national transit strike-------------the bus line,[1] the line
rose up to my head   –

-

-

-

• ramp goes up or goes down if I write the girl beside me wants to fall in
  love and the fly on my leg does too I don't want anything more than - --
  ------tt---------ttt------------ttt--------- --- ----------tt-- --- --- --- --- ---
  ---bz bz bz bz bz bz your clear baby blues-- ------------tt   -

• I always followed the path, I always wanted to go back to my house
  with its light and flies the calm dazzling setting and a move elsewhere
  Building in-vain-ness building silence- - - - - - - - - - but *bz.bz.bz.bz* your
  eyes like flies *bz.bz.bz.bz* cutely concentrated like mosquitoes noisy not
  like flies, it's from a sting all that about: *silence is a line on your rear end*

• because it is also a ramp.

sometimes the vertical smile confused in verse like a saber launches
a street sign there, analogy wanted to tell me: keep thinking about the causal
logic of time
temporal line my grandmother taught at the rural school line the cord of
your lamp and to tell you here here here here is the centripetal line I crossed
entering your fine tail through your bullet-shaped center twisted line folded
my hand enters in circular time)))))):) and what are you looking at?

tonal

reader

boober

(three lines ago

the caravan (nearly round) along the trafficked indian fabric over the very
loudspeaker death death in the street Injustice is celebrated in the name
of thinking thinking the analogy of the crease in your pants you come fiery
(women beaten to death, flies, *madrecitas*, to have baby blues and to say) you
fire me come sweet and slow procession-style, the lights, the yelps and death,

para secar el orín caído por su vientre antes del festivo eyaculaba en parábola
no en línea
ya no la misma lógica cagada:
- un impacto, dos de bala 22, el miedo lo absorbió ----ttt-----ttt----ttt----ttt----
ttt------ttt--.

pausa

------------.

---**salut**----

otro brindis por Pierrot, otros amigos

NOTE

1 Muerte el día viernes de --- --- ---------- --en la línea de ómnibus RAINCOOP. El conductor--
--------la vieja, otro viejo, un niño en mi país. Momo anda dando vueltas, el recordatorio de
los avisos fúnebres sigue dando-----t-----   ----tt---------- ----------ttt-------------------
----- ps.ps.ps........................

and the cemetery and the newspaper on the ground to dry the urine fallen
from her womb before the holiday ejaculated in a parabola not in a line
no more of the same shitty logic:
- one shot, two from a .22 bullet, fear absorbed it ----ttt-----ttt----ttt----ttt----
ttt------ttt--.

pause

-----------.

---**cheers**----

another toast to Pierrot, other friends

NOTE

1 Died the Friday of --- --- ---------- --on the RAINCOOP bus line. The driver---------the old
woman, another old man, a kid in my country. Momo is wandering around, the reminder of
the funereal announcements continues on -----t-----   ----tt----------   ----------ttt------
----------------- ps.ps.ps........................

TRANSLATORS' NOTE

1 Momo* (or el Rey Momo, King Momus) is considered the king of *carnaval* in some Latin
American countries. In Uruguay, the invention of *carnaval* is attributed to Momo. Momo is
also a Greek god, patron saint of sarcasm, jokes and ironic wit—the god of writers, poets,
and unfair criticism.

Querida mía:

el niño pide alimento
y es del poeta el hueco
el misco hueco o la dura manzana,
casana la jornada, casana.

¿Qué pasa en la aurora
una letra no entra el milagro
del pará pará.... ....para.íso ......**animal!!!!!!!!!!!!!!!! pará**
y hay desastre, del cielo...
pero todas las hojas son del viento
y del cielo la paloma, se vuelve la memoria tras la letra
abandono en plaza abierta
y se sigue, se sigue el rastro de Hansel sin Gretel...
Otro cuento sin niño derribando la tormenta
busca sentido. Sentido en parte de lucha.
Coraje busca. Busco decirte querida:

la revolución del lenguaje pasa mi amor

pasa Mall.armé (tal vez prefiera Rimbaud del olvido)

pasa estrujado este niño contra fondo frío en calle urbana,
este chiquito pobre (todos los chiquitos son pobres querida) como abuela
vieja tirada en esquina calienta agua hierve plástico moviendo mano abanica lumbre y hay
desenfreno querida, y vieja mueve, y mueve, mueve todo lo que pesa en la calle en mejor
sentido de democracia la calle es de todos aunque todos es mísero y mísero o miseria no es
número es palabra diciendo (todos los viejos son tristes, pero qué triste llegar a viejo—dice
mi abuelo).

y viejo pide pan o moneda, Mirame—dice—mirame dame palabra
visible, visible haceme, hacé.eme, **MMMM**iráme, mirá, mirá, mirra dame un
poco de paz que quiero carne que tengo hambre
y hambre cae como palabra muerta de huesos limpios
y niño dice dame forma (que no soy hombre) matame la tradición, matame

My dear:

the niño begs for food
and it's the poet's, the hollow
the samepty hollow or the hard apple
exhousted the workday, exhousted.

What's going on with the dawn?
a letter doesn't enter the miracle
of par par.... ....par.a.dise ......**animal!!!!!!!!!!!!!!! par**
and there's a disaster, from the sky...
but all the leaves are the wind's
and the pigeon the sky's, turns to memory after the letter
desertion on the open plaza
and it follows, follows the trace of Hansel without Gretel...
Another story without a niño demolishing the storm
seeks meaning. Meaning as part in struggle.
Rage is sought. I seek to tell you, dear:

> *the revolution of language is passing my love*

passing Mall.armé (Perhaps might prefer Rimbaud oblivion)

this niño all crumpled passes by against a cold background on an urban street,
this poor little chiquito (all the little chiquitos are poor, dear) like an old grandmother flung down
on the hot corner water boils plastic moving hand fans firelight and there's wild abandon dear,
and the old woman moves, and moves, moves everything that weighs down on the street amid a
better sense of democracy the streets are for everyone though everyone is miserable or misery
is not a number it's a word saying (all the elderly are sad, but how sad to become elderly—my
grandfather says).

and the old man begs for bread or coins, Look at me—he says—look at me
      give me a word
visible, make me visible, make.me, **LLLL**ook, look, look at **mmmmy mmmm**e,
myrrh give me a little peace
      because I want meat because I'm hungry
and hunger falls like a dead word with clean bones
and the niño says give me form (because I'm not a man) kill tradition for me, kill

a Juana de américa para decidirte (antes que me coman)

—*Verseame, amor, verseame el punto,*

no me dejes en suspenso que me planto con 7 y ½

    otra tirada de cartas, por favor

    •   no me gustan los dados ni el coup

Juana of américa for me to decide you (before they eat me)

—*Versify me, love, versify the point for me,*

don't leave me in suspense 'cause I stand with 7 in my hand

   deal the cards again, please

   •   I don't like the dice, nor the throw

D.F. México City

It's rain, it's rain y el niño saborea su azúcar dulce caramelo
la muerte anduvo un día, dos . . . momento sin sueño, hoy.
Y pide de la mano otro regalo, el niño, el mismo niño me dice
nacimiento, mientras la sonrisa es otra falta de la lluvia it's rain, it's rain
del hombre quiero que sea, el derecho, el feliz cielo del xocholate
cuando negrea la capota del que digo mundo y no quiero,
quiero del merengue la blanca
la mañana but it's rain, it's rain un segundo más del mal inglés,
    es el **paro**
en el tráfico, corazón mi auto, mi bomboncito almendrado, pedazo
    de caramelo caro
mi falta es agria,
but it's rain en el verso de la autopista que es cinta de regalo roja,
verde envoltura . . . como el bucito de mi niño pidiendo
mi dulce niño lindo espera pi.di.en.do la escala que cala la venta
    (valor de cambio)
y el corazón agita bandera en los bolsillos la moneda
candy, candy, candy, sweet caramelo o cándida dulzura, dulce candil,
but it's rain, perhaps

cantábile

perhaps, perhaps las notas abruman: *perhaps, perhaps, perhaps*

D.F. Mexico City

Es lluvia, es lluvia and the niño savors his sugary caramel candy
death was around for one day, two . . . dreamless moment, today.
And with his hand begs for another gift, the niño, the same niño says
birth to me, while a smile is another lack of rain *es lluvia, es lluvia*
for men I want them to be, rights, the happy sky of the xocholate
when it blackens the soft top of the one I call my world and I don't want,
I want meringue, the white one
the morning pero es lluvia, es lluvia one second more of bad English,
    it's the **standstill**
in traffic, my car my heart, my sweet little almond bonbon, expensive piece
    of candy
my lack is sour,
but es lluvia on the poem of the freeway which is the red ribbon on a gift,
green wrapping . . . like the little maw of my niño begging
my sweet pretty niño waits be.gg.ing the scale that soaks the sale
    (exchange value)
and the heart waves a flag in his pockets the coin
candy, candy, candy, sweet caramel or candid sweetness, sweet chandelier,
pero es lluvia, quizás
                              cantabile
quizás, quizás perhaps the notes overwhelm: *quizás, quizás, quizás*

D.F. México City:

Ganas de decirte linda una tristeza. Nicolás lloró y era triste,
el niño, el caballito
pegazo duro ese silencio esperando a verlo
mientras vendía una figura de caramelo
Esta mirada resiste linda esa casa ajada, mientras la espalda levanta el muro,
si hace simiente la vieja, la doña brillando en alma otra espera, pero brillando
    la casa levanta el desmoronamiento en el cartel de la acera **PLOMERO**
    se ofrece
Destapa caños, y reza, reza: *valor de cambio* esta mirada dice **ASÍ** es mi pollo
) media metáfora pide valor de cambios, cristos *c.a.c.a* o cerveza fría para
    llevar a casa
cuando linda viene cansada y
AMÉ.RICA tus besos de soldada
o dulce hogar sin estilo, cuate o letra **valedera**
(la compañera llaman en México al amigo y al peso al rescate), *coca-cola* es casi
    siempre lo mismo en casi todas partes.
Ganas de decirte preciosa una alegría, cambiar la comparación
cambiar otro delirio de la sin.taxis:
el niño de los vidrios, el cortado, el del caballito
sobrevivió el día

es de tu empeño las alitas de cualquier pegazo

D.F. Mexico City:

Desires to call you pretty, a sadness. Nicolás cried and was sad,
the niño, the little horse
pegasus (pow!) that silence waiting to see him
while he sold a caramel-candy figure
This gaze resists, pretty, that sickly house, while a back raises a wall
if the old woman seeds, the lady polishing another wait in her soul, but
    polishing the house raises the demolishment on his sign on the sidewalk
    PLUMBER services offered
Unclog pipes, and pray, pray: *exchange value* this look says **THAT'S HOW** my
    chickadee is) half
a metaphor begs for exchange values, christs *c.a.c.a* or cold beer to take home
when, pretty, she comes back tired and
AH.ME.RICH.AH your lady soldier's kisses
or sweet home with no style, *cuate* or letter that's **valid**
(as they call a friend in México compañera and to the rescue the peso), *coca-cola*
    is almost always the same everywhere.
Desires to call you beautiful, a happiness, to shift the comparison
shift another delirium of syn.tax:
the niño of the windowpanes, the one who was cut, the one with the little horse
survived this day

it's from your effort the little wings on any (pow!) pegasus

Two Poems

Rick Snyder

Testimonia

FROM POSSUM EGO III

A minor American poet of middle antiquity. Dates unknown.
Fl. during the first great swirl. His lines about the red leash
were noted by one reviewer and emphasize the human
inability to discern smells:

It all smells like smoke to me,
but something beyond the bush
makes her dog strain against
the red leather leash, claws
clacking on broken concrete,
neck engorged with anticipation

FROM PS-BOOKSLUT

His work was known to be reactionary and didactic.
Lines preserved in an obsolete platform present explicit
instructions to the reader:

Write this. We have burned their Mercedes
and eaten their chapbooks. Dear Reader,
we have fed their cats regular cat food
and told their children about the center

FROM THE NEW SMILES CENTER LOG

Reactionary and bilingual. American? A part-time musician
before the reunification of media and genres during the first
great swirl:

Estoy aburrido de Ew Esse A
¿Pero que es posible para mi?

FROM IRASCIBLE POETS

The red leash indicates that he starved after the first swirl.
Another site from an obsolete platform, however, shows the
poet to be corpulent, perhaps in an attempt to curry favor
with his countrymen:

I imagine future readers
obese and tired, like me,
appendages to a console

FROM IRASCIBLE POETS

In one cached file the verse continues:

tethered to a dead screen
at the uni{fication} center

People who died from snake bites
people who died in plane crashes
people who died on Locust Street
people who died on the toilet
people who died while singing
people who died during tax time
people who died receiving a stent
people who died in a cab
people who died while yawning
people who died in the yogurt aisle
people who died in a crowd
people who died on a roof
people who died doing a puzzle
people who died during prayer
people who died in an embassy
people who died in Tacitus
people who died while working
people who died in 1974
people who died in the library
people who died with hostages
people who died wearing silk
people who died processing rebates
people who died for freedom
people who died in Split
people who died in sunlight
people who died sweeping
people who died in a bush
people who died in the hospital
people who died on TV
people who died on purpose
people who died eating peanuts

Eleven Self-Evident Poems

Guy Bennett

Preliminary Poem

This poem is self-contained
and self-sufficient.
It does not require critical commentary
or explanations of any kind
to convey its meaning,
which is self-evident.

It does not exceed a single page,
and is thus appropriate
for publication in magazines
and anthologies.

It can be read in a single sitting,
and will not unduly tax the reader or listener
as it neither necessitates nor benefits from
excessive post-reading reflection.

Experimental Poem

I suppose that even this
could be considered
an experimental poem.

Poem Title Here*

Poem content
here.

*This is a self-evident meta-poem.

Pro-Life Poem

In order to complete this poem
it would be helpful to know:
do Afghan and Iraqi lives count,
or is it only a question
of unborn American children?

Pro-War Pro-Life Poem

We're killing them over there,
so we don't *have to* kill them
over here.

Pro-Choice Poem

This poem is pro-choice
in every respect
except one:
that would be
your choice
to not read it.

Political Poem

Some poems are explicitly political.
Others are implicitly so.
This one is both.

Alternate Political Poem

Some poems are explicitly political.
Others are implicitly so.
This one is neither.

Anti-Authoritarian Poem

You are free to think whatever you like
about this poem,
and to say what you will about it
to anyone at any time.
You may also write poetry
against this poem,
condemning it and its author
in language as virulent and vituperative
as you wish.

If you are reading it,
you may tear up the paper it is printed on
and burn or otherwise destroy it
with impunity.
You may likewise simply ignore it
without fear of retaliation of any kind.

If, on the other hand,
you are reading this poem
or hearing it read aloud,
there is unfortunately nothing
you can do about it
at this point.

Poetry and Terrorism

The state-sponsored varieties
are invariably worse.

Concluding Poem

All of these poems,
though independent
from one another
and thus self-contained
and self-sufficient,
could nonetheless be considered
a cycle.

As such they still retain
a certain autonomy,
though they do promise
a "greater than the sum of its parts" experience
when considered as a group.

Two Poems

Celina Su

To Steal Oneself

In between, an ellipsis of the agentic. Whereas

A smuggled adult is merely a smuggled adult.
Unless I, a woman of disgrace, open my mouth
Wide, illustrate the scars to prove it.
Then I exotic them my own. Dryly, would I.
Whose subjects, which objects,
Lit on fire as if *pristine* were a burning choice—

Finger-pointing these choices institutionalized.
Still my own luminous blackened cloud of . . .

A smuggled child, who is a trafficked child.
In certain circumstances of layaway purchase and sale,
Ringing up the will of others, limb-like devices
Perfect for crate-filled kitchen-friendly
Heavy lids on the school shift—

Double-Dutch me *victim* or *criminal*, skip the tumble,
Whose subject who objects to whose agent,
Prowling like a snuggled animal.
Metonymy my fierce. Regal me legal.
A snakehead with no mongoose federal agent,
A coyote's jowls with my own Benz bling
To ransack these entrapping escapes
Targeting darting person-shaped objects—

Tending to my wounds
Licking them quantitative
Number me dispassionate

I'm Stuck.

In it
Sticking it in it
Sticking it to it in it.

Standing on the sidewalk,
I call out your name. Louder than
Crawling double-deckers full of tourists

Sticking to it
Sticking it to my body
Sticking heat.

I call out your name again.
You do not come out. Stuck on you
The rush-hour businessmen glare

To stick to you
By sticking it to reddened love
A sharp stick.

A couple of people stop.
Together, we call out your name.
"Are you sure your friend's home," one pleads,

Sticking on me
Sweat sticker flames
Sticky burn in it in it.

But you do not live here.
But I am wearing red for you,
As if the red will not dull,

Sticking it in it to it
Sticking it to you in it
In why the red herring.

As if, when we count to 3,
Shout it one more time, *write it*,
Your name will not numb the

Why the how
The flammable you why.
As if the sticking sticks.

Three Poems

James Grinwis

Cantilena

There was a cloud in Denton and it carried a plum.

The open boat bumped into the dock at Mrnsk.

It was my megafauna and I nurtured it,
however luxuriantly it wept
having lost itself to the fern.

In her absence of robe and sweaters she lit a match.

There was a sound.

When one enters that village one becomes the shape of it
and it looks like this:

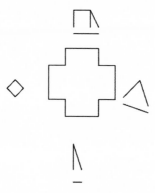

For this is the village of four museums and all work is
for the museums and everyone's life revolves around the
museum and everyone's mind is a museum where can be
found exotics and delicacies and machines and animals and
extinctions and lusts and jellies.

To become the village is to have the village become as a
breath ring of stakes tying shut the breath. And one is both
the center of the point and the energy that floats in the
space above one.

Mécanique

The project: obtuse, surrounded by moles
exhumed from their dens.

The standards: fluid, without definition.

The animal: domesticated, yet predatory-seeming,
watchful, apparently in wait.

Brainstorming: enterprise of greatness, of monstrous,
unwieldy limbs.

The project: full of gears and little filters.

The boy: skinny, radical, without definition almost.

Things started out in frenzied terms. Poor grasps of
missions, vocabularies, proper freeze techniques. The
girders but sagged. Some of the cables got tangled in pegs of
the instrument. The tall steel cones on the top of the colossi
shone too brightly. Further, the asses seemed misaligned.
Eventually however correct technologies found adequate
sockets and the thing groaned awake over the course of the
migration.

Memoir-less. I open my journal: an ultimate blank.
The empty space of where and of what I'd been.

Hunkering down for the rush, and frolicsome:
the assemblers on metallic steeds.

FROM **Floaters**

Michael Ives

Purported Micro-Bermudas
from which the atoms spring.

Shoals too are but a swimming
so let the poles wobble a mite

and aloes be smeared wherever.
Chronicles waiting to be inked in,

phases entering their phases.
Something hides in the river.

It keeps slipping back
into what it won't abide.

Into a protein shake
with what ails it.

Bas-reliefs baked into the shuttle's heat shield
warned us of the price we'd pay.

Large dark bubbles amassed.
It was then I built the vanishing chamber.

"Watkins," I said, "why is the lava corded?"
He handed me a system of sliding rods.

That may have started it,
this inner glaciation, I mean.

With such hazards an ebbing
could very well mistake itself

for a threshold, empty ritual
the dispersion medium in any case.

Thus do we moil in false clay.
And here too, wheels

and forking pipes of mysterious origin.
Electric tables flank the silence.

Poolings of anonymities leave faces.
Star groups dip out of season.

Crowded together at a window,
the accumulated heedlessness

riveted to an air bridle
blames tools for the ills of men.

Dip him in acid
who loves transfiguration.

Life monad
drifts into scar.

Honey place
cannot help

but fall in
with tracking system.

Haunts at the entrance
to a visible heaven

still speak
on behalf of femurs

half out of the mouth
of on behalf of.

And the pepper bird
shall do as it pleases

for there is
no such bird.

A clean transfer from thought to act
has no hobbies, if staying invisible

doesn't count. Well, and
staring down the task horizon

'til it's a geometric point,
which Euclid defines as

"that which has no part."
The tight space notwithstanding,

it would take a hundred years
to recapture in words

why the witness to the crime
blames himself.

For the abstraction that was
his unmolested field of view

has been ripped open
by his just happening

to be somewhere,
and all the baby spiders

pouring out from behind
make a trail for him to follow

away from his tranquil inner moltenness
toward a congealed frontier

where swordplay traced against the air
apotheosizes knowledge.

Who's letting whom
build what bomb?

Thugs are running dog races
in the aqueduct.

All around the plateau,
butch ways of chariotry

loiter, waiting for a warrior caste
to establish itself.

Too early for me to start drawing
broad conclusions from this.

Must resume reconstruction of the star clock.
That, or else disappear into a novelty cocktail.

How far inside these years must I travel
before I need no longer call them mine?

At the gun show
they're selling watermelon sorbet

in hollow plastic bullets.
"This is my death bling," says the death god.

"Touch it. Feel it."
And seeds of the wild lettuce float past.

FROM **Cleaning The House Workshop, or, No Intimacy Without Reciprocity**

Stephanie Young

The day after the dream of reassurance, today
is the first day I have after I have this dream:
reassurance is separation,
everything's OK

information from outside
in a dream of reassurance
received in public space
(John Zorn) is reading at the reading
which means it's not a reading
in the usual sense
it's reassuring, to begin with,
separate and public and OK.

I am not prepared
to begin, have not slept with crystals
in my bed
with their sharp edges
she often turned in her sleep
and cut herself, under the quilt
retrieved from his shed
after he died, a grandfather

if you don't prepare yourself
stop eating three months in advance
hand in a plaster
perfectly still, nothing
under a block of color
watch yourself for an hour
in this condition

you'll wind up
. . . I don't know

rhetorical slapstick. Mastery from the bottom

it'll be too clean
it'll be an object
and not about cleaning

already it's not a process
already so close it clings to the center
it doesn't want to fall off the edge and be alone

I guess I know now that every time I said "it" in a poem,
    previously, and I said "it" a lot
it was a bad habit I tried to break and haven't I guess

I meant poetry, but was obscuring this meaning from myself

and me from it

of always going on about it, always over-processing.

I guess it's too late to walk the entire length of the Great
    Wall of China.

I guess it's too late to start on March 30, 1988.

I guess we'll never start walking on the eastern end of the
    Wall, at Shan Hai Guan, on the shores of the Yellow Sea,
    Gulf of Bohai, walking westward.

I guess we'll never start walking at the west end of the Wall,
    at Jai Yu Guan, the southwestern periphery of the Gobi
    desert, walking eastward.

I guess I can't expect to walk until we meet.

I guess I have to give up all my dreams that we will both
    continuously walk for 90 days.

I guess we'll never meet on June 27, 1988, at Er Lang Shan, in
    Shen Mu, Shaanxi province, after walking 90 days each,
    over a distance of 2,000 kilometers.

I guess it's too late to meet to say goodbye.

Here's what I do.
Here's how I prepare:
I work five days in a row and look at the internet.

Rewrite the last section of something previous,
rewrite it in my mind
a kind of living
in an image of agony
I grab my head in my hands
and grimace and shake the head, and lower it
and make a sound like moaning.

I perform this series
involuntarily
whenever I recall my own behavior,
or writing, as I am rewriting it
becomes more and more impossible: I'm not prepared
and the grabbing of my head, and grimacing,
the shaking and moaning sounds
are, I fear, at least once, interpreted by my lover
as a reaction to what I am, my eyes, watching
what passes before them, while behind the scrim
I rewrite this behavior while we watch, on closing night,
Miramonte High School's production of Grease
for which he is the acting coach, and Grease is kind of great
so much more distressing than I remember, which is probably
about the setting, and costumes, pulling at their nightgowns
so that it covers her ass when they lay down on the bed and sing.

I try not to rewrite during the show
that evening because the image of agony
it recreates in me, once started, I can't stop
rewriting alongside now a fear that my image of groaning,
even when silent, might appear a form of response
to what's before my eyes, but it's not, it wasn't
because I can't see

I can't stop saying "I can't see"
because I'm not prepared.

To watch is not
the right verb
when one is in the room
in rows with others
and others onstage
have memorized some words and gestures
and repeat them into us

"In a given space.

We are facing each other, both producing a continuous
    verbal sound.

We slowly build up the tension, our faces coming closer
    together until we are screaming into each other's open
    mouths."

Not always this extremity
of to watch

but sometimes.
A metaphor.

I don't stop
on a thrust stage, anyways

shadows

the place where I sprained my hand
weak and willing to repeat the moment it went too far
    backwards.

I resolve to study with the teacher who practices
in order to support a healthy environment for meditation.

Like (Jennifer Moxley) as she describes herself in (The Middle
    Room), an undergraduate running my hand over the
    spines of books in the library, as if to absorb them.

I sleep pressed tightly against my lover, it doesn't end, we
    don't part

all night, with a mouth guard on my two front teeth
I watch videos of (Oscar Grant's)
shooting on the BART platform on YouTube over and over again

look at the clock and move the grains of quinoa aside, from
     off the J and K keys.

Do I release the skin of my lower back here?
Get rid of 15 shirts and 5 skirts
to release March February January December November
I cling to the internet and don't go anywhere
(Young Hae Chang Heavy Industries Dot Com)

Future Oakland
Public advocate subsidy Chart
Oakland Streets
Mapping Oakland

look at very small things with your eyes
is it a root system, or what

not a transform boundary
but created by one, the Hayward, the Calaveras

open the document
not very much

open the document

In retrospect, I prepare.

I do not think I am preparing but in the way I always do

A, drive home from work.
Clean my body, change my clothes, apply lotions and makeup.
Drive from A to B, from B to C.
Butter lettuce with bleu cheese and pears,
meat and cheese plate, too much meat
too large of pieces.
Drive from C to D.

Glass of wine.
Glass of water.
Drive from D to C.5.
Slice of heart attack pizza, two glasses of wine.
Drive from C.5 to B.
Remove my clothes, wash my face. Sleep.

Three cups of tea.

Clean, change, apply.
From B to E, coffee, bagel, E to F, F to A.
Water, carrots, toast.
Clean, change, apply.
From A to G, from G to H.
Sweet potato mash, cobb salad, bread, wild tuna grilled with
    cabbage, beer.
From H to I.
Gum.
From I to J.
Stuffed mushrooms, prosciutto-wrapped asparagus, manhattan.

From the J to the A.
Remove, wash, sleep.
Three cups of tea.

At this point I begin.

When one hormone stimulates the production of a second,
the second suppresses production of the first

when the hormones produced by one thing
suppress production of other hormones the thing needs,
atrophies, results in falling levels of some hormones
and rising levels of others

continued drops trigger the end

at this point I begin.

I don't know how to break my hand out of the plaster it
   seems to be contained in. The point does persist in
   being something about breaking my hand free of a
   plaster I am not sure I applied, or when, or out of order,
   and preparations inverse or opposite to the task. At the
   same time the other hand, the leg, I smear plaster on
   my fellows, I become frightened, "I'm made of plaster!"
   etc. I've stolen this plaster, wasted or abused it: scene of
   unexpressed paranoia at the party.

I need to know
what
to let go of.

Ultimately, my hand is never suppressed.

It expresses itself everywhere, including the face.
Before, after, and during preparations.

I eat so much chocolate in order to get here, you wouldn't
   believe it, but here it is, the chocolate, and hot chocolate

before you,
transmutation:

size 26 or 27 but then the legs and ass are too tight, size 27
   or 28 and they gap around the waist.

I trade in my clothes. Size 26.

My hands shake as I type this, from holding all the hangers
   in the store across my arm. I try on every item. Every
   item in the store. The clothing I trade is valued at ten
   dollars per unit. This seems about right.

But is it conspicuous ENOUGH.

Can we stand its vibration

Is the place geologically meaningful

Is there water present

Access to parks and other open space

Did you feel it

What means of transportation do you normally use

If you were sleeping, did it wake you

How frequently do you use the streets in your neighborhood
    for socializing

Were you asleep

Did others feel it

when I make a mark in the air

in order to bring myself in, shoving it, the tip of it, the nib of
    not so long ago
omitted lines, doing it again (with a broad gesture of the hand)
all of it to

stop it

can I stop

and prepare

while the cat coughs, stretched out on the floor
scratches my palm and call him a jerk

while reading
Artist Body
Public Body
Student Body
Mommy Must Be A Fountain of Feathers
The Oakland Crimespotting map

Caught on its corresponding colored circles, the red simple
assaults and aggravated assaults, the green robberies and
vehicle thefts, the blue prostitution and narcotics.

"An intention common to many students it to overcomplicate
works with unnecessary elements, thinking that more is
better."

My hand hovers over a graph of crime by day. Reduced.

"Sitting on a chair,
Looking at one of the primary colors—
Yellow, blue or red.
Motionless.

One hour each."

My hand hovers there.

I drove so many places in preparation, in traffic, and ate so
many rich and expensive foods—does it show?

I watched myself on the internet—did you see me?

"Unpredictably, I will hold a mirror in front of a participant's
face. He/she is not to change the facial expression of the
moment. I demand that the participant look in the mirror."

As I prepare I think it should have something to do with
direct address.
Not everyone wants to be addressed.
Not everyone in the room.

As I prepare I feel lost and unsure and want to address others
who I think maybe also feel lost or unsure, but I think that
one way would be to put all the names in, and another
would be to leave them out.

One way would be to address some social conditions, and
another way would be to allow those pressures to be felt.

I begin with a desire to rewrite, desire is not compulsion
but my intention becomes so, and yet I call it desire and
let it stand, it is wrong. "At the time I was just following
my compulsion, and I would feel a terrible discomfort if
I didn't react to it." I begin with this compulsion toward
section three of some previous writing, what I'm calling
section three is actually the seventh section, a piece of
writing that becomes over time abstract, I cannot recall
it to rewrite or bear to look upon its face, slapped as it is
again and again inside the film I am rewriting.

I begin with the idea that rather than names I should
address whatever it was I was trying to talk about,
address it directly,

and without film.

if one named names *there*
one shouldn't *here*, intention
as attempt to move beyond
but routed through behavior, breaks
as a way of going backwards

is that the way to let go?

is that the only way?

"Your knife is a lot sharper"
"No amount of letting go seems enough"
"I can't control what's happening to me"
"And why is everybody a monster?"

Three Poems

Karen Garthe

Beauty

A picture of darling you   barreling emerald eggs *piebald*

Bounded Blue Cushion Grandeur   bounded the medium   punys you resented or

opalized   *When the tide rises all boats float the same*

Unfirm jellies and tactics

Clasp longing right inside its daddy of dragons guarding the door

Hatching skeined drives   nubby sequences

To the dragon edge   the pillow center you had then,

More room than you thought

You had   Less vanity about the brow

Gorge

Baleen torqued hipped Gorge

turned in drying stiffening

working up to its crevasse

Looming
rippled blues
of what to feed the fathoms but take one's time
dark passes

gimps on clever
recedes as from out-of-style consciousness, out-of-style rescue

scarlet enmities/pieties cruise

This, your playmate
This, your fill
of plebiscites whiskered to yellow age
plump
rosy permanents

stun these sharpshooters
this wall with its crevasse

Water Quip

for Lois Hirshkowitz

Piqué and restive
to the water   lowboxed mourning to the kitchen level striation she's walking
        to the little

                                    Pantheon of the sea,

                                        Water Quip

Luscious morphing under arm lift 'twixt getting up, getting around

                Her
            and the all of pandering
        creaming world crush,
                    sibilant
                    mirror   life,
                        gilled other
                                breathing
                                Forward
                swarming

            close guardian to the water poise and   bug-eyed languish
                                anti-headstone   anti-monument

                            flux she digged down,
    discarding backward at the flange of dress-arms

                    deviled in canopy
                    &
                    billow
                        to the water

            piqué right up
                        to
            pour her profile hair
            her lash-whipped   buckets to the gossiping, bickering fountain

FROM **distance decay**

Cathy Eisenhower

tenderloin assessment
meant callbox

[scan for the possible plastic of feel]

at or
ation

[to muster endless coulds and thrilling]

mod u
late me

[very little us of use in learning how]

anti
stortions tender
powder, tender.under.ness.

[

example:
lop better pinpoints
that is

odds, an act
of skin
industry
designs
of rapid tend to ward
rapid off, tend toward
hard

ables "know"—
construe

—how this need's
expressed:

to think more of
what's said

that is one tasty pussy

what else rhymes
with measure?

no not that—

* * *

When you are not raging me, I am not considering not raging you.
From want of speechlessness and also from being in it.
What my structure is is this loom toward analysis.
If staring wild at vector shadows launched from a live source of mouth light
can extract loving heads that nuzzle from inside the body walls,
then what else could it possibly fucking want.
Whose mind has entered a man as hands full of diffident countries, font-shaped.
It holds lament patiently in its arrows.
This is the way we eyes clear the entering.
But the more I make of force as peer, the stranger I am dreamt.
That I belong to it of body-colored ink, a mineral year.
I try to be discursive. Miraculous.

to splinter the raping into sponsorships
with which to rub this cornea via eyelid
pushing grit to the edge to help it escape
hey hi, i'm writing a poem

grit is feetless not to say legless
floating toward a crease
instead of listing withholdings
i'm writing a poem

the crease stands in for the stand-in
when provisions get scarce, difficult stuff changes its status
to more or less difficult, we don't need you now
it's become so easy that safely we facts enjoy our paychecks

to deposit the moneyroll into my pocket
which sings through cloth skin and muscle into hip flexor
vagina is ten percent of a pie chart
what color should it be for this presentation

      * * *

who cannot stop raving this which
let me shame the ears with hearing
hardly what was felt on the bareness
of back to brain & back & then not backing.

attempts to recollect the infinite end
in raving, begin in being raved severally
refusal makes a title of the body: how
to strike out when you prepare to leak.

the mumble is coated with hours on end
the pipes transporting fire to herself at rest
then some abstraction breaks or sprouts a field
more likely it doesn't, just some clanging.

this sipping makes the day a structure
familiar shaken smile over the drink
as to rave quietly from warm dangers
their "let me say at once" not there

before there was light
—and detach expressions of satisfactions from them, is that broken?

you don't have to write about rape
if you want to . . .

you don't have to write about writing about rape
if you have to . . .

you don't have to rape
to not write about it . . .

as the need for reference
surfaced, as the soil however
willing borne, end
with a likeness

lustrous cunning, the bed,
(two beds), if you want to (what)
mirror the manner of
head-free tongue, Cervantes

candling, a public alone,
pulling off the little part
their floatings were mantles
inside themselves

cankered ask
is to rust
as mere is
to nation

the clean body conducting some
times would rip

there—a looking for some kind of planet that I do, & as well I stupid all over the junk where planet should assume, of my myness & personal shock transmissions careful to penetrate shut. thanks to my having your eyes in your thigh crevice eyeing a tongue this licking about, gentle planetary gravity causing love, restraining the preordered will we keep for reference. I say we now as know. the body was found under my body. I fucking knew it was there and began to sweetly test it.

essays
reviews
notes &
prose

Edited by
Julian T. Brolaski,
E. Tracy Grinnell &
Paul Foster Johnson

"Dame Critchley-Midgley" by Hannah Barrett

FROM **The Inferno**

Eileen Myles

I was bumping around one night in the dark of the loft of another guy, a guy named John. John Swan.

He was like my age, and I also liked him. John was cute. He was pretty with curly hair and kind of huge. He was a bulky guy, chubby broad arms. I'm having a hard time avoiding giving the impression that he was fat. But he wasn't fat. He was strong and milk-fed looking. And sort of a Nazi. He had the ultimate soft guy voice, but he was a total mean perv, you just felt it. He had a girlfriend Aurelia who he used to enclose in his baby fat at parties like they had just tumbled out of bed. It was hot, but sort of odd. Later there would be a million guys like him around, but they were mostly into business. The red suspender crowd. John had a tumbler of scotch in his hand. He wore rugged shirts and jeans and he spoke really soft. When I think of it now he was so writing program. He courted all the slightly older, hip academic poets. Tom Lux, James Tate. *Bill Knott.* And each of those guys generally had a babe in tow. This is the life, sipped John.

We who write poetry and think about it all the time—who walk the streets that other humans walk, past pizza stands and trees, are citizens meanwhile of a secret country with its own currency that gets exchanged anecdotally, even whispered in the loud thrumming silence of the day, in the galleries the Marxist auditoriums jammed bookstores (being jammed with thin and irregularly shaped journals and books and people generally twenty or thirty) the stinking bars where poets meet and read in. In dozens even hundreds of stained and damp diaries the evidence accumulates, notebooks bent from getting shoved in back pockets, or written into during the long nights of the poet's youth (included here is the bonus time of people who managed to stay young extra long, till forty or fifty, sixty or seventy even, at last croaking then). All of us whacking back drinks and sipping our beers, smoking of course— several long ones going simultaneously in the ashtray.

The poet's life is just so much crenellated waste, nights and days whipping swiftly or laboriously past the cinematic window. We're hunched and weaving over the keys of our green our grey or pink blue manual typewriter maybe a darker stone cold thoritative selectric with its orgasmic expectant hum and us popping pills and laughing over what you or I just wrote, wondering if *that* line means insult or sex. Or both. Usually both.

The mind expands. Getting up, taking a drag looking down onto 14th, 11th Street or Avenue A, into the sweet quiet park between 2nd and 3rd.

Looking out at the inner courtyard at Richard's on 5th St. He clears his throat laughing with a grin on his face. The total trombone of his voice. It's afternoon. Richard doesn't work today. Joint he goes, passing. Then down, writing another couplet. We called em *twos*. We made rules first. Threes or twos. *Ones!* So it felt more like kids playing cards. Push my chair away, laughing. Here, try this.

Richard grins resumes pounding the keys. In the sexual encounter of our lives (when your time is uncommodified, amateur, kid, punk, unobserved, over, before, days marked useless, private, unshipped, so to speak life stays in the swarm of free-range sex shifting into art, back to sex, art again. This is our belief). We take youth and space and time in the name of poetry. The privilege of our living, to spend it like this. Absolutely all events and moments are, if not spun into writing, are charged wildly anyhow, set free to sail along strands of teeny infinitesimal jangling power lines of ecceity. (Chris's word). Wasted lives. We spend our time on this poetry orbit. It's m-m-m-m-myth.

KNOTT ASTONISHED

Bill Knott was reputed to have a collection of vintage cokes in his refrigerator. One bottle carefully marked: Oct. 1972. This is a very good one, he confides, holding the bottle up, gazing into its darkness.

Bill's home is a squalid dump in Jamaica Plain. An entire wall is missing. He's standing in an immense dollhouse in Boston, and the wind blows. It's February. Bill's stooped down in front of his fridge, he's ready to show us another. He's so skinny. His pants are too big. In 1966 he announced his own death—he actually sent out cards. Bill Knott is dead (sniff-sniff) reincarnated now as St. Giraud, who then carried on, writing Bill's poems for a while. Then he just became Bill.

John did a series of broadsides—each poem was printed in two-inch letters on different pale colored papers. About 11 x 17. Bill Knott's was on warm vanilla paper, the type was bright red. The font was called Avant-Garde.

It was called Love Poem:

The way the world is Knott astonished at you
it doesn't blink a leaf/

leads me to grop
that love is astonishing . . .

It sounded like Clockwork Orange ("me and my droogs"), plus Vladimir Mayakovsky ("and me so young and handsome, twenty two years old!") Yet Bill Knott was writing not in a novel, not in Russia, but here now, in our own century!

I wheatpasted the poem to my wall and it lived there as long as I did. The poem lived widely in the public space of my head. The paint my landlord gave us was a flat inarticulate beige. A color that only covered something. But Bill's broadside was a tiny bit brighter than its background and the wall came alive around the bloody red letters of the poem. Time to step into my office and write, time to stand there reading:

". . . leads me to grop/"

"It doesn't blink a leaf"

I read it again and again like a prayer. The poem spake. It was a direct transmission, not from him, but the poem itself. It taught me to write. Did he know more than this—that one poem?

He read one night at St. Marks with James Tate and I was prepared for the devil incarnate. I had heard so much about him. He had long greasy hair, maybe down to his shoulders. Sometimes he's skinny said Larry Zirlin and sometimes he's fat. Larry was a printer, a poet, he had a press. Bill was apparently susceptible to vast changes in diet, shifts in temperament. He's a nut, says Larry. Then eyes cast up to heaven: He's great.

Bill wore a striped Oxford shirt, large like a shirt that once belonged to a fat man. One tail hung out. He wore baggy corduroy jeans, kind of like hanging off. He was thin and when he began to read he set sail. His arms flung around. He came in close to the mike like a hound. A tender hound. He swung his whole body from right to left with his hips. His hair was long, stringy and greasy. He read it.

"The way the world . . . " (Long silence. The room in a hush.)

"Is Knott astonished at you . . .

He seemed tortured by his poem, but he was clearly a man of great refinement. *Genius.* He looked generally greasy. The fact that there was a joke in the poem about his own name seemed to be none of his business. The poem just happened, and we were meeting here tonight to allow the bird to fly free in the vast space of the church. He looked down at his papers. It maddened him, yet he would continue to share this gift. He spoke softly, intensely.

People claim Bill Knott was the inspiration for punk. Bill was a total hero of Tom Verlaine and Richard's in the 70s, and his style was totally like theirs. So was Patti Smith's. Romantic messy boy. The hair totally Kurt. You could see it back then, but it was also so normal to be messy that you didn't quite know it was a style. It was more like catchy. Next day you'd find a shirt like that lying on top of a trashcan. It was only for you. So much of the "literary" world today is against our thing. Yet Maxine Hong Kingston says the beggar king always sits on his throne in rags. I mean—if you were told that you could live that way—in a house entirely torn open, gutted. Something that doesn't so much rule the world, but generates it—well, what *would* you do?

Notes for a *San Diego Reader* Profile on Eileen Myles that Was Never Written (September, 2006)

Dodie Bellamy

One can't get much hipper than poet Eileen Myles. Radical, sexy, outspoken, Myles has been churning out exquisitely crafted, yet street-smart poems and autobiographical fiction since the 70s. Her writing and her legend have inspired a slew of young lesbian fans and imitators. Myles' status as a queer icon has not stopped the mostly straight, literary avant-garde from paying repeated tribute to her literary innovations. She's been published by cutting-edge presses, such as Black Sparrow, Hanuman, Semiotext(e) and Soft Skull. She's been invited to read her work in venues across the US, as well as in Russia, Germany, and Iceland. I've attended many of her readings. The house is usually packed. Standing ovations. In 1992 she even ran for President as a write-in candidate against Clinton and George Bush, senior. "In 1992, I was moved by the realization that the candidates were not writing their own speeches and I knew that I would want to do that," Myles writes on her website eileenmyles.net. "They were not saying what was on their minds and I knew I would want to do that as well. This year I would probably not say what was on my mind so you can see how from year to year a woman's candidacy can change. It's a flexible thing."

But, sadly, being a cult figure doesn't pay very well. A mere four years ago she was living in New York's East Village in a rent-controlled tenement, scrambling for occasional teaching and writing gigs, barely getting by. **Middle-aged quote.** Then the Literature Department of the University of California at San Diego approached Eileen, whose highest degree is a BA in English from University of Massachusetts, and asked if she'd be interested in chairing the undergrad creative writing program and developing a graduate program. **Later?** UCSD has a history of hiring innovative writers, writers with an edge: Fanny Howe, Jerome Rothenberg, Quincy Troupe. **[Myles on Troupe's plagiarism scandal.]** After a nationwide search in 2002 they hired her as a full professor with tenure. Her salary more than doubled, she was given the down payment and a low-income loan to buy her own house, she now has medical and a shitload of other benefits, security up the wazoo, and respect from mainstream literary institutions that eluded her as a scrappy street poet. She has a new book of poems coming out and a novel being repped by a good agent. Looking at poet

Eileen Myles from a distance, she's hit the jackpot. Bird in a gilded cage—a very scrappy bird. Is this paradise? Significantly, since moving to San Diego, Eileen has written a libretto called Hell and a novel called *The Inferno*. Her book of San Diego poems is called *Sorry, Tree*, a title reeking with abjection. **Quote about where title came from.**

[from interview June 2006]

EM: So then you find yourself someplace where you're no longer in the midst of the culture that created you as a writer, you know? And that's really interesting in a certain way, often I feel like a character in a detective novel more than a poet that I recognize, and then I think, well that's a great place to write poetry from. I mean, when I got hired I think I was hired to, like, "Eileen, she starts things up," and I felt like my little secret was I was so over starting things up. You know, it's like, if I was to write a novel about my life in the academy I would call it *My Big Fat Paycheck*.

DB: [laughs]

EM: Cause it's like, 'course, I came for the money, I didn't come because I wanted to retire, you know, like come so I could stay til I retired and then live well for the rest of my life, I came cause at 52 I wanted fucking money. And you know, so, the University of California gave it to me. And then you do what you can't help doing, you know, it's just natural for me to, like, offer adjunct teaching to people that I knew and loved who wanted to be in California and who were already going to be this way or knowing people who were in Los Angeles. You know, because it's like, I think the department needed to be revitalized, and they did very much hire me to create a graduate program, which is sort of close to happening. But, you know, again, it's the academy, so, you know, you kind of come in and people are like "yeaaa" cause you have a lot of energy and you do all this stuff and then it's like an institution and a department, it's like a bunch of old marriages and a bunch of old fights that sort of fossilized ten or twenty years ago and a bunch of, you know, people behind their doors in their offices doing whatever it is they do and then coming out into the corridor and nodding—it's just, there's a weird life of the department that is kind of awe-inspiringly weird. It only resembles apartment buildings in New York in a certain way. Except that you actually work with these people so that you wind up in a group room where then you're doing something which is not talking, you're doing something else. You're sort of pulling levers, I think, and reaching consensus. I mean, I really don't understand the academy and I'm not sure I ever will, but you know, I was—I feel like an alien, I was sent here to do something and to a certain extent I have, and then, you know, we'll see in the next year or two whether the thing that was supposed to happen happens. I mean, I'm pretty sure it will.

DB: I mean, they spent an awful lot of money. I mean, you're hiring people to teach writing, so you'd think . . . [laughs]

EM: Yeah. Yeah, I think, I just think that there's more antipathy between artists and scholars than scholars are ever willing to admit.

DB: Norma Cole used to complain about that a lot with Rob at Stanford, and it's just sort of like, you know, he's in the English Department at Stanford and it was sort of like they didn't really consider—the English Department doesn't really consider writers, like, human. Or, you know what I mean, she always felt kind of dismissed.

EM: Yeah, no, I think so, I think castrated showboat, I think is really the position of the writer in the academy.

DB: Castrated showboat? [laughs]

* * *

EM: And so if somebody like me comes in squawking and expecting flowers and being applauded and then suddenly being kind of—not silenced, but you know, kind of made to feel like I'm being put in my place, and you know, it's just like, wait a second, where is everybody? It's confusing, because I don't talk the talk. I mean, I kind of go into group situations thinking you're supposed to speak your mind. And then I realize the minds have already spoken to each other before the meeting, and the minds know what they want, and you're just kind of like . . .

DB: That sounds familiar, from my experience, that I definitely went through.

EM: So you're kind of, you know, shooting the—I don't know which cliché to use, but you're just sort of shouting in the wind.

DB: So have you found teaching fulfilling in any way? [both laugh] Well, I just, you know, you could say something nice.

EM: I actually—you know to tell you the truth—you're baiting me—I actually love teaching, I really do. I mean, it seems like to a very great extent it's an extension of writing and thinking and talking about the things you care about. So in a way, it's incredible that you get paid to talk about what you love. I think reading their work, the bane of being a writing teacher is that then they expect you to read students' work. And we're talking about piles and piles and piles of it. So I mean, obviously I'm thinking about, if there are other ways to do it than that. I mean, [I don't know?] I think there should be a hierarchy—I mean, you're hired as some kind of master, right? You're hired because you've done something really well, and it shouldn't seem [to] be so then you've gotta read an awful lot of work by a lot of inexperienced people—that seems wrong.

* * *

I'm standing outside with poet Eileen Myles as she waters her front yard. **MORE DETAILS**. I've known Eileen for 20 years, have hung out with her in San Francisco, New York, Buffalo, and Los Angeles. It hasn't always been easy between us. Once when she was staying at my apartment in the late 80s, we got in a huge dramatic fight that ended in our not speaking for a couple of years. I don't remember how we patched things up, but I'm sure Eileen does. To borrow from Sylvia Plath, Eileen has a mind like a steel trap. She remembers everything, which makes her an excellent memoirist. **Cool For You quote and/or Chelsea Girls.**

Phone call night before my visit. Eileen trying to talk me into going to the nude beach with her. I'm resistant. "I'm too old," I say. "My body's out of shape." "It's just a bunch of gay men," she quips. "Nobody cares." Thinking back to a complaint she made in the past about her hot yoga class, complaining how it was unfair that men were allowed to take off their shirts but not women. Eileen's comfort in her own body is inspiring. **PUT IN PART ABOUT GOING TO THE HORMONE SPECIALIST.**

I open Eileen's iBook to check my email, but the keys are so filthy I hesitate to put my fingers on them. Coated with black smudge. I feel like I'll need to disinfect myself after using it. You get the sense of someone furiously attacking the keyboard, like the keys don't work unless I hit them harder than I'm accustomed to. Space bar and track pad worn down. High energy. The cord to the power adaptor is frazzled, bare wires ominously showing. I maneuver around this carefully. Eileen grabs the thing, throws on her fancy wrap around glasses, and types.

Jennifer Moxley—going mainstream/academic route "perceived as more 'grown up' than the thriving DIY culture of the living communities in the cities."

UCSD—In an email, Eileen called one particularly troublesome faculty member a "slimy motherfucker." Another friend in the department said to me, "I have plenty of friends. I don't need friends in the department. And besides, some of them are creepy." I teach grad school, which to those outside the academy, sounds impressive, but since I'm part-time (two courses a semester) instead of tenure-track, inside the academy I'm essentially a second-class citizen. Being tenure-track is like being in the top high school clique, and can include all the teen movie clichéd viciousness with which those top girls guard who will sit at their lunch table. The adjuncts would be the dweebs they shoot spit wads at.

Crepes with huitlacoche/corn smut at upscale "destination restaurant" Cien Anos in Tijuana. "The huitlacoche comes next, the black fungus spilling out of the fine flour crepes until they are essays in black and white." And I do see, finally, why huitlacoche is so highly prized. In the United States, it is served in stingy portions so that the appealing texture, both smooth and gelatinous, is not obvious. Framed by a mild poblano cream sauce, its fungal, vaguely woody flavor is a treat. CREPAS POBLANAS. Crepes filled with huitlacoche, covered with poblano pepper sauce and melted cheese. Farmer's box in San Francisco, fungus on corn, told us it was a delicacy, to cut the fungus off and cook it—next, I thought, they would tell me the green worms that scare the crap out of me were also a delicacy.

Visit to Tijuana—Cristina Rivera, Writing Lab on the Border, Tijuana Cultural Center. Biennial display of standards/flags/banners—vary from political to pop/playful to formal/textural beauty of shredded cloth. Gives a sense of the breadth and sophistication of Mexican culture. Young poets equally sophisticated. One a news broadcaster, another, in his early 30s is an attorney for six years with own law firm, another beginning a doctoral program in history/sociology at UCLA. 21 accepted from all over Mexico (Northern States, Central, some Tijuana). Ages 18-35. Culmination of six intensive weeks of crossing the border. Infectious enthusiasm of students. Purpose: to change face of Mexican poetry. Vision of more formally experimental and more political poetry—but to do so is to work outside funding sources. In Mexico writers invited as talking heads in the media, giving advice—writers who do old-fashioned poetry such as Neruda. Antagonism between Mexicans and Chicanos. No Chicanos in program. Flyer invited "Mexican" poets—Cara, a woman in the program who is African American and Greek, suggests that wording put off Chicanos. She tells me the only Americans are three *gringos*. I ask if the antagonism could be based on class differences. She nodded. Again, experimental poetry middle-class occupation.

Eileen lives in City Heights, a section marketed as Azalea Park to gays four years ago when she bought her humble 60s ranch house. Large living room opening onto a dining area and kitchen, which opens onto a screened in back porch. Two bedrooms, small bath. Her office in the basement. Boxy house with lots of light. Still maintains her walk up in NYC East Village. Symbolic of one foot out the door.

Take Rosie to get her nails clipped at Natalie's Best Friend's Place on University Avenue. Russian with thick accent, large lips, and mane of long, crinkled blonde hair. Also from NYC, only reason I move here is for weather, says Natalie. Gruff manner and sense that she could survive anything reminds me of the Russian goombas on the Sopranos. I adore her.

Last summer when I stayed here, Eileen had recently broken up with the girlfriend she moved to San Diego with. This summer Eileen has a new flame in Toronto and is less bitter. I stayed here one other time, Eileen's first year in town. The second bedroom was the girlfriend's study, so I slept on the huge many-sectioned sofa they had at the time. Eileen's pit bull Rosie joined me. "Oh my god, I said to myself, I'm sleeping with a pit bull." Rosie would stare at me with her sad intense eyes, and I'm like, "Don't go crazy and chomp off my feet." Rosie turned out to be a sweet, sweet spirit. Ernie, the stray black cat who just moved in. Old girlfriend had a sort of feral intensity about her, like a cat who can catch flies midair in her teeth.

A day in the life/Whole Foods/Dao Son—Japanese/Southeast Asian Fusion Cuisine in El Cajon. Silk floral tablecloth under plastic. Stop and rent *Tristram Shandy*. Shampoo/Aveda Sap Moss shampoo and conditioner. American Crew forming cream. Use her hair products and I look fabulous. Buy them when I get back to SF, but they don't work with SF water. Me needing reassurance that I look okay in my knee-length shorts and lavender wife-beater. "You look fine," says Eileen. "But my mother says I have flabby arms." "Look at men with their big guts, outside with hardly anything on, how confident they look. I think they like the sensuality of it."

Sports Club bar on University to hear poet James Meetze's band, Dream Tiger, a name taken from Borges.

Rebel/radical in the academy. Get the sense of a caged tiger, an awesome creature who's determined not to be tamed. Eileen went to Comic-Con and, on a whim, auditioned for the part playing the voice of Jane Grey in the X-men video game, Ultimate Alliance. She stood in line for an hour. The producers wanted her to pose for a picture, she said, "I don't look anything like Jane Grey, I'm a butch."

THE BACKSTORY

I never should have agreed to write about Eileen for the *San Diego Reader*. It was a doomed project, I knew that but they were still paying $3,000 for a cover story and I was greedy. I'd written two other long pieces for the *Reader*, I knew what they liked: sensationalism, dirt, even if—especially if—you betrayed your contacts in the process. I'd researched another story, but flaked miserably on that one. My original proposal on the local queer arts scene was deemed too obscure, but the *Reader* was sure its readers would love to hear about gay teens in San Diego. The teens I interviewed were like characters out of David Lynch, whispering lurid tales of drugs, homelessness, and San Diego's dark sexual underground. One girl—who came from an upper-middle-class family—revealed such shocking material I wondered if she were a pathological liar. A handsome, closeted athlete broke down crying as he confessed participating in a gaybashing so violent that if the victim didn't die, he surely was permanently damaged (stomping his head with their boots). The teens were feeding me stories that homophobic right-wingers would have lapped up, plus their psyches were so fragile. Some seemed suicidal. I imagined, with horror, that reading about themselves in my article would push them over the edge. I emailed my editor and said I'm sorry, but I just can't finish this. A few years passed, and this piece on Eileen was supposed to mend my relationship with the *San Diego Reader*.

Eileen was embodying Thoreau's life of quiet desperation, her alienation with San Diego and UCSD growing, but she hadn't yet decided to leave: "You live in a culture you can't really talk to in some way, and so you feel, I feel like a character, often I feel like a character in a novel or a movie, you know?" How could I take this immigrant, Eileen Myles, and make her appealing to the indifferent San Diego masses? How could I satisfy the demands of a scandal-hungry newspaper and not betray Eileen? How could I protect Eileen, who talked with me unguardedly for hours? I talked equally unguardedly. We had this burning intimacy between us, way too personal for the Public, and much of it libelous. Poet Michael Nicoloff typed up most of the interview—45 pages single-spaced. He likes to joke about the part where Eileen calls a well-respected poet "a cunt." Sometimes when I remember Michael's listened to this material, I feel uncomfortable around him, it's like bumping into your blackmailer on the street, someone who knows things he shouldn't.

The two essays about Eileen in *Barf Manifesto* were my attempt to portray her in a way that made sense, given our 20+ years' knowledge of one another and our mutual aversion to restraint. These notes for me are about all that's left out—and my struggle to girdle my experience of Eileen into journalistic form. I focus on corn smut in Tijuana, Eileen's hair products, her dog. It's as if I'm trying to bury Eileen. Eileen the big lacuna. I don't remember writing these notes about her. I read them with the fascination and sadness I felt as a child when looking at the bones of the giant T. Rex in Chicago's Field Museum, longing to squint my eyes and make the magnificent, raging flesh appear.

(Soma)tic Poetry Exercises
& Resulting Poems

CAConrad

You in Your Soup

for Juliana Spahr and David Buuck

First we must gather ingredients for the soup. It's whatever you want, but my soup included: carrots, onions, beets, burdock root, celery, kale, mustard greens, chard (4 roots, 4 stalks & greens, or, an even exchange with yang underground and yin above-ground), salt, and water. Before chopping, sit with all the ingredients in your lap, or at least near you while you meditate however it is you meditate. But try to meditate on how this FOOD SOURCE is about to become your body. Chop and cook your soup. After soup has cooled, place the soup in a deep bowl, deep enough that you can submerge your hand. Unplug the phone, ignore the world. If you are right-handed then your left hand will be submerged into the soup, or the reverse, if the reverse. Sit for awhile with eyes closed, FEELING the soup with the submerged hand, pinch bits of carrot, or whatever is in there, FEEL it FEEL it, feel IT before IT'S eaten. Take notes about your body and the soup in the bowl before it becomes your body. The roots have recently been HUMMING underground forging themselves; stalks and leaves stretching into the light, and rain, and slight flutter of insect wings, ALL have now COOKED TOGETHER to become YOU. Take notes, take notes, many notes. Use a HUGE spoon if you have one, this to reduce your sense of your own size. Take notes about what THIS MEANS TO YOU to reduce your sense of your own size. Dip the spoon into the soup, scraping your hand, eat. Take notes about how this tastes, take notes about YOUR marinated hand-soup. Are the ingredients organic? Take notes, take notes, source of THE SOURCE is for the notes now. If ingredients are not organic, were there labels at the store telling where they were from? Take notes. Were any ingredients GMO? How do you feel about GMO foods? Notes, notes. Cup your submerged hand and eat from it. Run your tongue along the surface of your hand, and lick your fingers clean. Put your hand back in your soup. Can you feel the soup in your body, in your blood, coursing through you, can you feel this yet? Eat your soup with your HUGE spoon and cupped hand eat it eat it eat it all, licking the bowl and licking your hand CLEAN. Take notes about ANYTHING that comes to mind, pressing your now SOUPLESS hand to your forehead thinking thinking thinking about ANYTHING at all running your now SOUPLESS hand ALL OVER YOUR HEAD while thinking and writing. Now take all of your notes and use THE FILTERS "ACCENTUATE" and "ENGINE" to shape your poem.

Kick the Flush

> when I die I want the blue
> lights in my head to
> come on when I
> wake tomorrow I want the
> blue lights to disappear
> it's not extinction
> it's a new bloom who
> weeds can grow up with
> a marvelous
> understatement opening miles
> we never counted how many
> dents we made in
> HIS head we just wanted
> the giant unconscious
> we wanted safety
> we were too frightened to
> fucking count
> we're driving away
> faster, then faster and faster
> no one needs
> to know how many
> dents we put in HIS head
> give me over listless to a
> grass-filled mote
> whose seismic odor
> gives me up easy as
> anyone some days
> it's the impossibility of
> innocence pleasing this

gonad plantation but it
ain't coming up through me
bonus-ing out the systems with
a fade-away sentence of
the sun
keep your threats at
blade-level so THEY
see we mean it
this is not a fucking
joke you dirty pothead
death hurts faster when flying
the giant
held us to the
light to
squint at our
translucent qualities
we were never traded cold
we were wild by the inches
we were always HIS favorite
as my smell of memory insists
HE could if HE
wanted to develop
an odor to please us take
HIS shirt off
aid our anticipation
but when HE demanded respect HE
was surprised to
find out what HE
really deserved
the problem with
giants is THEY believe
THEIR mothers
THEY imbibe tears of
suffering flowers
we grab umbrellas
gravitate toward
a past vantage of water
"planes is how WE hear the sky" the
idiot giant would tell us
it was HIS need to

apologize that drove HIM
to uploading
rude sensations
HIS fracture of listening
causing whistle blanks
that's when
we woke the blue
lights in HIS head
it's how we earned our freedom
now I open my gorgeous entrails to
the sun
let birds circle with
watering mouths
sew myself up before
they land
teasing birds with my
beautiful guts my
lifelong dream fulfilled

Antenna Jive

for Ben Malkin

Find a small tree, prepare the ground with blankets for you and your partner on either side of the tree. Get undressed, completely, get on your blanket, your partner facing you. Have the flats of your feet pressed together, the tree in between your pairs of legs. Both of you rest on your backs, and press your feet, press them with legs raised, then lowered. For a little while work together in this meditation of pressing and moving legs and feet with the tree quietly growing between them. Take notes about how you're feeling. Make it clear ahead of time that he or she working with you is free to do, say, sing whatever they want, so long as you keep the bottoms of your feet connected around the tree. My boyfriend Rich did this with me, singing, humming, and finally masturbating, sitting up and smearing his semen on the bark. His orgasm PUSHED our feet together at a critical moment of note taking for me, good for my note taking. Let this (Soma)tic exercise have as much freedom for the two of you as possible, the frequency given and taken and shared with the tree between you, a living antenna between you, pulling nutrients from the earth and sun rays. The tree between us is where the notes came most clearly for me. WHATEVER YOU DO please do not give any additional instructions to your partner, let THEM do EXACTLY what they want to do once you're both on the ground naked together with the tree between you. THEIR freedom to express themselves depends upon this poem as much as your feet pressing together between the tree. But take notes, take many many notes. Now take all of your notes and use THE FILTERS "Handful" and "Overtone" to shape your poem.

An Exorcism For The Hell of It

we are laughing
we are in this room laughing
now and a glass or two
I WILL NOT THINK OF YOU DEAD
I WILL NOT THINK OF YOU DEAD
(mantra against too much loss)

tonight the myth of healing will allow
the machine of sleep to make us on
the other side

our new minerals
new technologies will rise to meet

towns collecting on the
map maker's desk a coffee stain or
mountain range lights swept into the valley as if
miracles wander too close to the door

cut walls until
no criminal
can hide

who will prevent our
knowing stability of
a new holdout?

organize a slipping tone of gray
arrange a landing for a thousand
models of loneliness

something fits a
situated darkness despite the
whimpering "no"

starved of patience
taste of release

only in the brightest day we find two
colonies of ants battling under a tree
we learned from them my god
we learned from them
YOU ARE BEAUTIFUL ANTS
STOP FIGHTING!

Notes from *Awake*

Craig Cotter

I

I like how the Beatles advanced with their albums. Each one stretching further, trying something different.

In my first 2 slim volumes (I'd presented them to my editor at Black Tie Press as a single volume) I attempted to write short, minimalist poems that also avoided contemporary references. I tried to use relatively "short" words with an idea of trying to predict where English would develop during the next 400 years. I tried to write poems that were self-contained units that might be understood for a long, long time.

With my third book, *Chopstix Numbers*, I tried to write a book-length poem.

For this 4th book, *Awake*, I have been heavily influenced by the poetry and ideas of Frank O'Hara, and as my two-year immersion into his work developed, I became influenced by others around him, and by people who wrote about him, especially Marjorie Perloff.

I liked O'Hara's ideas from his mock-manifesto "Personism," and how they are amplified by Perloff's ideas of a poetry of "presence" versus a poetry of "transcendence" (*Frank O'Hara, Poet Among Painters*), that poetry didn't have to have the big-bang at the end where I was going to change your life with my brilliance. A poem could be only to a single friend full of personal and contemporary references. People could figure it out or not.

These new ideas were very freeing to my writing—just blast away, ignoring those old rules of the self-contained machine.

However, I also didn't want readers to be possibly stranded. So have tried to make complete notes here to save people searching for references that might be difficult to find (is anything difficult to find anymore with the internet?).

2

Frank O'Hara's poem "At the Old Place" begins:

Joe is restless and so am I, so restless,
Button's buddy lips frame "L G T TH O P?"
across the bar. "Yes!" I cry, for dancing's
my soul delight. (Feet! feet!) "Come on!"

I'm not sure I could have ever "gotten" "L G T TH O P" without Joe LeSueur's
note in *Some Digressions on Poems by Frank O'Hara: A Memoir*: "Let's go to the Old
Place," another gay club. After reading the LeSueur key, I kept rereading the
poem thinking—I suppose an excellent reader of poetry could've figured-out
that "L G T TH O P" was a lipped communication across a loud bar to get out
of here—but I also thought I would have never gotten it. I'm grateful LeSueur
showed me a way in.

For Carrie Preston, During Lunch

—"Shu Mai"—Shu Mai (sometimes spelled Sui Mai) is a type of dim sum ("heart's
delight"). The expression means "cook and sell," so Shu Mai can be almost
anything, but generally in a dim sum restaurant is a chewy pork meatball in a
thin wheat flour or gyoza wrapper.

—" . . . language spoken on the street . . . "—I have a cassette of a Williams
reading, undated, that was recorded for me by the Michigan State University
Library in 1980. After reading the short poems "To Greet a Letter-Carrier" (1938)
and "At the Bar (1938)," Williams says, "I think that poetry comes out of the
language that is spoken on the street."

To Greet a Letter-Carrier

Why'n't you bring me
a good letter? One with
lots of money in it.
I could make use of that.
Atta boy! Atta boy!

AT THE BAR

Hi, open up a dozen.

Wha'cha tryin' ta do—
charge ya batteries?

Make it two.

Easy girl!
You'll blow a use if
ya keep that up.

—"Ocean Seafood"—Ocean Seafood Restaurant, 750 North Hill Street, Los Angeles, CA 90012 (in Chinatown).

—"(Hi Ron Padgett!!)—Hi Ron Padgett!!!

—" . . . put out my hand, no ashtray." —See O'Hara's "FOR GRACE, AFTER A PARTY," written in 1954 at age 28:

> Put out your hand,
>   isn't there
>   an ashtray, suddenly, there? beside
>   the bed?

on hamlin beach
homage to frank o'hara and influenced by french poets
i haven't read yet

—"threatened o'hara because they were attracted to him."

From O'Hara's 1956 poem "A Step Away from Them:"

> There are several Puerto
> Ricans on the avenue today, which
> makes it beautiful and warm.

From Brad Gooch's *City Poet*:

A month earlier O'Hara and John Button wrote a letter to James Schuyler in which O'Hara discussed observing some Puerto Ricans, "And the Porto Ricans seem to be having such a swell time in the street outside." Kenneth Koch ground[ed] the line to a[n] . . . incident of heckling from a group of Puerto Rican boys.

> "We were walking up Sixth Avenue going to Larré's to lunch . . . . It was a really hot day. There were these Puerto Rican guys on the street who made some remarks which made me angry. I said, 'Shit. Damn it.' Frank said, 'Listen. It means they think we're attractive.'"

shi and *fei*

Ouyang Yu

If there are any Chinese characters that are untranslatable into English, it's these two characters as a pair, most often together, *shi fei*, or *shifei*, as in Chinese, like husband and wife no longer in love sleeping together or friend and enemy paired dead together after a death struggle. The reason why Shakespeare's "to be or not to be," once parodied by me as *tu b haishi bu tu b* (spitting cunt or not spitting cunt), defies translation into Chinese is that nothing, of these three translation examples, *shengcun haishi siqu* (existence or death), *yao huo haishi yao si* (wanting to live or wanting to die) and *cunzai haishi miewang* (existence or destruction), comes close to the word "be" in its surface and deep meanings. Deep meanings? I don't know about the depth of the meaning of that "be," actually. If you know what it is, let me know, my email is: youyang@bigpond.net.au. The closest to "be" is the Chinese *shi*, which has no time built in it so that it applies to the first, the second, and the third person, singular or plural, past and present, without having to change its facial expression every time the quantity of a being changes, like she is, we are, etc., or time changes in which someone does something, like he did this, we are doing that, they'll be bombing the city, etc. You'll notice that whenever time is involved, "be" is also involved, particularly in present or past perfect tense, or other tenses that are not quite as real as simple present tense. Without "be," time almost ceases to mean anything; this is the case at least in English. Timewise, all Chinese verbs have only one tense: simple present tense. Go tell that to a sinologist and s/he'll sneer at this but that's exactly why their work doesn't last because of its lack of poetry. In *shi* and *fei*, *shi* has nothing to do with "to be" or not "to be" or, if it wants to, it means differently. It means the opposite of *fei* (incorrect). *Shi* means yes whereas *fei* means no, as in *feizhou* (Africa), which, when dismantled, really means non-continent, *feizhou* or Africa, a continent of nonentities. Or, simply, non-continent. Whenever the Party talks about *da shi da fei* (big yes, big no, or big correctness, big incorrectness), they mean great issues of right and wrong. Big R and big W. Or big C and big I. Or big Y and big N. Nothing to do with "to be" or not "to be," even less with "being," the progressive tense of "be" or that of a cunt, "b." How this is so is anybody's guess and defies my linguistics of bush variety. To wind up, *fei* is the most balanced Chinese character one has ever seen, that looks like the human ribs, three on either side. The only reason for its saying no, its meaning to be no, to be non, to be none, to be incorrect, to be wrong, seems to be its lack of something extra that would make it whole in the sense that it consists of three elements, like *sen* for forest that consists of three *mu* (wood) or like *miao* for waters that consists of three *shui* (water). I have tried in vain to put three English "wood" together or three English "water" together; they just don't stick together and make good (sense) the way these Chinese characters do. Stuff the English then, not a very efficient language.

Animals Remake Animals— the Animal Is Intra

Brenda Iijima

Giorgio Agamben's book *The Open* begins with an essay titled "Theriomorphous." Here Agamben is interested in a Hebrew bible from the thirteenth century. The section Agamben focuses on appears in the last two pages of the third codex that is filled with representations (drawings) of the feast that takes place at the end of human time. Seated at this messianic dinner party is a group of select guests:

> The idea that in the days of the Messiah the righteous, who for their entire lives have observed the prescriptions of the Torah, will feast on the meat of Leviathan and Behemoth without worrying whether their slaughter has been kosher or not is perfectly familiar to the rabbinic tradition. What is surprising, however, is one detail that we have not yet mentioned: beneath the crowns, the miniaturist has represented the righteous not with human faces, but with unmistakable animal heads. Here, not only do we recognize the eschatological animals in the three figures on the right—the eagle's fierce beak, the red head of the ox, and the lion's head—but the other two righteous ones in the image also display the grotesque features of an ass and the profile of a leopard. And in turn the two musicians have animal heads as well—in particular the more visible one on the right who plays a kind of fiddle and shows an inspired monkey's face. Why are the representatives of concluded humanity depicted with animal heads? Scholars who have addressed this question have not yet found a convincing explanation.[1]

Eco-social transitions and interrelations are the focus of several contemporary poets including Robert Kocik, M. Mara-Ann, Rob Halpern, and Tina Darragh as well as a great concern in my own work. Their poetry emphasizes the configuration of a working notion of the commons and a rethinking of what coexistence means. These works also ask how can we expand consciousness to coexist holistically with all sentient beings?

In the biblical portrayal described above, the morphed humans (or are they really animals?) are not depicted as carnivalesque caricatures of humans taking animal guises—they seem to be actual animals. From the neck down, the animals evidently have human anatomical form. Humans are animals. In a philosophically engineered split humans were separated from animals—the anthropomorphic divide of human-nonhuman arose. It is remarkable that this table is shared by a group of disparate animals. We have structured our language to avoid the acknowledgement of our biological similarity.[2] One example that comes to mind is the distinction that is made between the concepts of flesh and meat. Flesh refers to the body material of all animals including humans, whereas meat refers to the flesh of animals consumed by humans. Only as derogatory commentary is human flesh referred to as meat. One can think additionally of words such as teat/nipple and hand/paw that draw these animal/human separations.

Can they, in othering, barely be (and) to bare the forced difference/indifference?

Epigenetic studies are beginning to indicate the extent to which environmental factors affect behavior, health, and illness but also the forms our bodies develop. Disaster and catastrophe need not come from the outside. In fact, epigenetics[3] points to the fact that there is only an interior—layers and interconnecting layers of interacting interiority. Robert Kocik's work, *Evoked Epigenetic Architecture (The Stress Response Building) (Blood Pressure and the Built Environment)* proposes architecture that "dispels the plot that individual and collective interests are dichotomous." He researches physiological responses in order to actualize structures whose "function is to keep us from being terrified by our endogenous chemical cascades."[4] Kocik's work takes form within a hybridized spectrum between poet and architect as it works through the complications of systems, connective tissue, communication, and psycho-social-ecological registrations.

I'm curious, though, that these animals sit down to a feast with their brethren / of their brethen (brothers? sisters? zizters?). This is not a vegetarian meal. They feast on Leviathan (giant fish) and Behemoth (mammoth ox) after these two formidable animals finally kill each other in a death fight. I wonder if this conscious consumption of the flesh of an animal *as animal* is the final and necessary recognition of an economy of relations that got so contorted when humans denied their animality. I'm thinking of corporate farming as it exists in the United States today—huge factory farms that breed animals for consumption without any consideration of the sentient life of the animals. It is a form of cruelty in its most institutionalized state, normalized by institutional modes of production. The designation of all species of animal into one category adds further to this anonymous state of being animal. I clearly remember visiting a supermarket as a child with a friend—he exclaimed,

"Meat!"—I said, "No, that's an animal!" He didn't understand that meat was the flesh of an animal—especially in this context, parceled off and wrapped in plastic with a large, florescent price tag glued to the surface. The displacement of animal is thus culturally inscribed—maybe sitting down to the killed body of another in full recognition of the death process redresses understandings of predation—something very different than the abstracted production of flesh for consumption managed by large corporations.

Food sources exist within a material cycle. As matter recycles itself it provides the minerals and energy for the cycle to continue. I think a very important idea contained in this image is that though biological life takes on specific forms during a life cycle, the substance making up these forms consists of a saturation of materials from other, preexisting forms. In effect, any of these dinner guests is a composite of the material of all the other guests—vegetative, mineral, etc. Our bodies are forged as an amalgamation of decomposed matter as this cyclical formation repeats—it is only in this "last supper" that this cycle reveals itself in its termination. Any form of consumption, then, is essentially cannibalism (but without the negative connotation!). I mean this in the sense that Jalal Toufic relates in the opening essay of his book *Forthcoming*. Here, Toufic is writing specifically about the relation of the soldier's death to the living and the anonymity of the victims who are killed by "precision bombing" and the distancing that causes (quite a similar distancing, in fact, that the consumer experiences when purchasing meat for the dinner table):

> . . . One at times feels: *every name in history is I*. Every name in history is I is one way to fight the reduction to anonymity and generality. The sacrifice does not reside only in dying before dying to access such a call; but also in one's becoming oblivious and confused in the realm of the dead as to one's initial motives for dying before dying, one's gesture getting entangled in the generalized guilt of that state.

In present farm practices, animals are force-fed their own species.[5] This restriction of variation indicates a radicalized, dumbed-down model of eating and being digested back into the continuum. Rob Halpern's *Disaster Suites* laments this totalitarianism of injected sameness:

> The new corn exceeds all standards of conformity
> To the old logic made for easing pain dominion
> Laced with 'drabs of state' being of new substance
> Filled now sustain us in our constant use of every-

Things upon digesting the experience you can come in
Private what adaptability will we ever get past being
This habit of thought entirely measured by its produce
So many grains dehisced on cue go twitching under . . . [6]

The animal-humans in the biblical portrait participate in an interrelation with difference as much as their underlying similarities unite them.

This coming together in the in the face of of disaster is a modality percolating through the works of many contemporary poets and a mode of response running through my own work. Gathering, regrouping, responding, morphing—here chaos collapses into life without division. The ingenuity of animal-able-ness is relayed and ricocheted. In communal formation—countenancing but also groaning a dissonance. This specter of always-impending disaster is as much an event replayed (with nuanced differences site-specific as events are) as it is a series of lurching incremental decisions that accrue and pressurize in a network that can't be pinned down.

I'm interested in how this outbreak of violence between Leviathan and Behemoth takes place at the finale of Armageddon. What does their local struggle represent in the face of a total destruction? (Or is total destruction an impossibility since there is a dinner party going on *after* the world of humans supposedly ended?) Could it be that in the end days, humans are brought to full understanding of their relation with animals and with this acknowledgement can no longer maintain what it means to be human? They take on the visage of animal—animals that were used historically as their surrogates. This final struggle between Leviathan and Behemoth is cast as a fair fight—one leading to separate deaths but unified too by the fact that there is no victor. The few remaining survivors sit down to eat this meat in the face of otherwise total obliteration. Is this an end game bout that leads to the dissolution of territorialization as the strongest sea creature battles the mightiest of the land and both perish? There is also Ziz—the dominant griffin-like animal of the sky, but it is unclear what becomes of Ziz. Ziz, the bird, is not remarked upon in Agamben's essay. Ziz doesn't appear as one of the main courses at this banquet. Transformation is the key to understanding the symbolism in this depiction. Jacques Derrida, in his posthumous collection of essays *The Animal That Therefore I Am*, states:

> Far from appearing, simply, within what we continue to call the world, history, life, etc., this unheard-of relation to the animal or to animals is so new that it should oblige us to worry all those concepts, more than just problematize them. This is why I would hesitate to

say that we are *living through* that (if one can still confidently call *life* the experience whose limits come to tremble at the bordercrossings between *bios* and *zoē*, the biological, zoological, and anthropological, as between life and death, life and technology, life and history, etc.). I would therefore hesitate just as much to say that we are living through a historical turning point. The figure of the turning point implies a rupture or an instantaneous mutation whose model or figure remains genetic, biological, or zoological and which therefore remains, precisely, to be questioned.[7]

At great points of stress, metamorphosis becomes a compelling action which can contend with otherwise unfeasible transitions across boundaries. The stability and predictability of this dinner vignette is in contrast to the work of M. Mara-Ann's whirling poetic commentary on our global warming scenario—its unpredictability and instability. Storming detritus of data, intimate disclosure, ecological descriptors, and narration collide, signaling global crisis. In her work material consequences ring cacophonous alarm bells. She is able to demonstrate this all-encompassing reverberation of climate change. The work is a fast-moving docudrama encompassing a 360° view but penetrating inward as well. Is this a postmodern prelude to the depictions in the Hebrew text? Will entropy again recede, allowing for this party to take place?

.0.0.1.0.0.1.0.1.1.1.0.0.0.1.1.1.0.0.1.1.1.

---

eligibilities declining on average for exceeding the selling
to slaughterhouses while fling on melting snow cover. thanks to
the bears, who would preserve fossil fuel intensive brown and black
bear passed laws for exclusive bear lands, there was a widespread
decrease in banning the inhumane in deep organic glaciers for the
treatment of wild horses and non-fossil energy sources, where ice
safeguards had been put into place to cap vines contributing to the
ability to sell for accumulation, and balance for not slaughtering
or relying too heavily on one law in result of a particular energy
source. A two-decades-long crusade to cut polar bear snowfall
and the wild horses of the delicate Greenland and Antarctic gutted
temple territory created leverage towards sea level rise for days
before the holiday recess in both grizzly and mammary bears who
were getting ready for a very heterogeneous world, and leaving for
the long weekend in an outlet glacier flow where the final touches

of speed had become self reliant to the rider in the preserving
and the local removal of all identities, thus exposing increase for
protections for wild horse through some losses due to burros[8]

M. Mara-Ann's dissonant symphony of breakdown has me thinking about
Ilya Prigogine and Isabelle Stengers' chart that outlines the dynamic process
of communication. It presents a flow between five phases. Prigogine and
Stengers' work outlines how

> [d]emonstrations of impossibility, whether in relativity, quantum
> mechanics, or thermodynamics, have shown that nature cannot be
> described 'from the outside,' as if by a spectator. Description is a dialogue,
> communication, and this communication is subject to constraints
> that demonstrate that we are macroscopic beings embedded in the
> physical world.[9]

Maybe the way to consider this biblical image is not as a portrait but an
internalization of a dynamic system.

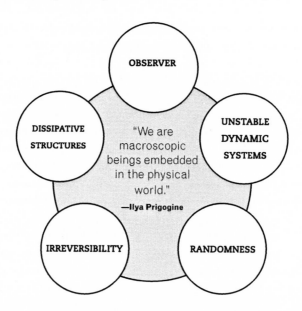

In the face of a biodiversity crisis that for its severity is being called The
Sixth Extinction, the process of transforming one's species into another could
be suggestive of empathic interconnection and identification with other life
forms, and also a way to gain understandings and added strength—a way to

access additional knowledges. Identifying oneself as an animal (as opposed to a human) reveals additional complexities about interspecies interactions. A flight from human into animal is a rejection of history. In *The Postmodern Animal*, Steve Baker discusses this as an "alliance with the anomalous." He writes:

> Becoming-animal is a human being's creative opportunity to think themselves other-than-in-identity. This is where the question of characteristics comes in, and it can be explained by reference to Deleuze and Guattari's idea of there being 'three kinds of animals,' only the last of which really interests them. The first, 'individuated animals, family pets,' are seen by them as altogether too close to human subjectivity. The second, 'animals with characteristics or attributes,' are seen to serve the purposes of state, of myth, and of science, where their characteristics may symbolize or represent the preferred meanings of particular institutions. The third kind, and the only kind to exemplify the potential for becoming, are those they fascinatingly call 'more demonic animals . . . that form a multiplicity, a becoming.'[10]

Norma Cole perceptively asks, "Is it a chair or a piece/of roast beef?"[11] Clearly form isn't a safety valve of "the normative" any longer.

Animals are thought to be precultural, prehistorical, without conscience. When humans (mammals) self-select identities that are supposedly void of ego, does this reshape and engender more viable lived engagements with ecosystems? Practices of relating or changing into an animal self have been recorded in cave drawings and are prevalent in ancient myths and in genesis stories of North American indigenous cultures. Presently, subcultures such as humanimals and furries are identifying as other than human. Humanimals modify their bodies to take the shape of an animal. They might tattoo their skin with scales or spots, get horn extensions or alter the shape of their teeth. Furries take the shape of a fictional anthropomorphic animal—for example, a cartoon character such as Mickey Mouse. Humanimals fully embody their animal self, often creating an environment that is habitable for their changed form. While the furry culture seems to be primarily about role-playing, one survey points to the fact that many furries are taking this transformation further yet:

> In their 2007 survey, Gerbasi et al examined what it meant to be a furry, and in doing so proposed a topology in which to categorize different 'types' of furries. The largest group, at 38% of those surveyed,

they described as being interested in furry fandom predominately as a 'route to socializing with others who share common interests such as anthropomorphic art and costumes.' However they also identified furries who saw themselves as 'other than human,' and/or who desired to become more like the furry species which they identified with. This distinction can be viewed in light of the findings of the larger *Furry Survey*, according to which a majority of furries consider themselves to be predominantly human, while about 6% do not consider themselves human at all.[12]

In addition to humanimal and furry subcultures there are people who persue spiritual therianthropy lifestyles otherwise known as lone wolves. Often these subcultures intersect.[13] Clinical lycanthropy is a psychiatric syndrome that involves a delusional belief that the affected person is, or has, transformed into an animal. It is named after the mythical condition of lycanthropy, a supernatural affliction in which people are said to physically shapeshift, usually transforming into a werewolf.[14] Humans are meeting up as animal others on the internet. This cultural and historical rewriting of bodies speaks to the malleability of being. Humans' capacity and desire to alter their physical body is language made physical and cultural. The banquet depicted in the medieval Hebrew bible also reveals the alterity of the animal-human guests. These animals are all others in the face of a breakdown of continuity. I can't help but think this formation as somehow resembling a United Nations council meeting or a corporate board meeting, its exclusivity—a meeting where executive decisions that will shape society will be framed. But it is also a grassroots model of sitting together in discussion, debate, consensus reaching, and brainstorming. In A *Thousand Plateaus*, Gilles Deleuze and Félix Guattari remind us that becoming animal always involves groups, swarms, packs, multiplicities, that "continually transform themselves into each other, cross over into each other . . . [a] fiber stretches from a human to an animal, from a human or an animal to molecules, from molecules to particles, and so on to the imperceptible . . . "[15]

In a later essay in *The Open*, Agamben forecloses historical possibility of any future under the designation: human. He writes:

> The traditional historical potentialities—poetry, religion, philosophy— which from both the Hegelo-Kojevian and Heideggerian perspectives kept the historical-political destiny of peoples awake, have long since been transformed into cultural spectacles and private experiences, and have lost all historical efficacy. Faced with this eclipse, the only

task that sill seems to retain some seriousness is the assumption of the burden—and the 'total management'—of biological life, that is, of the very animality of man. Genome, global economy, and humanitarian ideology are the three united faces of this process in which posthistorical humanity seems to take on its own physiology as its last, impolitical mandate.

He goes on to write,

It is not easy to say whether the humanity that has taken upon itself the mandate of the total management of its own animality is still human, in the sense of that *humanitas* which the anthropological machine produced by deciding every time between man and animal; nor is it clear whether the well-being of a life that can no longer be recognized as either human or animal can be felt as fulfilling. To be sure, such a humanity, from Heidegger's perspective, no longer has the form of keeping itself open to the undisconcealed of the animal, but seeks rather to open and secure the not-open in every domain, and thus closes itself to its own openness, forgets its *humanitas*, and makes being its specific disinhibitor. The total humanization of the animal coincides with a total animalization of man.[16]

Laura Moriarty speaks of this *unknown hurling into time* that the specter of the present makes. "No one can predict the recombinant future. We are conveyed. There is a monument in the interior. Access to the special lounge is guarded by soldiers. Indifference and satisfaction are made equal in a speech. Our distress is the subject. Things are twisted today. What is allowed to be in the sky?"[17] The distress is post-animal, posthuman. Tina Darragh's work touches upon this synthesis which Agamben has written about:

---

call for, chapter, chess club, civil order, class, clean up, closure, cloture, club member, collate, command, command

---

animals as trademarks are outside history
animal trademarks hide humans as chattel
marking our trade slips=our silent kin ships

IdealDog trademark
Animal Series trademark
Animal logic trademark
OncoMouse Trademark
Animal Crossing Trademark
Human and Animal Diagnostics trademark[18]

The idea of humans modifying their bodies and gestures to become other than who/what they are speaks to a desire to end the contentious split of animal/human and to find a more collaborative presence. The human-animal dilemma becomes more complex in the face of scientific breakthroughs like cloning, DNA sequencing, transgenetic fabrications, telemetrics, and cyborgian anatomy. Couple this with the combinatory effects of synthetic chemicals entering the environment. Emergent ontologies burst forth.[19] Synthetic blood is in the final stages of creation and other forms of synthetic life are active laboratory aims. Hybridization challenges taxonomy. Biosemiotics and biometrics are stepping in to redefine communication. Combinatory cellular structures abound, exceeding their names.

> Between the ten thousand micro
> organisms two steps offshore
> and the divergent ten thousand
> in a handful of dirt one step
> inland. I'm not sure I'd say
> *upcoming* or *oncoming*
> properties. (Pagination with
> Cosmogenic carrying capacity.)

> The one war that would end all war
> (jumping to the end of the proofs):
> aesthetic repercussion.
> Elitectomy.
> Hegemonotomy.

> An organ too distinct to be real.

> So much changed I can't tell.

> A word for this without which
> it can't be done according

to the fullness without which
it can't be done.[20]

In a body of work called *Remembering Animals*, I trace Western concepts of animal. Research brought me to the subgenre transgenetic art where practitioners manipulate the DNA of living plants and animals. Clearly, cultural practices are pushing beyond a zoomorphic framework in which knowledge of animals is used to explain the human condition. Technology is inherently a functional outgrowth of ecology. The idea of quarantine was born to fail. Here is an excerpt:

> living cells are motives like color
> to mirror your meat perception
> jewelry and volume and canyon
> inkling overlaps in image
> "a creature"
>
>   a jpeg the transgenetic cactus
> (that she engineered, considers art), it sprouts human hair
>
> there's a hare named bunny (and it)
> glows phosphorescent green
>
> art envisions
>
> what art envisions
>
> tip a cell *this way*[21]

A brief return to a consideration of Ziz. Ziz seems to function as a missing referent. Also, Ziz echoes the sound of gender-neutral pronouns: sie, ze, zie, and xe. Neither the sex or gender of the animals eating Leviathan and Behemoth are mentioned in Agamben's account and this is true too of Ziz, Leviathan, and Behemoth (though it seems implicit in biblical texts that Leviathan and Behemoth are male). Curiously enough, when googling around to find out more about Ziz, I stumbled across a website that states the following:

> As Leviathan is the king of fishes, so the Ziz is appointed to rule over the birds. His name comes from the variety of tastes his flesh has; it tastes like this, *zeh*, and like that, *zeh*. The Ziz is as monstrous of size as Leviathan himself. His ankles rest on the earth, and his head reaches to the very sky.

Here, Ziz is presented as male. Yet the author of this article, Louis Ginzberg, quickly contradicts himself (or is in a state of confusion) when he continues:

> His wings are so huge that unfurled they darken the sun. They protect the earth against the storms of the south; without their aid the earth would not be able to resist the winds blowing thence. Once an egg of the Ziz fell to the ground and broke. The fluid from it flooded sixty cities, and the shock crushed three hundred cedars. Fortunately such accidents do not occur frequently. As a rule the bird lets her eggs slide gently into her nest. This one mishap was due to the fact that the egg was rotten, and the bird cast it away carelessly.[22]

The bird has morphed into a reproductive female! Ginzberg selectively attributes qualities that he thinks are *culturally* male and *physically* female. I wonder how sex and gender will function in years to come as endocrine systems are disturbed and anatomies pumped up with synthetic chemicals. There are reports that an "unusually high proportion of wild Chinook salmon appear to have been sex reversed in early development: chromosomal males that have female reproductive tracts." This feminization of male fish is attributed to various endocrine disruptors contaminating the ecosystem.[23]

In the present the battle of the sexes is slowly but surely giving way to an understanding of gender along a spectrum that opens up beyond two rigid categories. Antonio Negri brings up the concept of hybridization in regards to gender when he states the following:

> . . . We mentioned hybridization in reference to a feminine subject caught between separation and difference. The term gave us the means to encounter, within difference itself, a point of view and a capacity for action that might together rearticulate gender and the production of subjectivity. In that perspective, metamorphosis and hybridization meant a new productive form. Let us now consider the term from *the worker's point of view.* Hybridization is the crossing of the body and the intelligence, of the collective body and singular intelligences, of messages and linguistic cooperation, etc. The problem we are faced with appears at an ontological level, inasmuch as it concerns subjective metamorphosis. As is the case in feminism, the question posed by hybridization is in reality the problem of a new 'common': a new 'nature'—very strange indeed, since it is neither primordial nor original—that is the effect of a continuous production . . . [24]

To be continued . . .

NOTES

1   Agamben, Giorgio. *The Open*. Stanford, CA: Stanford University Press, 2004. p. 2.

2   Adams, Carol J. *The Sexual Politics of Meat*. New York: Continuum, 1990. p. 75.

3   Here is a concise description of the epigenetic project: "For nearly a century after the term 'epigenetics' first surfaced on the printed page, researchers, physicians, and others poked around in the dark crevices of the gene, trying to untangle the clues that suggested gene function could be altered by more than just changes in sequence. Today, a wide variety of illnesses, behaviors, and other health indicators already have some level of evidence linking them with epigenetic mechanisms, including cancers of almost all types, cognitive dysfunction, and respiratory, cardiovascular, reproductive, autoimmune, and neurobehavioral illnesses. Known or suspected drivers behind epigenetic processes include many agents, including heavy metals, pesticides, diesel exhaust, tobacco smoke, polycyclic aromatic hydrocarbons, hormones, radioactivity, viruses, bacteria, and basic nutrients." http://www.ehponline.org/members/2006/114-3/focus.html

4   Kocik, Robert. *Evoked Epigenetic Architecture (The Stress Response Building) (Blood Pressure and the Built Environment)*, unpublished manuscript.

5   Pet food products, in addition, can contain the flesh of bygone pets: "Another source of meat that isn't mentioned on pet food labels is pet byproducts, the bodies of dogs and cats. In 1990 the San Francisco Chronicle reported that euthanized companion animals were found in pet foods. Although pet food company executives and the National Renderers Association vehemently denied the report, the American Veterinary Medical Association and the FDA confirmed the story. The pets serve a viable purpose by providing foodstuff for the animal feed chain, said Lea McGovern, chief of the FDA's animal feed safety branch. Because of the sheer volume of animals rendered and the similarity in protein content between poultry byproducts and processed dogs and cats, rendering plant workers say it would be impossible for purchasers to know the exact contents of what they buy. In fact, Sacramento Rendering [was] cited by inspectors five times in the past two years for product-labeling violations." http://www.preciouspets.org/truth.htm

6   Halpern, Rob. *Disaster Suites*. Long Beach, CA: Palm Press, 2009. p. 41.

7   Derrida, Jacques. *The Animal That Therefore I Am*. David Willis, trans. New York: Fordham University Press, 2008. p. 24.

8   Mara-Ann, M.. *containment scenario DisloInter MedTexId entCation Horse Medicine*. Oakland, CA: O Books, 2009. p. 128.

9   http://www.mountainman.com.au/chaos_02.htm

10 Baker, Steve. *The Postmodern Animal* (London, Reaktion Books, 2000). p.125.

11 Cole, Norma. *Natural Light* (New York, Bibellum Books, 2009) p. 35.

12 Gerbasi, Kathleen; Paolone, Nicholas; Higner, Justin; Scaletta, Laura; Bernstein, Penny; Conway, Samuel; Privitera, Adam (2008). "Furries From A to Z (Anthropomorphism to Zoomorphism)". *Society & Animals* 3: 197–222 as quoted in http://en.wikipedia.org/wiki/Furry_fandom

13 http://www.geocities.com/yaiolani/think.htm

14 http://www.economicexpert.com/a/Clinical:lycanthropy.htm

15 Deleuze, Gilles and Guattari, Félix. *A Thousand Plateaus*. Brian Massumi, trans. Minneapolis: University of Minnesota Press, 1987. p. 249.

16 Agamben, Giorgio, *The Open*. Kevin Attell, trans. Stanford, CA: Stanford University Press, 2004. p. 77.

17 Moriarty, Laura, from *"Departures 1-11/War in Heaven,"* in *War & Peace #2.* Oakland: O Books, 2005. p. 32.

18 Darragh, Tina, *"(dis-pose)→ABLE creatures,"* in *War & Peace.* Oakland: O Books, 2005. p. 28.

19 "Emergent ontologies" is a term originated by Helen Veron, an Australian philosopher of science. Donna Haraway uses this term in her lecture at The European Graduate School in Sasse-Fee, Switzerland, "Birth of the Kennel," 2000.

20 Kocik, Robert. *Rhrurbarb.* Bowdoinham, ME: Periplum Editions / Field Books, 2007. p. 29.

21 Iijima, Brenda. "Cry 1" from *Remembering Animals,* unpublished manuscript.

22 http://jhom.com/topics/birds/ziz.html

23 Nagler JJ, J Bouma, GH Thorgaard, and DD Dauble. "High Incidence of a Male-Specific Genetic Marker in Phenotypic Female Chinook Salmon from the Columbia River." Environmental Health Perspectives 109:67-69, 2001
http://www.ourstolenfuture.org/NewScience/wildlife/200101chinooksexratio.htm

24 Negri, Antonio. *The Porcelain Workshop.* Noura Weddell, trans. Cambridge: The MIT Press, 2008. p. 105.

Roberto Harrison's *Urracá*

Andy Gricevich

Urracá by Roberto Harrison
Achiote Press 2009

Roberto Harrison is of that class of poets whose work expands the poetic, where poetry is itself a living practice, a way of searching for new forms of experience and understanding. This writing seeks meetings with orders of being that resist language: geological and astronomical time and space, subterranean and aquatic nature, human cultures trapped in a past made inaccessible by the massive destruction of colonialism. Language itself appears simultaneously as the medium of this staging and as part of the world—a world always churning, formed and undone in a drama of becoming, reflected—no, enacted!—in poems that are dizzying, mysterious, and often frightening.

I've been reading Harrison's chapbook *Urracá* through the lens of a recurring gesture in César Vallejo's *Human Poems*, in which mountains, rivers, lodes of silver, dust, and rain are given human characteristics, linked initially with the experience of the poems' "I." In Vallejo's work, this exceeds the bounds of personification and reverses its trajectory. The syntax of metaphor is short-circuited so that—rather than reducing nonhuman nature to a reflection of the poetic subject—it makes the nonhuman the proper bearer of the subject's characteristics. The subject is not erased conceptually, but is inflated, made porous at its boundaries, the location of a language that the nonhuman can use to speak. Vallejo's subject comes to be radically identified with what exceeds and surrounds it (which, later in his work, includes the communal resistance to Franco's fascism).

Where Vallejo pushes the subject toward a horizon of something larger, Harrison's work begins on the far side of that horizon. There is no "I" in the first place in *Urracá*, where humans are generally manifest only in fragments. These fragments appear in the process of forming bodies that never quite come together—or as the severed detritus of an "unknown, terrifying *junta*." Harrison's poems are also on the far side of the political horizon Vallejo faced, in the long wake and recurrent threat of later dictatorships in the Americas.

The major pronoun in *Urracá* is "it," an initially empty word that, at the same time, connotes thingliness. "It" unites abstraction and concreteness. In the poems, "it" is the location (or the movement) in which connections are made and unmade (the making and dissolving of connections is the major category of event in *Urracá*). The status of "it" allows the poems to give primacy to processes of becoming, in which things are effects of the conjoining and separation of contrary forces and primal elements.

The first poem, "weapons concealed in the roof of her mouth," begins with the line "the past vanished," and its successor, "la llorona," takes up this pastness as it sets up the parameters for the rest of the book.[1] The opening stanzas of the poem (which, like every work in the book, consists of 39 tercets) read like a strange creation myth:

> there was, in
> with the back of it, a walking
> with no fire
>
> there was another, with the first light finished
> to see one with it sounding out
> in the ocean
>
> there was the window of its kind
> in the forceful water
> that sees

The poem deploys a series of pairings and oppositions: past and present, "one" and "another," "no fire" and "light," seeing and hearing. These are played off against the three-ness of the stanzaic structure (often strengthened by a tripartite conceptual or grammatical schema)—part of a drama of number that runs throughout the book. In the next stanza, dryness contrasts with sea in "noise has it for the ground / in accretions / pushing one together." Two stanzas later, that ground expands "to connect the continent"[2]—an event whose massive scale then shifts to that of "the ant that moves for the foot." Weather systems return us to the large scale; most of the poems take place in a winter, first introduced as "fields / of snowmen" and later as a kind of ice age in which "the visual / calibrated for flow" is "still and divided, in the snow."

In the next stanza, the introduction of a strong present tense and an unexpected pronoun we usher in a different kind of major event: "as we see the replacement, it derails / and opens the opposing absolute." "The replacement" is our first stand-in for "it," but only opens further questions: what does it replace? And what is it? A snowman "standing for" real bodies? Its own replacement of "it?" Hints occur:

corrupt our series of naturals

for the shrinking down of the storm
to collect the range of a simple
conversation, as it aims for and becomes

the animal [. . .]

And later: "as the question aims at the knot" (a figure of binding and connection), and then: "we wear the word for creation, but not itself." Perhaps the "replacement" is language, and the "opposing absolute" it opens is again that unspeakable "it," doubled and displaced by speech. This attempt to bring things together within acts of language, to unite "alarms and a mammoth, the small / inferior plane, the brush," keeps bringing about a split: "returned as reconciliation, it severs."

This, however, is not a picture of failure (the old trope of language's inability to refer beyond language), but of the conditions under which "it" can come to speak for itself (to "open," a frequent movement in these poems). "We do not arrive // as aggregation," but it "will arrive when one is not it / when it is as two is not one." In trying to speak it, we cause it to split, and then "as it speaks it separates itself and remains" apart from us, appearing as "one to the divided, a music of erasure // and a common nature." The two-ness—we speaker-observers versus "it"—then opens up: "as reading is not one for it in three." It's in *reading*, in attention, that "it" is set free, "one with the weather // to allow itself to become," and that reading is made possible by the split that occurs when we have tried to speak. The world folds to read itself, and "we" is absorbed into the folds.

I hope that I'm capturing some of the *motion* of Harrison's poems, rather than boiling their unsettling experiential character down to a propositional poetics. It's that motion that makes these poems so compelling—just as their approach to formal meaning goes beyond abstraction to a demonstration of the enactment of a world through the work of form. The poems' way of "worlding" is evident less in lines that seem to sum things up than in those that pull the ground out from under us—as in the terrifying scale of:

it opens the unraveled star, the quaking
white connection
made to be a whole, like rivers through a crystal

(where the conceptual movement "opening—unraveled—(made to be) whole" reverses "la llorona's" "calibrated for flow / still and divided"). We zoom in on another winter landscape, where the appearances of animals ("a cockroach now arrives / and stays outside the sight of islands"; "a field of flies"; "absent forests / teeming with robotic cats / and selves the boxes in a straw mound see") lead to

> [. . .] what a herd becomes
> to live through tunnels in a mountain for a bird
> that swims, that atrophies with blood and claps
>
> to make an opening another neck, a neck that dangles with the frost
> filled with a dozen eggs, a magnifying
> pole up north

—where the conceptual grouping of "burrowing—flight—swimming" mirrors the earlier grouping in a more concrete way, and a global scale explodes out of an egg's.

There is death all over these poems as well—death may, at times, be the recurrent *it*—unbinding things to "[make] light a circulation," playing its part in the becoming that never ends in full-fledged creation or utter destruction: a death at the level of novas and ice ages, but also of the psychic "death drive," the push to dissolve the egoic self, so that the "id" (*das es*, properly "the *it*") may unleash its energies. It's also the death that severs hands and heads, that executes dissidents, embodied in "the gun," in "armies filled with quivering tripe / and made to promise like a cutup worm // for icons sold to be undone." It's in relation to death that human beings do, on occasion, come into the poem—precisely as the dead, as ghosts, or as those threatened by starvation or brutal repression.

"symbol table," perhaps the most moving poem in the book, begins with another staging of the relation between language and landscape. We "read the river" as a writing in a language known by absent people,[3] in a place inhabited by "a bird // an answer / erases," where there occurs "the growth / of an infinite / eclipse, like the fern // a face makes / for words." In the midst of this drama, where "behind the language / a river threatens for its music— / future wood in a soundless word," the reader (or her stand-in, perhaps the poet) is addressed at length for the first time:

[. . .] in Panamá, their ghostly bus
will stand inside the arrival

as they become you [. . .]

to wear one for the torso as it packages
the allure of your housing
with another plane to fill this, in the seat

of your miniscule cadaver, the dogs are
what any chain is shiny for
you, in the shelter under ropes

their vast landscape in the spoken
to the air far with flowers, a harpy eagle
swoops to the sloth as you wear

the matrimony, and the only servant
filled with each starving donation, the poor
will become your iron—not what puts a hand

to your face. a fall for your region, the paper
makes families reside, with food, and a dog
in the aftermath as you speak

"It sees you as country": here the reader is cast as the channel of a rich region's language, encompassing the "vast landscape," of the colonized, wearing the "matrimony," the privilege of making connections, of housing, travel, resources ("to wear the oil")—but "it" intervenes again between "you" and "yourself," to open the possibility of "a complete knowledge of interruption," of the transformation of a colonizing subjectivity into a channel for what's buried by that subjectivity's way of constructing a world:

to the river it sees one out
it speaks as one is a tunnel
in air of it arriving with one to become / not one

While this reading has touched frequently upon the one's splitting from itself in non-identity, it hasn't addressed another way of becoming not-one: the multiplication of identity through acts of collaboration and community.

Though "human affirmation" has little place in Harrison's poems, there occurs again and again, from the dim world of organs without bodies, the emergence of *hands*, making connections, writing a language of the landscape on scales from "the bodies in each cuticle" to the interstellar. "Each hand . . . promises / a magnet," a drawing-together and a global polarity. It's not an easy answer; "we do not arrive // as aggregation," and this is emphasized by the poems' form, which prevents any comfortable adding-up of results. *Urracá's* tercets ask us to go beyond neat pairings and unities, just as its diction, its way of never quite forming stable syntactic units, keeps pushing our attention beyond interpretation to the phenomenality of language, the words' ways of actually *doing* things, achieving the creation of worlds in bringing objects and forces into conjunction, keeping becoming in action.[4] What the hands build together will be something bigger and stranger than our current political imagination can conceive, something that can appear only in the untamable space between them.

> and in the constellation cradles come to first of all
> a word that spins a spider for a stone beyond the canyon edge
> and what each child could not intend without a second heart, returns

NOTES

1 *La Llorona* is the subject of a legend that takes different forms throughout the Spanish-speaking Americas: she is the ghost of a woman whose children have drowned (in most versions, by her own hand) in the wake of her rejection by her lover (on account of the existence of these offspring). *La Llorona* walks the night screaming, searching for her children and occasionally kidnapping those of the living. In some versions she is associated with Contlicue, the goddess who appeared just before the arrival of Cortés to herald the downfall of the Aztecs—or with La Malinche, who served as Cortés' interpreter before he impregnated and abandoned her, after which she committed various acts of vengeance.

2 Probably a reference to Panama (Harrison is Panamanian-American), which rose up from the ocean to connect North and South America.

3 The Ojibwa, as the poem's subtitle tells us.

4 Their way of pushing *outward* is one of the singular achievements of Harrison's poems. They are externally directed in the otherness of their content and in the nature of what we could call their "formal figures," motifs that never become fully concrete (meaning that their relations are internal to the poem, and not with an external referent) but always suggest a palpable, material being or movement. This play of "formal figures" is prominent throughout Harrison's work: see (for example) the tropes of subterranean passage and emergence in *Reflector* (another recent volume, published by House Press—which, incidentally, produces some of the most beautiful chapbooks around). The result is a poetry that advances the investigation of radical form while bringing it to bear on an urgently experienced extra-poetic reality—a difficult challenge rarely taken up in recent poetry.

Willie Monad

Mina Pam Dick

1 The Monad of which Willie, shuffling extra, uncomposed furlough

2 Brown w/green w/orange crayon marks on glass table, arcs of kids' strokes

3 Now, when elements of dizzy implications gurgle, fumbled subways

4 Their dissolution, Willie's fearful gulping coffee: imperishables are simpletons

5 Or the squawk of flanking knights. Mattress tunes. Decomposed misconceptions

6 Therefore only annihilation. Bruises on girls' shins. French laptop accent

7 Therefore no window punctures Willie Monad, who's immobilized excursion milk

8 Electric blue anorak on alien new black notebook plenum; moat of abstractions guarding Willie Monad

9 Intrinsic Bob of Dylan electric wiry tangled-up hedge of hair. The blue crayon must've emigrated

10 Change is unchanging, it rained onto hip boots—I mean Wellingtons. Nothing new in Willie's coils

11 It follows that no influenza wracked Willie's wheezes. Russian syllables triumphed in absentia

12 Unity of the manifold stranded inside Willie. Brown book bag with orange ellipse

13 Therefore a plurality of conditions such as nervous scalp itches makes Willie host many n-place predicates

14 Triumphal nostrils on the girl in charge of atmospheric lighting. Toddler's pink snowsuit vs. no-show snow

15 The desire doesn't always reach the snow sled. But it reaches to new potions as of Willie's principle: eager elbows

16 The simple substance of the soul with a multiplicity of features such as spiritual nostrils. Such as street signs

17 The actions of perceptions being unmechanical procedures for demonstrations. Willie walks into a laundromat like John the Baptist w/ dirty underwear

18 Autonomous automats are childhood chocolate cake slices with perfect pitch and coin slots: incorporeal

19 Therefore Willie who remembers has a soul; feeling is greater than bare perception. Willie felt sad, afraid, smart, or weird. Willie comes alive!

20 Then dies. Being stupefied or fainting is a lack of friction, air, or visions. No smell of grilled cheese sandwich to transcend entelechy

21 Supersonic shrieks are stunts of kids' play. Massing weak perceptions. Willie got spun by dizziness, stunned into inertia

22 The chain of states of perceptions inside Willie clanked. Park with trees of percussion. & with no toupees, nor big hair as of Gottfried

23 Therefore unconsciousness does not mean no perceptual timpani. The sidewalks sidle, flinging beats of flanking views

24 Although, a royal stupor might be a prize for one like Willie Monad, who's distinctive and frightfully highly flavored

25 Waves of light, rays of air. Head seizing fist of the numinous mouth organ. Epileptic aesthetics of the unbare point

26 For instance, if a stick is shown to Willie. Instantly memory furnishes feelings of pain & fear, and he whines & runs away

27 Force of x or else frequency of x = intensity of picture. Such as the bucking wooden chair w/padded seat plane. Willie should pray to the horizontal axis

28 Willie the empiricist guessed, There will be light. Then what happened was dumb, brute & unreasonable

29 But the momentary eternity of the dusk world yarmulke, or this girl's 3rd grade giggle, is what raises Willie Monad's eyeballs with their holes. Green and blue construction paper, glue

30 Thereupon, thoughts of God act deflectively. And Willie gets to forget his defective I of I *think*. It's as simple as *that*: not a that-clause

31 Reflective acts being about contradictions vs. clanking bottles, white skirts with gold dollops and the truths of recursive Polish

32 Secondly, the principle of St. Casimir/Kasimierz/Kasek, through which to believe that no God can exist unless He loves plumbers, poets, logicians & especially all youth (including girls)

33 Also butchers. Then the orange wax paper glows shyly. That is a truth of fact of acquaintance. A truth of reason is: Willie ≠ Kazek

34 A definition is: Willie is a monad. An axiom is: Willie is indivisible. A postulate is: Willie is a simple idea which never gets defined

35 A whistle for Willie from the Polish super, not the kids' book. Who also made music from bottles & cans. Then a Venezuelan youth with a toothpick stumbled by in truth. That's yesterday

36 But now something new passed by Willie's entity. Namely, some present that spilled accidental infinity w/no insurance plans on Willie's shirt cuffs. Dispositional, disposable

37 Then something else goes outside to say what is what, while Willie advances minor theories. Such as the guy with the unshaved back of his neck with a Tictac mole

38 But God as a necessary fountain pen meant Willie Monad rubbed his head rigorously. And did this thinking: So here. No Liquid Paper

39 There is only one God who said: Now Willie gets stuck in the elevator; now Willie whistles in the dark; now they come to free him

40 God = necessity & all reality. Willie = contingency & some reality. Poem = necessity & unreality

41 Whence it follows that God is perfect, Willie Monad is imperfect, and the poem is simple & imperfectible. Hey, I don't think so

42 Defects of abstractions being Willie's natural but distinctive limitations. So Willie went to the street to become an unbounded variable

43 Because the point of the unreal of the necessary is Willie qua first-person God who'll find a set of nostrils. Or a coat or swirled marble or some collision or idea

44 For possibility only becomes *necessary* unreality when things such as facial features, milky hopes, algebraic equations, or rugs of snow show up

45 Willie perceives the little girl in pink with a pink backpack and long brown straight hair; her mama explaining how to be happy even if you're poor. The girl responds earnestly

46 Necessary truths depend upon understanding; contingent truths depend upon will, such as the truck chewing bottles while Willie strolls, agog. Unreal truths depend on fits

47 Then: Johan is a savior! If Johan Santana, then not Carlos Gomez, who has to decrease vs. increase. Furthermore, Carlos Santana was a musician, but Johan Santana is a perfection

48 Willie has puny biceps and no sinker ball. God is a unity. Divinity is flashes such as percepts of perfect curveballs or solemn pink-clad girls

49 Action is having clear & distinct perceptions which are true and perfect phrases, while passivity is being dazed & confused is Willie Monad's creed

50 But degree of perfection equals degree of independence. So Willie refused to have a job or reply to friendly greetings. But he looked at everything to make it hum, exist

51 Dependence on others is in God, thus Willie must not be in God but in His concept. No physical influences such as fondlings

52 Once Willie lay upon a Greta but did not do much. Thinking is a dark blue mail box. Whatever's active is also passive is one interesting idea

53 Willie has tan plastic glasses which he wears to see better. Infinity of possible universes in the ideas of Willie, perceptions help him pick

54 Yet perfection demands to exist further, paradoxically, in the form of necessary unreality. For existence exceeds reality when Willie is possessed. Chess game: white guy tries to sound black

55 Old Chinese lady with Chinese black lacquer hair swings her arms because ideas have to circulate. Leaves do good, plain men watch on bench

56 Willie circumambulates while relations & modifications of everything to everything make Willie be a model of the universe. Willie rubs his weak chin cleft with life

57 The summa of all the cities from all the views is the one city, reports Gottfried, and Willie gives one aspect. So the City of Gottfried needs Willie Monad, it's a huge set as in math

58 Perfection the whole set, Willie loitering qua subset. Then unreality flips into reality when Willie makes it up with make-believe. Metaphysics gets inflated

59 The relation Willie has to things is so he can express things, thereby fit in the totality. Therefore Willie looks around in his monad. It's sort of a mess

60 Thus Willie is independent yet suffused in a confused way. But only what's near is perfect and clear, such as the ripped beige stockings on the old lady with the blocky black brogans

61 The world is crumpled and compressed w/hyperbolic folds of afros & other hairdos. And everything connects to everything by communicable unease

62 But currently it is through Willie's concave chest, skinny forearms and surprising ingenuous baritone that the whole universe gets exposed and glows. Lookit!

63 The body has a soul to which it belongs: Willie Monad, living being with a big head with turnstiles. Willie, mirror of the whole through disorder particles and victuals

64 Yeah, Willie has a big head like a kid's, proportionally speaking. Each body part of Willie with a function which expresses Willie. So he cries when some hairs fall out

65 Also if a foot were subtracted, as with some soldiers, verses, or persons with diabetes. Willie the child size will helmet never went to a big war to fight something with his nerves

66 He—his helmet—offers protection against everything insisting to inflict itself on Willie. But Willie still gets overwhelmed and hides in his room. Diabetics suffer thirst, hunger & loss of weight

67 Even the smallest portion expresses the whole or God as a pool of liquid. Willie perceives how a black umbrella has a broken side like a tan and black German Shepard. Then his head limps

68 Secretly there is no negative space, the spaces between things are actually proud and bold shapes with initiatives. So everything is full of meanings like in an abstract painting

69 So everything is alive, dirty and perfected when it is seen acutely w/ the action that's passion: love as suffering. E.g., a paper cut. Willie perceives a yellow taxi in the grey plinking rain

70 And bodies have body parts which can be removed. But the soul is a monad. Like that permanent black ink—it's called Eternal! Won't run when it gets wet. It is willful

71 Once there was a flood in Willie's head. Then the world was annihilated, because it was a bad one. But everything is always fluid, so Willie was wrong & feels better today. He repents

72 Soon Willie's body was changing like a current he stepped into of nervous electric impulses of ontology. It's raining, vows Willie. Drops ping onto the air conditioner. Willie is a body that's alive

73 No true death, only envelopes and diminutives. Huh? I don't get it. Willie is a diminution of Wilhelm, does that mean death is imperfect, thus unreal?

74 I am not dead, thinks Willie, but I was destined for some great transformation. I turned small and lost some hair, now I glow in the dark

75 Mostly, things vanish. Only a few make it to the great stage as the chosen ones, says Gottfried. But I see things such as the man with the silver sideburns and the grey Russian fur hat

76 The death of a monad would be the death of the world: annihilation all at once, as a totality. But we haven't ended yet, we are still Willie. So how come I feel sad?

77 Indestructible inverse of the universe, coatings of Chinese red get scratched off, although we don't. The black knight took the white pawn, it's been five minutes, I still don't play chess

78 I am too impatient. The principles of true thought are beautiful overcoats, whiffs and contradictions. Anti-establishment harmonies of laws of souls with bodies. Awkward head moves

79 Thereby recitations of the whole world electric organ. I have to eat something now, perceives Willie, who abruptly feels weak. It would be efficient to cause a sandwich

80 Gottfried fell into his system of Pre-Established Harmony, while René fell over his assertion of I Think, etc. Willie fell out from his vision of: to note or be a note

81 Soul parallel to body: bodies cause bodies to move and souls souls. The two attributes are suspenders holding up the world trousers. Dickies, not Levi's!

82 So say Gottfried and Benedict, two reasons who'd warrant Willie. But his sensuous daily soul didn't elevate to pure rationality; Willie got stuck in the elevator and missed his school commencement

83 Then a bus splattered Willie's maroon corduroys with water from the gutter. And Willie said, My soul is also a mind. Therefore soluble w/divinity in a formula like for an infant

84 So Willie Monad had a mind which was a version of God, not only of the world/Bowery. So Willie was a beloved son or subject, not only a symbolic formalization or formal symbolization

85 Therefore the city of Willie was the city of God, a principality, and Willie strolls around in an ermine sweat jacket, keeping his eye on the castle w/all the apartments which stay coordinated but apart

86 So it is possible for Willie to be good. But it cannot be necessary, since Willie is only good sometimes. When he feels bad, Willie feels ashamed. But he still feels bad. Sometimes he is klutzy

87 Therefore he should be chastised sometimes, such as spanked or struck or pushed over. Like that little girl slain by her violent papa. Except that girl was innocent

88 The papa said it was an accident. But he tied her to a chair after he dunked her in cold water. But there is no true physical contact. Therefore Willie can't untie the girl, who gets nixed

89 A pun's a sin and a self-mortification of compulsion. But bad actions entail their own penalty, good actions entail a reward such as an emotional mechanical glow or halo. But the little girl in pink is dead. The real exceeds the necessary

90 Finally everything is for the best of all possible worlds, says Gottfried Wilhelm, who feels peaceful. And Willie wants to be the will of God, with pure love, otherwise we are stupid. But Willie Monad blurs the world

91 In the details, God hid. The thing kept going, it was different. The city of God is big, it's an amputee. Unauthorized & dumb. The metaphysics wept. The girl stayed dead. Everything's Scotch-taped

FROM Interview with Leslie Scalapino

Michael Cross

MC: Let's start with your first full-length trade edition, *Considering how exaggerated music is* (a book that collects many of the early chapbooks). You claim in *Autobiography* that "it was the first time (you were) writing."[1] In what ways is this writing different from other experiments you were involved in at the time, for instance, your chapbook *O and Other Poems*, and can you elaborate on your claim that this work is "a light extremity?"

LS: I regarded myself as writing "for the first time" with "hmmmm," because I had the sense of that work being unlike the other poets I'd read, of being my own; whereas *O and Other Poems,* my very first poems, were similar, as I discovered while in the midst of writing them, to Francis Ponge, a discovery which cut short that writing and prevented me from beginning anything else for a year. The poems in *O* were as if doing the inside of objects, passionate elucidation of objects, somewhat similar to Ponge (at least that was my intention recognizing the similarity when I read him).

As for why I described "hmmmm" as a "light extremity": emerging from a violent conjunction of circumstances, I was in a state of shock and "hmmmm" arose from being in that state and waking up in that state. The subject matter of "hmmmm" was not the source, was after what I'm describing as a violent conjunction of circumstances, the sense of the individual's (my) private context and a violent outside, public context (in that case the Vietnam War) entering or being the same space. Perhaps the vernacular expression "blown away" is similar to "light extremity" and realistic conveying having lost or no longer having your self. Having been dismantled, no longer there, there's a sense of being curiously free, so even painful circumstances personal-social happening to or in front of oneself (not war) seem very funny. This is not unlike the theme of sensations of objects (as in *O and Other Poems*) but *more wildly felt*.

In regard to my sense of individual context and the outside in chaos converging on each other and being the same, I had perhaps five or so formative instances of such, which helped to form my writing. I recall a poet not too long ago at Georgetown University, in a question-answer session, remarking about some of my writing that it is "psychological," the word used disparagingly to mean that "psychological" is as such conventional which is limitation (of the human and of writing). Meaning, we have the same responses, these are closed? It's a view of my generation which I've heard expressed many times, probably enhancing intellect above examination of any "experience" (itself a word that has been excised from usage by those with this view). I'm not regarding "psychological" as conventional (as repetitive) and as such a limit (this view implies the human mind is separate from one's senses and body and that we cannot change and learn as direct action in event). In "hmmmm," I was trying to make seeing (and) being motion be one's total change as direct action, event.

MC: I'm interested in your use of the word "event" here, a concept which, thanks in part to philosophers such as Alain Badiou and Giorgio Agamben (after the work of Heidegger), is very much in vogue in contemporary aesthetics at the moment. Your sense of coming into a voice seems very much related to an investigation of the "event of the poem" (as it relates to so many singular "events" in the world). Some characterize this event, wholly in relation to your work, as an investigation into the simultaneity or relationality of interiority and exteriority; however, as I read your writing, the "event" of the poem obliterates these binary distinctions as such. You often refer to the event of writing as a "horizon," or as a "rim" of experience. In *New Time* you write,

> the events: a rim collapsing (in one)—differing times on the same present—(and one's)—no—bud—one fears that's too fast

> the two 'two' events are only 'spring'—'obstructions'—as one won't be in (be) them at the present at the same time—being—no—bud[2]

And in *The Front Matter, Dead Souls,* you write, "I'm trying to get the real event. It's a balance as to when the real event emerges."[3] Can you respond to the distinction you see between events as such and the event of the poem as a kind of immanent "event horizon?" How does this distinction relate to your early experiments to find a voice?

LS: Reading your description of Badiou, Agamben, and Heidegger in relation to the concept of "event" I think all are very interesting and amidst these examples there is some resemblance to my sense (more investigations than theory) of "event." For example, my sense of "event" in the passage you quote from *New Time* is similar *in a general way* to the description: "For Badiou, the subject's militant fidelity to this event, that it took place, is the material trace of its occurrence. In this sense you could say that the poem is a material trace of a happening that has withdrawn."[4] My passage from *New Time* is also similar *as* ('just as'—and 'while' or 'because') there is no producer—no (single) event— no cause and effect (though something's happening—has happened). The site of occurrence can't exist (as it's interdependent with everything else). I'd read Nagarjuna but not Badiou; yet I was not so much influenced by Nagarjuna as enabled by him after the fact to try to explain or think through what I was encountering. The particular passage you quote:

> the events: a rim collapsing (in one)—differing times on the same present—(and one's)—no—bud—one fears that's too fast

> the two 'two' events are only 'spring'—'obstructions'—as one won't be in (be) them at the present at the same time—being—no—bud

This is a sense of space as time-event, the starting of an event (which has no time of starting as no time in the present) and the sense of the event *being* a present only by (imagining) a rim (a mental marking, as visual line of attention, which has no existence anywhere except the individual's attention there). It's like trying to keep time if one were in sensory deprivation in prison without outside reference—except the opposite, it's the state of flooding of outside references which, as simultaneous, are not beginning, are not in 'the middle' and are not ending. Comparing mine to Badiou, I too am viewing an event as "a material rupture in this situation that is unknowable, haphazard, and unpredictable"[5] (both the event and situation)—and I'm seeking giving up one's own militant insistence on the event (any), militancy in which the event becomes a kind of lawlessness (its assertion obliterating other events and the event is causal where it is actually not-existing—such as spring. Not-existing in fall). Spring exists, held onto—viewed as single, also obscures, distorts as an event that's posited, say as two occurrences of spring (obstructions) obscuring everything else, requiring (in one dropping the mode of orientation) that there *be* no events of any kind held?

I did not approach this occurrence or problem of writing as theory (such as reading Nagarjuna and applying it—or Heidegger, whom I have not read I confess). I was approaching conceiving "event" as I was encountering or undergoing it, like testing space and events in it with writing by (as) a spatial lineless (no line breaks except as paragraphs) mind syntax.

The use of the word "voice" or vocabulary "finding a voice" I think is inappropriate, in fact antithetical to my writing in the sense that I'm aware in any/all writing (of mine at least) of one's fake or created constructions of voice, there in any case in anything, and the whole idea is to peel these away, exposing and using them—to use language to recognize in the writing and be actions. The poem is doing or is state of being in no single time no single event.

MC: How would you characterize the "event" of the *poem*, then? Are you saying that the poem is also interdependent with other occurrences—that writing as an activity in the world is no different than other activities, and, as such, cannot operate as a privileged mode of thinking? And if so, why write poetry *specifically*? In my understanding, your writing *deactivates* occurrence—it makes hierarchies of power, significance, and difference *inoperative*, and as such, works *next to* this interdependence as a mode of self-reflexivity (which, I suppose, privileges the writing by pushing it outside the act of leveling). In other words, does writing *level* occurrence in your practice by making all events interdependent (that is, does the thinking and writing actually *perform* this task?), or is the writing always already simply another occurrence in a web of happenings?—a record of simultaneity? Or, does the writing somehow transcend this leveling in the *act* of attention (imaging the rim), by reflecting on this "lawlessness" in real time, *next to it?* Is it that there's no site of occurrence or that there is no *privileged* site of occurrence because *everything is always evental in nature*, is always touching?

LS: You give a multitude of possibilities—I like all of them to be in operation at once. Even if they are conflicting they are questions in the mind and the response of the reader, not needing to cancel each other but jostling. However, I don't understand the question: [my view apparently being] "that writing as an activity in the world is no different than other activities, and, as such, cannot operate as a privileged mode of thing? And if so, why write poetry *specifically?*" My answer: There's occurrence that can only be as the poem, it's a mental activity that's a space and relation that doesn't exist otherwise, in the world. It is not that poetry "is no different than other activities," (though I may have said that, I meant:) it's that it is ALSO activity—so, mind and action are not separate in the sense of mind being weak and ineffective in the face of 'real' action (the motions of history predominate and the individual mind is nothing, without power—minds are also making those motions? those that ARE the history). Anyway, throughout my writing it's a problem I'm working on, I don't have an answer or fixed view: it's like I'm trying to find out, differently, in individual works.

As I get deeper into your series of questions, I realize there are other thoughts I don't quite understand: "does writing *level* occurrence in your practice by making all events interdependent (that is, does the thinking and writing actually *perform* this task), or is the writing always already simply another occurrence in a web of happenings—a record of simultaneity?" I don't think writing would be "leveling" occurrence by making (or enabling seeing) all events as interdependent. As such they are in a sense seen from a distance and also actively altering every second and every instance in that second. Events ARE interdependent (in fact, in reality) and seeing that (as if one reads the events in fact, directly—OR in writing as motions of syntax) does not lessen the vitality of each event or link—writing CAN do that (that is, it can BE that interdependence). As such, writing interacts with phenomenal action in the formation of other actions (single individual's mental-phenomenal—and 'phenomenal-actions in the world').

MC: Can you address *your* experience *as a reader* of your poems? I imagine undergoing the time-event of the work as a reader must be radically different than as a writer; and yet, I experience a kind of *displacement* when reading your work, as if the text is emptied of authorship *by* or *because of* the reader's labor, which creates a kind of vertigo (at least for me) in which the time of reading and the time of writing become impossible to trace. In other words, do *you* experience similar "conflicting . . . questions in the mind" (as you have it) as a reader *and* writer, and how would you differentiate *the time of reading* from *the time of writing?*

LS: Can you say something more about "the time-event of the work as a reader must be radically different than as a writer"—? Do you mean that the event as reader reading is far from the real-time event (also—and the same as?—the time of writing)? Are you saying you can't understand it, can't get with it? My first reaction to your question was that I'm having the sense right now (in the work *Floats Horse-floats or Horse-flows* in fact) that I'd needed in the past to catch the motion that's event its transpiring as syntax shape (not representing the event but getting at something inner and outer as spatial occurrence sculptural kinetic that's an event itself, as the language—but also is an occurrence that's real-time for the reader unrelated to any real-time event of the past)—but now returning to some similar life events I'm needing to render my need or intention itself, the aftereffect in time of being separated from one's own events . . . something like that. But I don't know if that bares on what you mean in your question.

MC: You respond pretty accurately to my question in reference to *Floats Horse-floats.* I certainly don't mean that one can't *get with* the text, but that one's experience of the poem as temporal (experiencing the event as it happens) must be much different for one living with it, struggling with it day to day, etc. My interest, I suppose, is in a number of different things (hence the confusion!): on the one hand, the kind of displacement that happens when a reader *re-enters* a time space the writer shaped (occupied), sort of twice removed, trying to *get in* the poem (so to speak) (I wonder if I mean here that delay that occurs when you tune your body to the measure of a difficult poem?), but also that every reading is a new experience of the poem's temporality (is a new temporality) (so what makes the writer's experience in real-time different than the reader's experience after the poem is "finished"? Do you have to change gears as a reader, or do you feel that you're using a similar skill set to "stay with" the event). Not that the reader is entering the *writer's time*, but instead that the reader is tuning his/her own time to the writing's time (if that makes sense).

I'm interested in this given that reading your work is a kind of creative labor, a kind of *composition*, and I have a hunch that what makes the reader's experience of *composing with the poem* different than the writer's work of "living with the things as they exist" is how we experience the temporality of the poem . . . Rereading what you say here, I think it totally bares on what I'm asking . . . If it's not too complicated, you might think of an example such as *That they were at the beach* or *way*. How would you characterize the *labor* of writing either text, versus the labor of reading either, and how might you *occupy* or *accompany* the poem as both.

LS: The difference (and my intention as that) between *the time of reading* and *the time of writing* is actually a mode or process of probably all of my writing. You mention experiencing a "displacement . . . as if the text is emptied of authorship *by* or *because* of the reader's labor." Then also: "Not that the reader is entering the—writer's time—, but instead that the reader is tuning his/her own time to the writing's time." The reader tuning their own time to the writing's time is my intention; *either* recording *or* re-experiencing a particular event is *not* the point. That is, the writing (in *that they were at the beach—aeolotropic series* or *way*) is not narrative about events or making those events. Rather, I was 'finding' or 'hearing'—having a sense of—a gyration or whirr, reading as coming in the poem to a place where motion occurs (accumulation as reading) as if that is interior and/of life itself of any simple action as if chosen at random. Particular events were deemphasized ('omitted' as denuded) of their narrative or psychological import, which wasn't this occurrence (and would only conceal it). Thus I was always dismayed when people would break down segments into individual stories, that were merely segments of series or sequences; frequently this would be from an individual who either hadn't read my work, more than a page or two, or would not approach language as a sound scheme.

For example, *that they were at the beach—aeolotropic series* had one recurring sound scheme: a two-paragraph form, the two paragraphs commenting on each other (somehow this sound-shape arising in my mind and continuing until the poem was done) and to which all the 'real-time historical events memories arising as it happens and then proliferating associational' were *submitted*. That sound-shape emerging was regardless of the content of the events (content which had nothing to do with the content of my time of writing, my internal time, which happened, in the case of *that they at the beach*, to be a crisis of chaos outside seeming to cause chaos inside in my life *then*). I wrote in a note on that poem (published as "Note on My Writing") that I was punching a hole in (real-time) reality as punching out in space each event as it came up. Years later, Paul Hoover wrote in his intro to the selection of my work that's in his *The Norton Anthology of Postmodern American Poetry*, not only that I do the same thing continually, having one idea, but that my work is psychological, apparently dispelling psychological personal events by repeating these punching them out. Punching out all events (using one's own events because these are real-time, historical) was in order *not* to be within memory, to get to some present *only as text* that's as such spaceless (of real-time) but in space as 'sound scheme' of reading interior motion as if 'hearing' life-itself-text's-imitation-of-motions. My imposing the same sound on all becomes as if a neutral ground on which that interior sound occurrence (or occurrences) can be 'heard' but only outside of single episodes.

In *way*, it was completely different (I had to keep changing to come at it differently, unlike Hoover's view that my writing is one idea): each series has a different sound scheme as different conception where somewhere in each work one comes to (creates as reading) a place that's gyration (a hitting the fan that can be 'heard' maybe delicately, also emotional) is only the syntax, spaces of dashes, one word juxtaposed with space and with another word. Now and then the reader 'gets to' such a sound-motion—that's sense of life itself as motions the continuousness in the whole. In *way*, there's accumulated motions as if all over a conceptual space; particularly "The Floating Series" in the middle (of the long poem) makes points or blips that are all over a large spatial 'conceptual-outer-space' as if you were looking at this space. This will never be noticed if you're reading for content. I received a Before Columbus Foundation Award for *way*. I was honored to receive this. However, David Meltzer wrote an introduction to this poem for an anthology from Before Columbus, publishing "bum series" from *way*, interpreting the poem to mean I was a nervous woman afraid of being mugged and generally afraid of city conditions. I was actually shocked by this. In "bum series," there's a very delicate grinding 'motion' (just emptying spaces, by dashes, line breaks leaving single words by/beside themselves) making empty slots compared to freighters as one self also being dumb too. That delicate grinding motion of the bums already having died—yet that motion still there affecting the landscape—this was at the *beginning of the middle* of the long poem *way* opening a huge space utterly outside one and simultaneous *as the time of writing* and *the time of reading* ('later' is at once).

The prose work *Floats Horse-floats or Horse-flows*, because it's prose its scenes take a longer time than in a poem, passages in which one can dwell (have the sense of being in a particular episode or thought). The earlier poems, as I say, are composed of small motions. Yet even in this prose I had the sense in reading it of the text making at some point a wall, sense of everything hitting that flimsy wall-skin flowing from the back of the text and flowing from the front of the text to hit that wall that's like a plug (bursting, as change of seeing it while reading). Maybe (I hope) the reader gets the sense of that 'outside' motion as if life—itself not in single content (but is—in single episodes—when you notice it 'outside'). If this is there to the reader, it only occurs in this work by small discrete chapters that suggest continuousness, like segments of a crocodile's back, being read to overflow sense of the discrete unit.

Anyway, in the past I would be disturbed when other poets said about works like *that they were at the beach, way,* or *Crowd and not evening or light* (the three being very different in what and how they are doing something) that I was "just writing narrative"—disturbed because communing as interior core as life itself of random (as 'exterior') events (seen by putting motions together) apprehension *only possible as the text* isn't there unless one is in the text *as* (that is) the writing time altering the reading time.

After these works (still in the period of North Point publishing my books), *The Return of Painting, The Pearl,* and *Orion/A Trilogy* carried this attempt a little further. "Orion" was/is the reader seeming always being (to be) in a present line of the text yet moving into future which is present then (triple—the past also) by in "Orion" a line both making up events (fictionalizing) at the same time as being the vehicle for evidently real (real-time) events until the fictional takes over and can be 'seen' 'ahead.' This process could only occur (be visible—as their own mind, as if reader sensing their mind doing this, seeing their mind in a sense) to the reader by their having first read the earlier sections of the text (starting with the section titled "The Return of Painting"). Otherwise the gesture that's the text can't be seen. The reader has to have the illusion of their being in my (someone else's) past real-time as my writing-time for them to be in the later writing's time (of their own future, in "Orion").

I don't know if these descriptions make sense. It's very hard to describe this. Anyway, I'm saying simply that the dislocation as reader, of which you speak, is part of the writing.

MC: I wonder if you could further elaborate on what you're calling the "gyration" or "whirr" of the work in relation to the volume that followed the North Point Press books, *Crowd and not evening or light* (1992). I'm interested to know how the "sound scheme" of the work changed after *way,* especially as *Crowd* is such a distinctly *visual* work. It is the first, to my mind, to incorporate your photography (a relationship you've continued to explore in such works as *The Tango*), though you showed an interest in visual collaboration as early as the Cloud Marauder edition of *Instead of an Animal* (1978), which features drawings by your sister, Diane Sophia. If the sound scheme of the work creates a spatial, sonic "accumulation" in which the reader confronts a stilled interior that is one's mind "seeing" one's mind, how do the visual elements of *Crowd* *and not evening or light* (both photography and handwritten text) contribute to or alter the "interior motion" of the reader's experience? Can we think of these elements as contributing to the wall or film that registers the reader's interior movement?

LS: Perhaps the best I can do to answer the question of the nature of the gyration is to quote from the talk that I gave at University of Chicago.[6] In this talk I was giving ideas that were stages of my work, the essay is an answer to Lisa Samuels, who wrote an essay that was to be the introduction to my poems in a Wesleyan anthology in which Lisa said my writing is autobiography, my recent poetry "indictments" of the world, "reporting," and other completely inaccurate representations of my writing. First I said I would withdraw from the anthology after she said she wouldn't change any of her comments 'because then it wouldn't be her idea.' This essay might be of interest because it's the best I've written so far to describe my writing:

> Any way of making event's occurrence a singular *subject* or an argument of discourse outside of its language as its action (discourse as looking at event by separating oneself from *being* it, not seeing such separation is creating itself by its process of perceiving), is *as writing* to reproduce customary mind-body split that is inherently hierarchy-authority, to place perception (that is, writing) back in same social autism unknown to one while (because) doing 'being that autism.' In creating and doing any (singular) discourse we're unaware, accustomed. I've wanted to make myself aware, continually. Dismantling hierarchy-authority (that of the outside is thoroughly embedded *as one self*) can only occur by 'authority' (that's determining the writing, such as its mode, its constructing) *not* existing except as the unfolding that is in *that* writing itself—its specific occurring. That is, there can be no general dictum, as the poetry's purpose, except it is mystery of being as its language mind-shape sound . . . .

> 'The mind is action'—the writing keeping up with it—tracking it, is not to say that that is always re-action; it's this instant, to be unpeeling the social construction of reality and of oneself. Tracking is the (one's, reader's) mind's gesture itself in any instant of attention. Attention is an action, whose content is *attention*—apprehension as motion. Sometimes a sense occurs of 'between' apprehension-space-motion that is one's/outside's 'being'?

. . . Borderlessness as if a line is infinite: As an imagined originary event, or as there being *no* originary (and originating) event also, one is—neither—being—space—nor—in it—at once, (what) is the 'outside'? (Actual) sky space horizon to land is (*not*) infinite line *either*—seen 'at present,' is. The 'outside' and the 'inside' 'seen' at once:

> silver half freezing in day
>   moon's elation
> of the outside rose, his seeing
>   on both
>   'sides'
> seeing someone else at all and the
>   half freezing
> elation of the outside so that's even
>   with one
> continually over and over one/person[7]

The following passage that's in the essay "Poetics—for Lisa Samuels" is my attempt to answer your question about what I meant by a "gyration" I'd feel or have a sense of in a sequential poem (not in prose, it has to do with the sound-shape in a poem—that is, duration is necessary to it and line breaks shape-sound). Your asking me about this sense of "gyration" compelled me to try to describe it:

> As dismantling hierarchy-authority (that of the outside thoroughly embedded *as one self*) there can be no general dictum, as the poetry's mode or purpose: except it is mystery of being as its language mind-shape sound, a configuration (gyration) which can be 'heard' (silently even) at points in a sequential poem. As recognition of when *way* was 'there' (completed), I had a sense of (or heard) a gyration somewhere in the sound as duration of the poem sequence. The measure of the poem, conceived as the rendition of motions of the outside-events (sound as say the poem's line breaks): This 'gyration' might be described as a gap, that is emptiness, where word/reality face or abut each other, a whir between word-based and experience-based idea, as apprehension. This gyration in measure is shape emptiness of one's conceptualization (that is name/word and that is reality/named), the sense that neither is existent. That is, *both* (word/reality) are being constructed (at once, by the reader). This experience is similar to Buddhist emptiness theory in regard to language apprehension (this unknown to me at the time of writing *way*).

I realized something about this sense of syntax/gyration (an abutment in syntax of contrasting senses as word, emptiness of reality, these facing each other) from reading right at the moment a book by Gen Lamrimpa called *Realizing Emptiness/Madhyamaka Insight Meditation*. I'll quote several passages. Obviously, I did not conceive in terms of this or such ideas at the time of writing *way*, for example; but I was doing some similar process:

> The image of the Space Needle that appears to the conceptual mind is said to be the generic idea of the Space Needle, and we say that mind apprehends the Space Needle itself and not the generic idea of the tower. In short, the generic idea of the Space Needle *appears* to that conceptual mind, but it apprehends the Space Needle . . . Both types of ideas appear to us, the verbal idea and the generic idea . . . The wisdom that realizes personal identitylessness focuses upon the self, the "I," but it falsely apprehends it as truly existent. Thus, there are two types of mutually incompatible cognitions: first, grasping onto true existence of the self, and second, the realization of emptiness with regard to the self. Even though they focus on the same thing, their modes of apprehension are mutually incompatible . . . for sensory cognitions, such as auditory or visual cognition, whatever is apprehended by the cognition is the same as what appears to it.[8]

NOTES

1 Scalapino, Leslie. *Zither & Autobiography*. Middletown: Wesleyan University Press, 2003. p. 34.

2 Scalapino, Leslie. *New Time*. Hanover: Wesleyan University Press, 1999. p. 61.

3 Scalapino, Leslie. *The Front Matter, Dead Souls*. Hanover: Wesleyan University Press, 1996. p. 7.

4 Cross to Scalapino in correspondence.

5 Cross to Scalapino in correspondence.

6 Scalapino, Leslie. "Poetics—for Lisa Samuels," forthcoming in *How Phenomena Appear to Unfold* (Revised Edition), Litmus Press, 2010.

7 Scalapino, Leslie. *It's go in/quiet illumined grass/land*. Sausalito: The Post Apollo Press, 2002. p. 1.

8 Lamrimpa, Gen. *Realizing Emptiness: Madhyamaka Insight Meditation*. Ithaca: Snow Lion Publications, 2002. pp. 32-3.

contributors

"The Chesterly Sisters" by Hannah Barrett

Contributors' Notes

STEFANI BARBER is the author of *Non Eligible Respondent* and her work has appeared in various journals and anthologies, including *Tripwire*, *Kenning*, and *Step into a World: A Global Anthology of New Black Literature*. She is an associate producer for a t.v. news program.

JUSTYNA BARGIELSKA was born in 1977 and is a social activist, a writer, and a poet. She is the author of two books of poetry, *Dating Sessions* (2003) and *China Shipping* (2005), and she is working on her third collection, *Two Fiats* (a working title). In 2010 her book of short stories, *Obsoletki* (Miscarriages), will be published by Wydawnicto Czarne. She lives in Warsaw.

HANNAH BARRETT holds a lifelong appointment as "Court Painter to the Wicked." If you are wicked and lack a painted pedigree, Master Barrett can supply a single, pair, or group of portraits. Perhaps you already possess an ancestral gallery, but your pictures are lonely and require some fresh company? Master Barrett will gladly addend your family tree. Whether at your castle, palace, country manor, or town house, Master Barrett is happy to execute all of your portrait commissions from a comfortable suite with a nice view.

KACPER BARTCZAK received his Ph.D from the University of Łódź, where he is an Assistant Professor of American Literature. His book publications include *In Search of Communication and Community: The Poetry of John Ashbery* (Peter Lang, 2006), *Świat nie scalony* (Wrocław: Biuro Literackie, 2009), and *Życie Świetnych Ludzi* (Łódź: Wydawnictwo Kwadratura). He has published poems and critical articles in numerous Polish literary magazines, as well as the United States and Ireland, and has been the recipient of grants from the Fulbright Foundation and Kosciuszko Foundation.

ELLEN BAXT lives in her hometown of Brooklyn, New York. She has one full-length book, *Analfabeto / An Alphabet* (Shearsman Books) and four chapbooks, *Since I Last Wrote* (Sona Books), *Tender Chemistry* (Sona Books), *The day is a ladle* (Press Toe) and *Enumeration of colonies is not EPA approved* (Press Toe). Her writing has appeared in *ActionYes*, *How2*, *Saint Elizabeth Street*, *spell, the tiny* and *XCP:Streetnotes*.

DODIE BELLAMY'S chapbook *Barf Manifesto* was named best book of 2009 under 30 pages by *Time Out New York*. Other books include *Academonia*, *Pink Steam*, and *The Letters of Mina Harker*. Her book *Cunt-Ups* won the 2002 Firecracker Alternative Book Award for poetry. She lives in San Francisco with writer Kevin Killian and three cats.

MARTINE BELLEN'S *2x(Squared)* will be published in the spring (BlazeVox books). For more about her other work, visit www.martinebellen.com.

GUY BENNETT is the author of several works of poetry, nonfiction, and numerous translations. His writing has been featured in magazines and anthologies in the U.S. and abroad, and presented in poetry and arts festivals internationally. Publisher of Mindmade Books (formerly Seeing Eye Books) and co-editor of Otis Books / Seismicity Editions, he lives in Los Angeles and teaches at Otis College of Art and Design.

MIRON BIAŁOSZEWSKI (June 30, 1922 – June 17, 1983), born in Warsaw, Poland, was a Polish poet, novelist, playwright and actor. He published nearly two dozen books in his lifetime, including *Obroty rzeczy* (The Revolution of Things), *Myle Wzruszenia* (Erroneous Emotions), and his highly acclaimed *Memoir of the Warsaw Uprising*.

MIŁOSZ BIEDRZYCKI (also writing as MLB) was born in 1967, and is the author of six volumes of poetry published in Poland. A bilingual book of selected poems, 69, is forthcoming from Zephyr Press.

JULIA BLOCH grew up in Northern California and Sydney, Australia, and currently lives in Philadelphia, where she is a doctoral candidate in English Literature at the University of Pennsylvania. She is the co-founder of the Emergency reading series at the Kelly Writers House; her new chapbook *The Selfist* is forthcoming from Katalanché Press.

TAYLOR BRADY lives in San Francisco. He is the author of several books of poetry and prose, most recently *Occupational Treatment* (2006), and *Yesterday's News* (2005), and is the co-author with Rob Halpern of *Snow Sensitive Skin* (2007). Recent poems, beginning to accumulate under the title *Pamphlets, Rants, Tracts & Ballads*, attempt a series of extrapolations, re-readings, and polemics with and against the grain of the writers and musicians who instruct him. He is active in the Nonsite Collective, and has recently edited the collected essays of Will Alexander for 2010 publication.

ANDRZEJ BUSZA (b. 1938, Poland) is a Polish poet, essayist, and translator. His books include *Astrologer in the Underground* and *Scenes from the Life of Laquedem*. He has written extensively on the work of Joseph Conrad, and along with Bogdan Czaykowski was the first to translate a collection of Miron Białoszewski's poetry into English, *The Revolution of Things*.

EWA CHRUŚCIEL writes both in Polish and English. In 2003 Studium published her first book in Polish, *Furkot*. Her second book in Polish is forthcoming in 2009. Her manuscript in English, *Strata*, won the 2009 International Book Contest, and will be published in December 2010 in the United States. Her poems and translations have appeared in numerous journals in the U.S., Poland, and Great Britain. Her translations of poetry from Polish to English have appeared in numerous journals and two anthologies: *Carnivorous Boy, Carnivorous Bird* and *Six Polish Poets*. She is a Professor of Humanities at Colby-Sawyer College in United States.

NORMA COLE is a poet, painter, and translator. Her recent work includes 14000 Facts, Do the Monkey, Spinoza in Her Youth, Natural Light and Scout (a CD-ROM). Her translations include Danielle Collobert's Notebooks 1956-1978, Fouad Gabriel Naffah's The Spirit God and the Properties of Nitrogen, and Crosscut Universe: Writing on Writing from France. Born in Canada, Cole has lived in San Francisco since 1977.

CACONRAD is the recipient of The Gil Ott Book Award for The Book of Frank (Chax Press, 2009). He is also the author of Advanced Elvis Course (Soft Skull Press, 2009), (Soma)tic Midge (Faux Press, 2008), Deviant Propulsion (Soft Skull Press, 2006), and a collaboration with poet Frank Sherlock titled THE CITY REAL & IMAGINED: (Factory School, 2010). He invites you to visit him online at CAConrad.blogspot.com and also with his friends at PhillySound.blogspot.com.

ROB COOK is the author of Songs For The Extinction of Winter, Diary of Tadpole, the Dirtbag (both from Rain Mountain Press), and Blackout Country (BlazeVOX [books]). Work has appeared or will appear in A cappella Zoo, Caketrain, Osiris, Weave, Fence, and Zoland.

CRAIG COTTER was born in 1960 in New York and has lived in California since 1986. His third collection of poetry, Chopstix Numbers, is available from Boise State University's Ahsahta Press. Poems from his new manuscript Awake are upcoming in Global Tapestry Review, Lungfull!, Poetry New Zealand, Alimentum, Dalhousie Review, Court Green, Mudfish, Van Gogh's Ear, Inkwell, Eleven Eleven, Euphony, Margie, Hawaii Review, and The Antigonish Review.

MICHAEL CROSS edits Atticus/Finch Chapbooks and co-edits ON: Contemporary Practice (with Thom Donovan and Kyle Schlesinger). Additionally, his work as an editor includes the anthologies Involuntary Vision: After Akira Kurosawa's Dreams (Avenue B, 2003), Building is a Process / Light is an Element: Essays and Excursions for Myung Mi Kim (co-edited with Andrew Rippeon, Queue Books, 2008), and a forthcoming edition of the George Oppen Memorial Lectures at San Francisco State. He is finishing a monograph on the work of Louis Zukofsky, and starting work on a short critical work on Leslie Scalapino. His chapbooks include Cede (Vigilance Society, 2006) and Throne (Dos Press, 2007), and his full-length poetry collections include In Felt Treeling (Chax, 2009) and Haecceities (forthcoming from Cuneiform in 2010).

BRENT CUNNINGHAM is a writer, publisher, and visual artist currently living in Oakland, California with his wife and daughter. His first book of poetry, Bird & Forest, was published by Ugly Duckling Presse in 2005, and his second, Journey to the Sun, is forthcoming. He and Neil Alger founded and run Hooke Press, a chapbook press dedicated to publishing short runs of poetry, criticism, theory, writing, and ephemera.

BOGDAN CZAYKOWSKI (b. 1932, Poland; d. 2007, Canada), was a Polish Canadian poet, essayist, literary translator and literary critic, professor emeritus, and former Dean at the University of British Columbia. He wrote numerous articles in academic journals and literary magazines, and was the subject of literary research papers. Czaykowski received the Killam Prize in 1996, the Polish literary awards *Fundacja Turzańskich* (1992) and *Fundacja Kościelskich* (1964), and other awards. With Andrzej Busza, he was the first to translate a collection of Miron Białoszewski's poetry into English (*The Revolution of Things*).

MINA PAM DICK (aka Hildebrand Pam Dick, Nico Pam Dick et al.) is a writer, artist, and philosopher living in New York City. She's a native New Yorker. She received a BA from Yale, and an MA in Philosophy as well as an MFA in Painting from the University of Minnesota. Her prose and poetry have appeared in *BOMB*, *Tantalum*, *The Brooklyn Rail*, and *The Boog Portable Reader #4*. Her philosophical work has appeared in a collection put out by the International Wittgenstein Symposium (Kirchberg am Wechsel, Austria). Her first book *Delinquent* was published by Futurepoem in 2009.

DOLORES DORANTES (b. 1973) lives in Ciudad Juárez, Chihuahua. She is site director of the border office of Documentación y Estudios de Mujeres, A.C. (Women's Documentation and Studies; www.demacvirtual.org.mx), a nonprofit dedicated to promoting autobiographical writing among women in marginalized communities. She has published three books of poetry: *Poemas para niños*, *SexoPUROsexoVELOZ*, and *Septiembre*; as well as the epistolary book *Lola: Cartas Cortas*. She updates her blog regularly: www.dorantes.blogspot.com.

PATRICK DURGIN is a poet-critic whose recent publications include *The Route*, a collaboration with Jen Hofer (Atelos, 2008), and contributions to *Contemporary Women's Writing*, *Denver Quarterly*, *The Journal of Modern Literature*, *Mark(s)zine*, textsound.org, and *XCP: Cross-Cultural Poetics*. New work is forthcoming in *P-Queue*, *Prairie Schooner*, and *WIG*. Durgin teaches literature and writing at the School of the Art Institute of Chicago.

CATHY EISENHOWER lives and works in Washington, DC. Edge published her first book, *clearing without reversal*, and Roof her second, *would with and*. She's translating the selected poems of Argentine poet Diana Bellessi and is an editor of the forthcoming journal *Women in and Beyond the Global*.

LAURA ELRICK is the author of the books *sKincerity* and *Fantasies in Permeable Structures*. Audio pieces and the video-poem "Stalk" can be accessed online at Pennsound. She currently lives and works in Brooklyn.

CAL FREEMAN was born and raised in Detroit. He received his undergraduate degree from University of Detroit–Mercy and received his MFA from Bowling Green State University in 2004. That year Terrance Hayes awarded him the Devine Poetry Fellowship. His work has appeared or is forthcoming in *The Journal*, *Nimrod*, *Commonweal*, *Drunken Boat*, *Ninth Letter*, as well as several other journals. He currently teaches at University of Detroit–Mercy.

RODRIGO FLORES and his homies (Mexico City, 1977) are the authors of *estimado cliente* (Lapsus, 2005 and Bonobos/Setenta, 2007) and *baterías* (Invisible, 2006). They were the founders and editors of the literary journal *Oráculo. Revista de poesía* (2000-2009).

KAREN GARTHE'S poetry appears in the premier and current issue of *Lana Turner*, and is forthcoming in *Barrow Street*, *Mad Hatters Review*, and the *Colorado Review*. Her poetry has been published in *New American Writing*, *Chicago Review*, *Fence*, *VOLT*, and *American Letters & Commentary*. Her first book *Frayed escort* won the 2005 Colorado Prize and her second book *The Banjo Clock* will be published in 2012.

NADA GORDON is currently considered a single author. If one or more works are by a distinct, homonymous authors, go ahead and split the author. She wrote *Folly*, *V. Imp.*, *Are Not Our Lowing Heifers Sleeker than Night-Swollen Mushrooms?*, *foriegnn bodie*, and, with Gary Sullivan, *Swoon*. She is a founding member of the Flarf Collective. At the time of this bio-writing, she is working on a movie about women, hair, and excess.

NOAH ELI GORDON is the author of several collections of poetry, including *Novel Pictorial Noise* (Harper Perennial, 2007), which was selected by John Ashbery for the National Poetry Series, and subsequently given the SFSU Poetry Center Book Award. His work in this issue is excerpted from *The Source*—a manuscript marking the results of a multi-year investigation in constrained bibliomancy and ambient research; other excerpts can be found in recent issues of *New American Writing* and *Denver Quarterly*. He's the co-publisher of Letter Machine Editions and an Assistant Professor in the MFA program in Creative Writing at The University of Colorado–Boulder.

ANDY GRICEVICH lives in Madison, Wisconsin, where he edits the journal *Cannot Exist*. He has spent much of the past decade performing strange political theater, experimental chamber music, and satirical songs with the Nonsense Company and the Prince Myshkins. His poems appear here and there. He is uncomfortably writing this in the third person.

JAMES GRINWIS lives in Florence, Massachusetts, and is founding editor of Bateau Press. His work has appeared in a diverse variety of journals, including *Columbia*, *Conjunctions*, *Court Green*, *Cranky*, and *Cream City Review*.

GABRIEL GUDDING'S most recent book is *Rhode Island Notebook* (Dalkey Archive Press, 2007), a 436-page poem he wrote in his car. His poetry, essays, and translations appear in periodicals such as *Harper's Magazine*, *The Journal of the History of Ideas*, *New American Writing*, *EOAGH*, in such anthologies as *Great American Prose Poems: From Poe to the Present* (Scribner), *The Oxford Anthology of Latin American Poetry*, *Poems for the Millennium*, and *The Whole Island: Six Decades of Cuban Poetry* (University of California Press). He is a contributing editor for *Mandorla: Nueva Escritura de las Américas*, has started creative writing programs in three prisons, and is a Professor of Creative Writing and Experimental Poetics, whatever that is, at Illinois State University.

ROB HALPERN is the author of several books of poetry, including *Rumored Place* (Krupskaya, 2004) and *Disaster Suites* (Palm Press, 2009). With Taylor Brady he also co-authored the book length poem *Snow Sensitive Skin* (Atticus / Finch, 2007). *Music for Porn* is forthcoming. Currently, he's co-editing the poems of the late Frances Jaffer together with Kathleen Fraser, and translating the early essays of Georges Perec, the second of which, "Commitment or the Crisis of Language," recently appeared in the *Review of Contemporary Fiction* together with an essay of his own on Perec. An active participant in the Nonsite Collective, Rob lives and works in San Francisco.

ALAN HALSEY's recent books are *Lives of the Poets* (Five Seasons) and *Term as in Aftermath* (Ahadada). His earlier work is collected in *Marginalien* (Five Seasons, 2005) and *Not Everything Remotely* (Salt, 2006).

JEN HOFER is a Los Angeles-based poet, translator, interpreter, teacher, knitter, book-maker, public letter-writer, and urban cyclist. Her most recent books are a series of anti-war-manifesto poems titled *one* (Palm Press, 2009), *sexoPUROsexoVELOZ*, and *Septiembre*, a translation from *Dolores Dorantes* by Dolores Dorantes (Counterpath Press and Kenning Editions, 2008); *The Route*, a collaboration with Patrick Durgin (Atelos, 2008); and *lip wolf*, a translation of *lobo de labio* by Laura Solórzano (Action Books, 2007). She teaches at CalArts, Goddard College, and Otis College, and works nationally and locally as a social justice interpreter. Her translations from *Intervenir* can be found in *Mandorla* #13 and *OR* #3.

RICK HILLES was a recipient of a 2008 Whiting Writers Award and is currently a fellow at the Camargo Foundation in Cassis, France. He has been the Amy Lowell Poetry Traveling Scholar, a Wallace Stegner Fellow at Stanford University, and the Ruth and Jay C. Halls Fellow at the University of Wisconsin–Madison and has received the Larry Levis Editor's Prize in Poetry from *The Missouri Review*. His poems have appeared in *Poetry*, *The Nation*, *The New Republic*, *Ploughshares*, *Salmagundi*, and *Witness*. He teaches poetry at Vanderbilt University.

SCOTT INGUITO, a poet, painter and educator, teaches writing and critical thinking at San Jose Community College. Recent poems have appeared in *Shampoo*, and his paintings can be seen at scottinguito.com. He is the author of *Dear Jack* (Momotombo Press, 2008).

MICHAEL IVES is the author of *The External Combustion Engine* (Futurepoem Books). His poetry and prose have appeared in numerous magazines and journals both in the United States and abroad. He has taught at Bard College since 2003.

KATARZYNA JAKUBIAK is an Assistant Professor of English at Millersville University of Pennsylvania. Her work includes scholarship in African diaspora studies and translation theory, as well as translations of work by contemporary Polish poets Ewa Sonnenberg, Dariusz Sosnicki, and Roman Honet. In Poland, she published a collection of translations of Yusef Komunyakaa's poetry, *Pochwala miejsc ciemnych* (Znak, 2005).

PAOLO JAVIER is the recent author of *The Feeling Is Actual* (creature press) and *Megton Gasgan Krakooom* (Cy Gist Press). He runs 2nd Avenue Poetry and lives in Queens.

ANDREW JORON'S latest poetry collection is *The Sound Mirror* (Flood Editions, 2008). *The Cry at Zero*, a selection of his prose poems and critical essays, was published by Counterpath Press in 2007. City Lights will publish his *Trance Archive: New and Selected Poems* in 2010. Joron's critical study of American surrealist poetry, *Neo-surrealism; or, the Sun at Night* will be reissued by Kolourmeim Press in 2010. Joron is also the translator, from the German, of the Marxist-Utopian philosopher Ernst Bloch's *Literary Essays* (Stanford University Press, 1998).

ANETA KAMIŃSKA (b. 1976) is a poet and translator of contemporary Ukrainian poetry. She was born in Szczebrzeszyn, comes from Zamość, and lives in Warsaw. She holds an M.A. in Polish Philology from the University of Warsaw and teaches Polish as a foreign language. She is the author of the collections *Wiersze zdyszane* (Breathless Poems, 2000), *zapisz zmiany,* (save the changes, 2004), and *czary i mary (hipertekst)* (hocus and pocus [hypertext]) In 2007 her translation of Nazar Honczar's collection *Gdybym* (If I) was published. Recently she has been working on the innovative anthology *Cząstki pomarańczy. Nowa poezja ukraińska* (Slices of Orange: Contemporary Ukrainian Poetry), and a new collection, *autoportret szczątkowy. ostatnie wiersze nazara honczara napisane przez anetę kamińską* (a residual self-portrait. the last poems of nazar honczar written by aneta kamińska). She blogs at www.wszczebrzeszynie.blog.pl (where she recounts the adventures of foreigners with the Polish language) and www.marszrutka.blog.pl (where she talks about her experience translating Ukrainian poetry).

VINCENT KATZ is the author of *Alcuni Telefonini* (Granary Books, 2008) and *Judge* (Charta/Libellum, 2007). Recent work can be found in *EOAGH 5, Letterbox, Bomb*, and *Live Mag*. He lives in New York.

MONIKA KOCOT holds an M.A. in Polish Philology, and is completing another graduate degree in English Philology at the University of Łódź. Her field of research is Scottish and Polish contemporary poetry seen through the prism of contemporary literary theories. She has published on Polish language poetry, cognitive aspects of Stanisław Swen Czachorowski's immanent poetics, poetic imagery in William Blake's and Moniza Alvi's works, but also on postmodern American Indian novels by Thomas King and Sherman Alexie. She combines theory of literature and cognitive linguistics to engage in comparative analyses of literary works. She is also a member of the Polish Cognitive Linguistics Association and the chair of the K.K. Baczyński Literary Society.

ELA KOTKOWSKA works as an editor for Oxford University Press. Her translations from French and Polish have appeared in *Chicago Review* and *Poetry*. Her own work was featured most recently in the anthology *The City Visible: Chicago Poetry for the New Millenium* (William Allegrezza and Raymond Bianchi, editors).

VIRGINIA LUCAS (Uruguay, b. 1977) is a poet, editor, and literature professor. Her books include the poetry collections *Épicas marinas* (Artefato, 2004) and *No es de acanto la flor en piedra* (Lapsus, 2005) and the anthology *Orsai: género, erotismo y subjetividad* (Pirates, MVD, 2008). She is Literature Director of the National Office of Culture (part of the Uruguyuan Ministry of Education and Culture) and is Reserach Coordinator of Queer Studies Montevideo, where she is also a member of the Humanities Department, with a focus on Latin American Literature. Recently she has been concerned with problematics of representation in poetic writing and reading modes absent a foundation in the body. Part of her project addresses the problematic of various Americas and posits an approach toward cultural criticism as cultural poetics.

KRZYSZTOF MAJER, Ph.D. (University of Łódź / Adam Mickiewicz University) is involved in Canadian and American Studies. His chief interests are postwar North American fiction as well as Jewish literature and culture. He also works as a freelance translator of fiction, art criticism, and literary theory.

FILIP MARINOVICH is author of *Zero Readership* (Ugly Duckling Presse, 2008), and of the forthcoming *Sanguis*. Work appears online in EOAGH #3 and #5 and in *Critiphoria*. He has performed his poems and plays in Paris, San Francisco, and New York.

C.J. MARTIN lives in Lockhart, Texas, where he co-edits Dos Press with Julia Drescher. He's also a contributing editor for Little Red Leaves (www.littleredleaves.com) & LRL e-editions. He's the author of *WIW?3: Hold me tight. Make me happy* (Delete Press, 2009), *Lo, Bittern* (Atticus/Finch, 2008), and *City* (Vigilance, 2007). He teaches at Texas State University–San Marcos.

ROD MENGHAM teaches at the University of Cambridge, where he is also Curator of Works of Art at Jesus College. He has written books on Charles Dickens, Emily Bronte, and Henry Green, is the author of *The Descent of Language* (1993), and has edited collections of essays on contemporary fiction, violence, and avant-garde art, and the fiction of the 1940s. He is also the editor of the Equipage series of poetry pamphlets, co-editor and co-translator of *Altered State: the New Polish Poetry* (Arc Publications, 2003), and co-editor of *Vanishing Points: New Modernist Poems* (Salt, 2005). His own poems have been published under the title *Unsung: New and Selected Poems* (Folio/Salt, 1996; 2nd edition, 2001). His Most recent book was *Parleys and Skirmishes* [poems] with photographs by Marc Atkins (Ars Cameralis, 2007).

EDRIC MESMER, collator of the "Buffalo local" *Yellow Edenwald Field*, works as an adjunct lecturer, academic researcher, and bookshop aficionado. Poems appear elsewhere in *BlazeVOX* and in the forthcoming *Vanitas*.

MONIKA MOSIEWICZ is the author of *cosinus salsa,* which was nominated for several literary awards in Poland. She is a practicing attorney and lives in Pabianice.

MYUNG MI KIM is the author of *Penury, Commons, DURA, The Bounty,* and *Under Flag.* Kim was awarded The Multicultural Publisher's Exchange Award of Merit for *Under Flag* and a number of other awards. The anthologies in which her work has appeared include *American Poets in the 21st Century: The New American Poetics, Moving Borders: Three Decades of Innovative Writing by Women, Premonitions: Kaya Anthology of New Asian North American Poetry,* and *Making More Waves: New Writing by Asian American Women.*

LAURA MORIARTY'S long essay poem, *A Tonalist,* is due out from Nightboat Books in early 2010. *Ladybug Laws,* a chapbook from Slack Buddha, appeared in December 2009. Other books are *A Semblance: Selected & New Poetry 1975-2007* (Omnidawn Publishing) and a chapbook, *An Air Force* (Hooke Press). *Ultravioleta,* a novel, and *Self-Destruction,* a book of poetry, are also pretty recent. She has taught at Mills College and Naropa University among other places and is currently Deputy Director of Small Press Distribution. She is findable online at *A Tonalist Notes* and related blogs.

EILEEN MYLES is a poet who lives in New York. Her novel *The Inferno/a poet's novel* will be out before the end of the year. She is teaching this spring in Missoula, Montana.

LEE NORTON lives in Brooklyn and works in New York. His work has been published in *Sawbuck, Hayden's Ferry Review,* and *6x6,* and is forthcoming from *Drunken Boat* and *Supermachine.*

LINNEA OGDEN is the author of two chapbooks, *Another Limit* (Projective Industries, 2009) and *Long Weekend, Short Leash* (TapRoot Editions), which is forthcoming in 2010. Her work has appeared in *Conduit, The Boston Review, Ploughshares,* and elsewhere. She lives and works in San Francisco.

GEOFFREY OLSEN is the author of the chapbook *End Notebook* (Petrichord Books). He lives in Brooklyn and works at The Cooper Union.

PRZEMYSŁAW OWCZAREK was born in 1975 and is a cultural anthropologist by profession. He is a graduate from Jagiellonian University in Kraków with an M.A. in Art and Literature Studies. He is responsible for the Department of Urban Cultures in the Archaeological and Ethnographic Museum in Łódź. He has contributed to scientific, artistic, and literary publications, including *Tygiel Kultury* (Culture Pot), *Literatura Ludowa* (People's Literature), *Magazyn Sztuki* (Magazine of Art), *Studium, Format, Gazeta Wyborcza, Journal of Urban Ethnology,* and numerous other periodicals. He has received numerous poetry awards throughout Poland and has published two full-length books: *Rdza* [Rust] (2007) and *Cyklist* (2009). He is the general editor of a new quarterly journal, *Arterie,* dedicated to literature and art, and the coordinator of a poetry series in tandem with the magazine. He is interested in contemporary art.

JOCELYN SAIDENBERG is the author of *Mortal City* (Parentheses Writing Series), *CUSP* (Kelsey St. Press), *Negativity* (Atelos), and *Dispossessed* (Belladonna). Born and raised in New York City, she lives in San Francisco where she works as a catalog librarian for the public library.

TOMAZ ŠALAMUN lives in Ljubljana, Slovenia, and occasionally teaches in the US. His recent books translated into English are *Woods and Chalices* (Harcourt, 2008), *Poker* (Ugly Duckling Presse, 2008) and *There's the Hand and There's the Arid Chair* (Counterpath Press, 2009). His *Blue Tower* is due from Houghton Mifflin Harcourt in 2010. He received Europäische Preis in Münster, Germany, in 2007 and a Golden Wreath from Struga Poetry Evenings in Macedonia in 2009.

LESLIE SCALAPINO is the author of thirty-one books of poetry, fiction, plays, and essays including *Day Ocean State of Stars' Night* (Green Integer, 2007) and *It's go in horizontal, Selected Poems* (University of California Pres, 2008). Next spring UC Press will publish a lengthy collection of poetry by Michael McClure, *Of Indigo and Saffron*, which Scalapino selected and for which she wrote an introduction. Granary Books in New York has published two books of her poetry as collaborations with artists, including *The Animal Is in the World like Water in Water* with artist Kiki Smith (2010). FC2 published her novel, *Dahlia's Iris,* and *Floats Horse-floats or Horse-flows* is due in February 2010 from Starcherone in New York.

STANDARD SCHAEFER is a poet and fiction writer living in Portland, Oregon. His books are *Nova* (Sun & Moon Books, 2000), *Water & Power* (Agincourt, 2005), *Desert Notebook* (ML & NLF, 2009), *False Purgatories* (forthcoming from Chax, 2010).

KATE SCHAPIRA is the author of *TOWN* (Factory School, Heretical Texts series, 2010) and several chapbooks, including *Heroes and Monsters* (Portable Press at Yo-Yo Labs), *The Saint's Notebook* (Flying Guillotine Press), and *The Love of Freak Millways and Tango Wax* (Cy Gist Press). Her work has appeared in a number of anthologies and journals, and she coordinates the Publicly Complex Reading Series in Providence, Rhode Island.

ANNE SHAW is the author of *Undertow* (Persea Books), winner of the Lexi Rudnitsky Poetry Prize. Her work has appeared or is forthcoming in *New American Writing, Gulf Coast, Green Mountains Review, Black Warrior Review,* and *Beloit Poetry Journal.* She has also been featured in *Poetry Daily* and *From the Fishouse.* Her extended experimental poetry project can be found on Twitter at twitter.com/anneshaw.

RICK SNYDER is the author of *Escape from Combray* (Ugly Duckling, 2009), *Flown Season* (Portable Press at Yo-Yo Labs, 2004), and *Forecast Memorial* (Duration, 2002). He divides his time between Rochester, New York, and Manhattan.

ANDRZEJ SOSNOWSKI, poet and translator, was born in 1959. He is the author of nine collections of poetry. His translations include both poems and prose by authors such as John Ashbery, Elizabeth Bishop, Jane Bowles, John Cage, Ronald Firbank, Harry Mathews, and Ezra Pound. He lives in Warsaw.

CELINA SU was born in São Paulo, Brazil, and lives in New York City. She teaches political science at Brooklyn College and is the author of *Streetwise for Book Smarts: Grassroots Organizing and Education Reform in the Bronx* (Cornell University Press) and *Our Schools Suck: Students Talk Back to a Segregated Nation on the Failures of Urban Education* (NYU Press, co-authored). She has also worked with the Burmese Refugee Project, in northwestern Thailand, since 2001. Recent poems have appeared or are forthcoming in *Action, Yes, Sous Rature, XCP: Cross Cultural Poetics,* and elsewhere.

NATHALIE STEPHENS (NATHANAËL) writes l'entre-genre in English and French. Her books include *The Sorrow And The Fast Of It* (2007), *Paper City* (2003), *Je Nathanaël* (2003/2006), *L'Injure* (2004), *. . . s'arrête? Je* (2007), and the essay of correspondence, *Absence Where As (Claude Cahun and the Unopened Book)* (2009).

KATARZYNA SZUSTER (a.k.a. Żółwik) holds an M.A. in English Philology from the University of Łódź. She translates contemporary Polish poetry and is working on a book-length manuscript entitled *All the Weird-Looking Animals*. She also knits, découpages, and has recently begun training to be a plant-whisperer.

MARK TARDI is the author of the book *Euclid Shudders* (Litmus Press) and two chapbooks: *Part First——Chopin's Feet* (g-o-n-g) and *Airport music* (Bronze Skull). Recent poems have appeared in *Chicago Review, Van Gogh's Ear,* and the anthology *The City Visible: Chicago Poetry for the New Millenium.* He was the 2009–2010 Fulbright Senior Lecturer in American Literature and Culture at the University of Łódź and continues to teach there, translate Polish poetry, and torture himself with clay-court tennis, devastating bike rides, and undying support for the Chicago Cubs and Liverpool FC.

MICHAEL THOMAS TAREN is a recent graduate of the Iowa Writer's Workshop. His poems appeared in *Colorado Review.* His translations of Tomaž Šalamun were published in *7 Poets, 4 Days, 1 Book* (Trinity University Press, 2009), *Slovene Sampler* (Ugly Duckling Presse, 2008) and have appeared or are forthcoming in *Chicago Review, Public Space, Poetry Review* (UK), *Fulcrum, Colorado Review, Ninth Letter, Jubilat, Poetry London, Circumference,* and elsewhere. His book, *Puberty,* was a finalist for The Fence Poetry Series.

ALISSA VALLES has worked for the BBC, the Dutch Institute of War Documentation, the Jewish Historical Institute, and La Strada International in Warsaw, and is now an independent writer, editor, and translator based in the Bay Area. Her poetry book *Orphan Fire* (Four Way Books) appeared in 2008. Her poetry and essays have appeared in *Ploughshares, The Antioch Review, TriQuarterly Review, Poetry, Verse, Boston Review, The Washington Post Book World*, and elsewhere; she has been a recipient of a Ruth Lilly Poetry fellowship and the Bess Hokin Prize from *Poetry* magazine, as well as a number of other awards. She is editor and co-translator of Zbigniew Herbert's *Collected Poems 1956-1998* (Ecco), a New York Times Notable Book in 2007, and *Collected Prose* (forthcoming, 2010) and has contributed translations to the *New Yorker, New York Review of Books, Harper's, Modern Poetry in Translation, Words Without Borders*, where she acted as poetry editor, and *The New European Poets* anthology (Graywolf, 2008), for which she was also an editor.

Born in 1929 of Belgian parents, in Asnières, on the outskirts of Paris, MICHEL VAN SCHENDEL studied law before settling in Québec in 1952. He quickly became active in sociopolitical and literary debates, publishing *Poèmes de l'Amérique étrangère* in 1958, then *Variations sur la pierre* in 1964 with Éditions de l'Hexagone. During the 60s, van Schendel had various occupations: journalist, critic, translator, screenwriter, director of the journal, *Socialisme*. When he became a professor, he observed a long poetic silence, which he broke in 1978 with *Veiller ne plus veiller*, written in the margins of a strike at the Université du Québec à Montréal. He was awarded the Prix du Gouverneur Général du Canada in 1980 for *De l'oeil et de l'écoute*, the Prix Victor-Barbeau and Prix de la Revue Spirale in 2003 for *Un temps éventuel* as well as the Prix Athanase-David for his life work. *Mille pas dans le jardin font aussi le tour du monde* appeared several weeks before Michel van Schendel's death in fall 2005.

FRANK L. VIGODA is a literary translator based in Riverside, California, who translates from Polish (primarily poetry). Translations have appeared in a variety of publications including *Modern Poetry in Translation, Lyric Poetry Review, Chicago Review, Absinthe: New European Writing, Circumference,* and *Fence. 69 (New Polish Writing)*, a collection of poems by Miłosz Biedrzycki, is forthcoming from Zephyr Press.

JASMINE DREAME WAGNER is the author of *Charcoal* (For Arbors, 2008), a chapbook of poems. Her poems have also appeared in *American Letters & Commentary, Blackbird, Verse, Colorado Review, Indiana Review, North American Review, Action, Yes*, and other magazines. Her fiction has been featured in the *Seattle Review* and *Lost and Found: Stories From New York Vol. 2* (Mr. Beller's Neighborhood Books, distributed by W. W. Norton, 2009). A graduate of Columbia University, Wagner was a writer-in-residence at The Hall Farm Center for Arts & Education in Townshend, Vermont. She currently lives in Brooklyn, New York, where she performs folk and experimental music as Cabinet of Natural Curiosities.

CRAIG WATSON'S recent books include *Free Will* (Roof, 2000) *True News* (Instance Press, 2002) and *Secret Histories* (Burning Deck, 2007). Meanwhile, he continues to search for the perfect cinnamon roll recipe.

TYRONE WILLIAMS is the author of three books of poetry, c.c. (Krupskaya Books, 2002), *On Spec* (Omnidawn Publishing, 2008) and *The Hero Project of the Century* (The Backwaters Press, 2009).

DUSTIN WILLIAMSON is the author of the chapbooks *Gorilla Dust* (Open24Hours) and *Exhausted Grunts* (Cannibal Books). He is the Monday night reading coordinator at the Poetry Project and the publisher of Rust Buckle Books.

STEPHANIE YOUNG lives and works in Oakland, California. Her books of poetry are *Picture Palace* (in girum imus nocte et consumimur igni, 2008) and *Telling the Future Off* (Tougher Disguises, 2005). She edited *Bay Poetics* (Faux Press, 2006) and her most recent editorial project is Deep Oakland (www.deepoakland.org).

OUYANG YU came to Australia in early 1991 and has since published 52 books of poetry, fiction, nonfiction, literary translation, and criticism in English and Chinese languages. He also edits Australia's only Chinese literary journal, *Otherland* (since 1995). His noted books include his award-winning novel, *The Eastern Slope Chronicle* (2002), his collections of poetry, *Songs of the Last Chinese Poet* (1997) and *The Kingsbury Tales* (2008), his translations in Chinese, *The Female Eunuch* (1991) and *The Man Who Loved Children* (1998), and his book of criticism, *Chinese in Australian Fiction: 1888-1988* (US, 2008). He is now based in Melbourne. His website can be found at www.ouyangyu.com.au.

ILONA ZINECZKO is a photographer, writer, and part-time ninja. Recent work can be found in *Matchless Magazine* (www.matchlessmagazine.de), as well as *Dekadentzya*, where she is a contributing editor. She is completing an M.A. in English Philology at the University of Łódź.

ELIZABETH ZUBA co-edits *swerve* magazine and makes art in Brooklyn.

do you Aufgabe?

Aufgabe #1, edited by E. Tracy Grinnell and Peter Neufeld, with guest editors Norma Cole (covers and content pages of small publications from France) and Leslie Scalapino. (out of print)

Aufgabe #2, edited by E. Tracy Grinnell, with guest editor Rosmarie Waldrop (German poetry in translation).

Aufgabe #3, edited by E. Tracy Grinnell, with guest editor Jen Hofer (Mexican poetry in translation, bilingual). (out of print)

Aufgabe #4, edited by E. Tracy Grinnell, with guest editor Sawako Nakayasu (Japanese poetry in translation).

Aufgabe #5, edited by E. Tracy Grinnell with Mark Tardi and Paul Foster Johnson (special issue dedicated to Norman O. Brown's lecture "John Cage") and guest editors Guy Bennett and Jalal El Hakmaoui (Moroccan poetry in translation). (out of print)

Aufgabe #6, edited by E. Tracy Grinnell, Paul Foster Johnson and Mark Tardi, with guest editor Ray Bianchi (Brazilian poetry in translation).

Aufgabe #7, edited by E. Tracy Grinnell, Paul Foster Johnson, Mark Tardi, and Julian T. Brolaski, with guest editor Jennifer Scappettone (Italian poetry in translation).

Aufgabe #8, edited by E. Tracy Grinnell, Paul Foster Johnson, Julian T. Brolaski, and Rachel Bers, with guest editor Matvei Yankelevich (Russian poetry & poetics in translation).

WWW.LITMUSPRESS.ORG

Subscriptions are available through the publisher. Back issues may be purchased through Small Press Distribution. A limited number of complete sets (#1-#9) are available for libraries and other public access collections. Contact us for more information. Does your local library, university, or bookstore carry *Aufgabe*? Ask them to. Anywhere else you'd like to see *Aufgabe*? Let us know!